IMAGES
of America

HISTORIC FORSYTH COUNTY

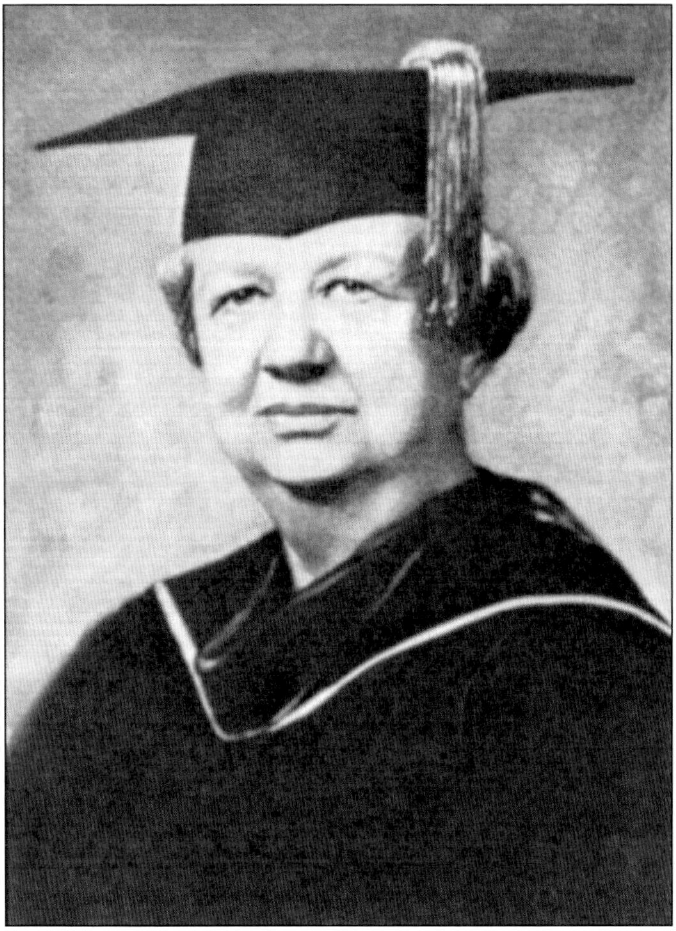

The inspiration of Dr. Adelaide Fries, the first recognized archivist and historian of the North Carolina Moravians, gave the author his first deep understanding of the day-to-day life of the Moravian people. She spent most of her adult life translating and compiling the massive collection of Moravian records. Without her dedication, this work and that of many others could never have been possible. (Courtesy West Salem Historical Association.)

ON THE COVER: The Winston-Salem Retail Merchants' Parade of 1948 was one of many Forsyth County parades of the 20th century. Since this was the largest county parade, participants in surrounding towns were also in attendance. One of the county's namesakes, The Forsyth Theatre (visible at top), oversaw the festivities. (Courtesy West Salem Historical Association.)

IMAGES
of America

HISTORIC FORSYTH COUNTY

Michael Bricker

ARCADIA
PUBLISHING

ISBN 978-0-7385-9787-4

Published by Arcadia Publishing
Charleston, South Carolina

Printed in the United States of America

Library of Congress Control Number: 2012942633

For all general information, please contact Arcadia Publishing:
Telephone 843-853-2070
Fax 843-853-0044
E-mail sales@arcadiapublishing.com
For customer service and orders:
Toll-Free 1-888-313-2665

Visit us on the Internet at www.arcadiapublishing.com

To my wife, Tommie, my guiding light, and daughters Alexandria, Sophia, and Vivian, my shining stars.

Contents

Acknowledgments

I would like to thank Leann Pegram and the Forsyth County Historic Resources Commission and Margaret Bessant, Forsyth County City-County Planning Board. They shared information about local historical landmarks and how preservation on a local level works for the betterment of the county.

I would like to thank LaNelle Church and Salem Baptist Church of Winston-Salem, Paul Mcraw of First Baptist Church of Winston-Salem, Piedmont International University, and Thomas A. Holcomb, member of West Salem Historical Association. A special thank-you goes out to Dr. Adelaide Fries and Bishop Ronthaler (posthumously). Without their dedication to the preservation of the Moravian culture and its history, this publication would not have been possible.

Another special thank-you goes to photographer Frank Jones (posthumously) for his dedication to his craft and for sharing local history with me when I was a boy in mid-20th-century Winston-Salem. As a collector of archival photographs, many produced by Frank Jones, I wish to acknowledge him for his hard work. I also want to thank the West Salem Historical Association for continuing to trumpet local history in the county. The following abbreviations are used in the book: West Salem Historical Association (WSHA) and Frank Jones (FJ).

I would also like to thank Arcadia Publishing for their assistance in the publication of this book, especially Lindsay Carter, Brinkley Taliaferro Gary, Erin Rocha, and Katie McAlpin.

Introduction

Nearly all counties in the United States have exact beginning dates. Forsyth County was an exception to the rule. Previous history books state that 1849 was the year of Forsyth County's birth, thus making it one of the youngest counties in North Carolina. Past authors and historians never questioned the date, since the town of Winston, North Carolina, began in the same year. Also, Winston became the county seat of Forsyth in 1849. After extensive studies of the Moravian Archives of Salem, North Carolina, I discovered the true date of Forsyth County's birth, 1754, and the circumstances surrounding it. The consulting agents drawn from the archives were the Moravian Council, the Church of England, and the newly elected governor of North Carolina, Arthur Dobbs, all of which confirm this date. The archives read, "We value nothing so much as liberty of conscience and the granting of an unlimited conscience to our people will prove a proper encouragement to transplant themselves from these and other parts to North Carolina. Therefore, we pray the land called Wachovia may be erected into a separate parish, and that leave be given to regulate the matters in said parish according to the rules, rights, and forms of our ancient Episcopal Protestant Church." In the 19th century, Adelaide Fries, the first true historian of Forsyth County, believed this as well when she dated the beginning of Forsyth County to the beginning of the parish of Wachovia.

At the time of the Moravian settlement of the Wachovia Tract, the Church of England was the established church, and each county constituted a parish. While individual freedom of worship was not usually interfered with, supervision was unpleasant to the Moravians, who had their own system of government for their congregations and towns. The Wachovia Tract was under the care of the church authorities in Bethlehem, Pennsylvania, and in mid-1759, they took advantage of the coming of Arthur Dobbs, the new governor of North Carolina, to petition for a special favor in the matter. The petition was taken to Governor Dobbs, who was told that without the privilege of ecclesiastical government in Wachovia, it would be almost impossible to induce more of the brethren to move there. Dobbs was most open to the request, and in October 1755, the General Assembly passed an act making Wachovia a district governing unit, Dobbs Parish. The success of the measure meant much to the new settlement, and ultimately, it had great weight in establishing the boundaries of the county. Dobbs Parish progressed through nearly a century before being recognized as Forsyth County around 1849. The Moravian land of 100,000 acres had existed under several other county names, such as Stokes, Surry, and Rowan. The petition of 1759 set the stage for the Winston Tract to be governed in an isolationist Moravian custom, uniquely independent of the respective county, be it Stokes, Surry, etc., throughout the 18th and 19th centuries until the creation of the new Forsyth County seat of Winston in 1849. With the establishment of Dobbs Parish, the late 18th and early 19th centuries brought challenges to the isolationist ways of the Moravians.

The surrounding land of the county/parish was filled with non-Moravians, many of whom were often left out of previous history books. The regulators were formed by Scots-Irish to the west of the town of Salem. These different conflicts and battles between the regulators and Tory/English hierarchy in North Carolina will be discussed in this book, with the town of Salem being caught in the middle. Famous Revolutionary War and War of 1812 individuals such as Capt. Joseph Winston and Major Benjamin Forsyth will be profiled. John Hauser of Bethania is another hero from this time. Most Americans have heard of the famous adventures of Johnny Appleseed. The county had its own version of this famous character. Like Johnny Appleseed, Henderson Lewelling planted fruits and sold wares throughout the future United States. However, unlike Johnny Appleseed, Lewelling founded new towns throughout the country and named each for his hometown, Salem. His final destination was Salem, Oregon.

Richmondtown was a county seat during the early Colonial period. The occurence at Richmondtown was a catalyst for Salem in adopting the concept for the creation of the central city of Forsyth County, with the establishment of Winston in 1849. Richmondtown later faded into obscurity because of one simple fact: the town was literally blown off the face of the earth several days after it was designated the county seat. Richmondtown is now a small hamlet to the northwest of Winston-Salem. When Salem established Winston, Salem always remembered what happened to Richmondtown, so preparation was made in case this tragic event repeated itself. Winston was created on separate Moravian land north of Salem for the county seat.

The images and text in this book cover the Civil War, World War I, and World War II, including Prohibition and the Great Depression, in Forsyth County. Through *Historic Forsyth County*, the author hopes to show residents and visitors the true richness of this area, which is not found in just a few individuals and which had a large influence on our state and the founding of our nation.

One

The Beginning of a Vision

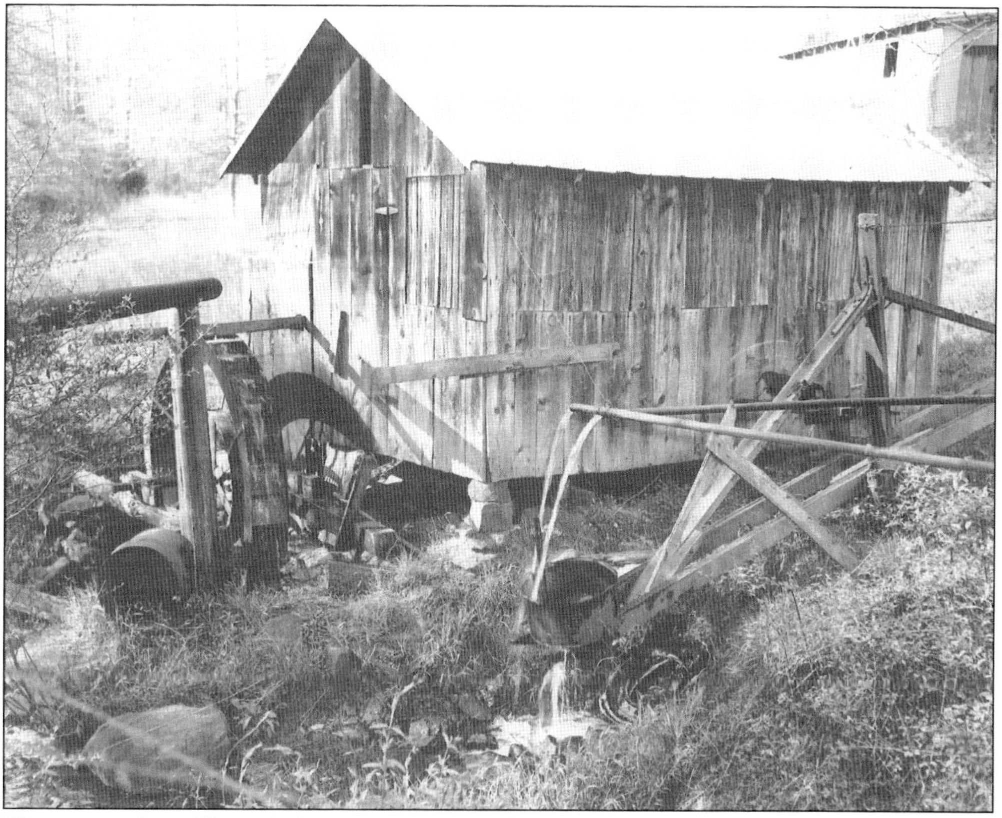

This image of rural Forsyth County conjures up the greatness of a frontier people. Whether they were Scots-Irish or Lutheran, Reformed, or Moravian Germans, the bulk of Carolina's backcountry settlers made extraordinary contributions to the piedmont cultural heritage. With little more than sheer determination and a dream for a better future, these Forsyth County ancestors transformed a wilderness. (Courtesy WSHA.)

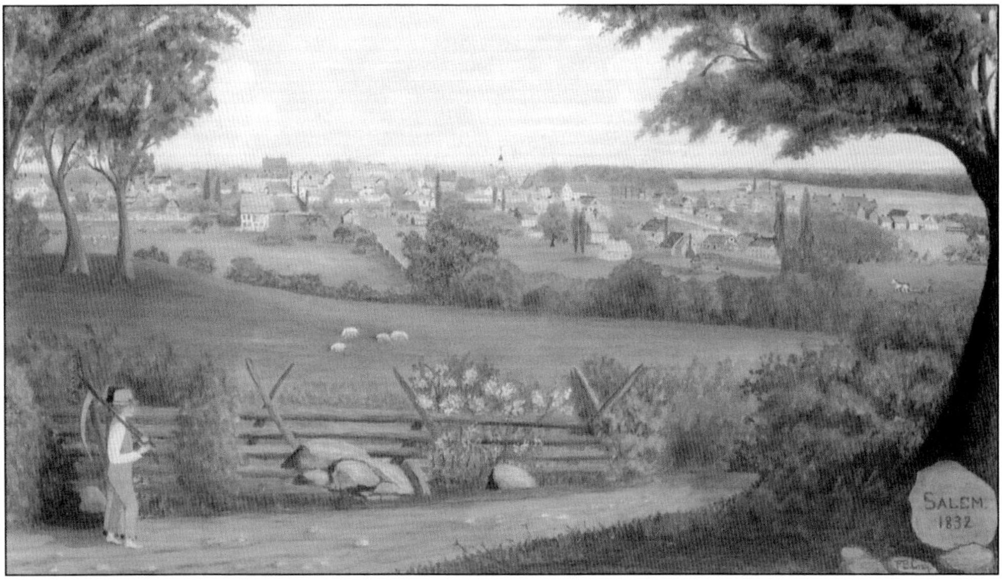

Initial settlers survived hardships on their journey. The Moravian Archives state that the forests of the western piedmont were "tractless as an ocean and uninhabited." The route to Dobbs Parish followed the Great Wagon Road from Pennsylvania through the Shenandoah Valley and Roanoke Gap into Bethabara. The Old Shallowford Road was cut to Salem by the Moravians. This depiction of the "Road to Salem," today's Broad Street, shows Salem in the distance. (Courtesy Old Salem Inc.)

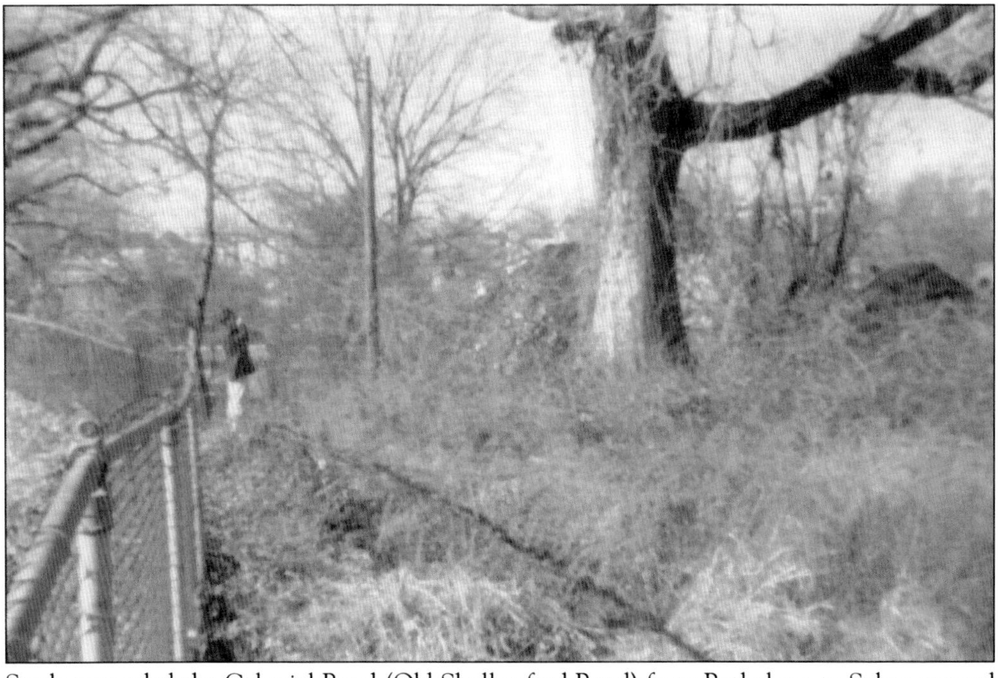

Settlers traveled the Colonial Road (Old Shallowford Road) from Bethabara to Salem around 1766. This road became a major thoroughfare to Dobbs Parish for more than 250 years. Thomas Holcomb took this photograph of a long-lost Colonial Road tree, which shaded settlers on their journey long ago. (Courtesy WSHA.)

The first builders arrived in Salem in 1766 and built this log structure. Only meant to be a temporary structure, it has stood for over 240 years and is located at Brookstown Avenue and South Liberty Street today. The craftsmanship of the early Moravians in Dobbs Parish could include the simplest of supplies, but they created a product that lasted more than two centuries. (Courtesy WSHA.)

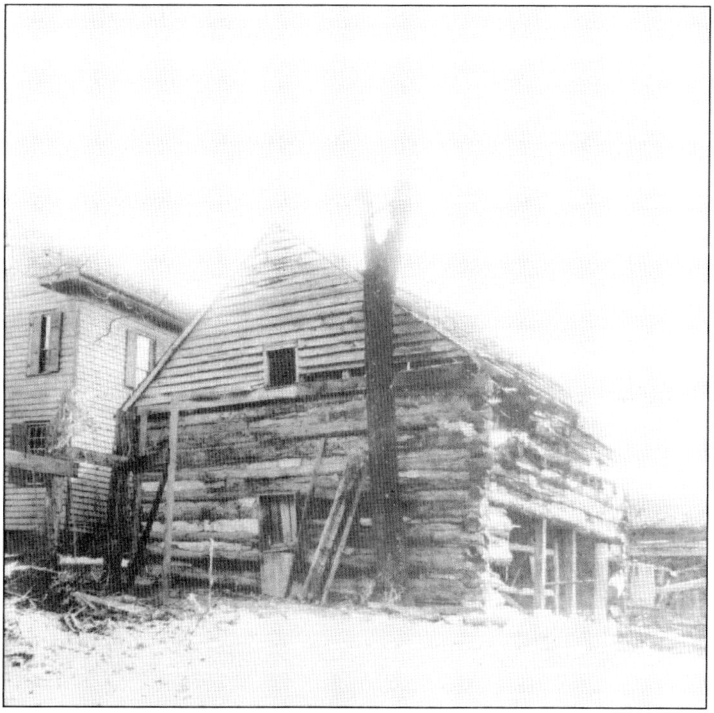

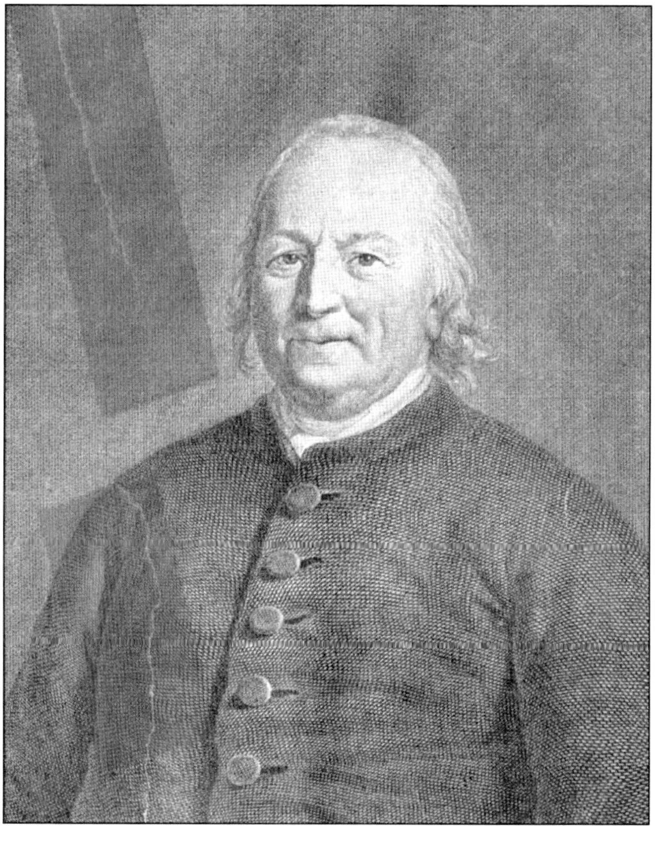

Spaniards arrived in North Carolina during the 1600s, but their expedition for the gold and riches of El Dorado was unsuccessful. In 1752, six Moravian brethren sought out their own El Dorado, searching not for gold but for religious liberty. The leader of this group was Bishop August Gottlieb Sprangenburg. The record states that Bishop Sprangenburg located 100,000 acres in one tract in Anson County. Even though Dobbs Parish was shown to be in another county, the bishop and his people were confident that Dobbs Parish had been and would continue to be the land of the Moravians' true expressive identification. (Courtesy WSHA.)

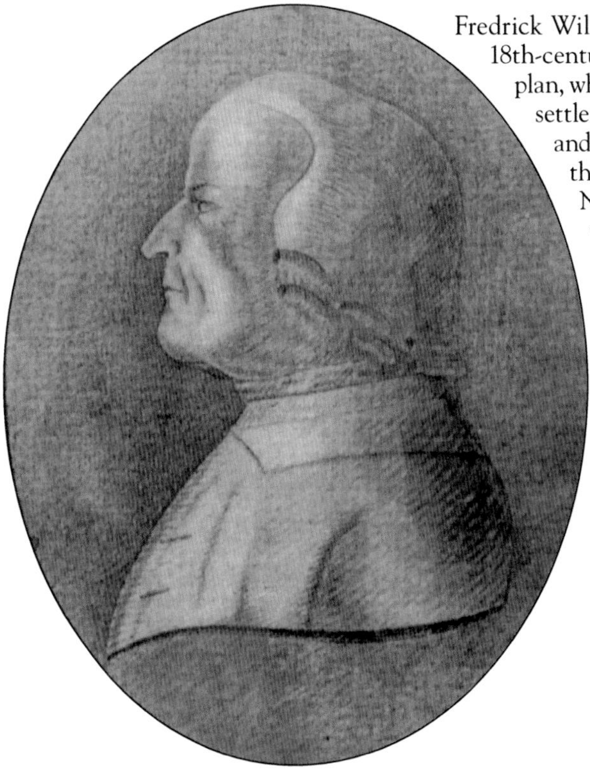

Fredrick William De Marshall, shown in this late-18th-century pencil drawing, created the Marshall plan, which laid the foundation for the Moravian settlement of Salem. He oversaw the financial and business affairs of the Moravians, making the settlement the most successful in rural North Carolina. In 1773, Dobbs Parish was threatened by division. Brother Marshall led the charge to the General Assembly to keep Wachovia as one parish belonging to one county. Dobbs Parish survived.

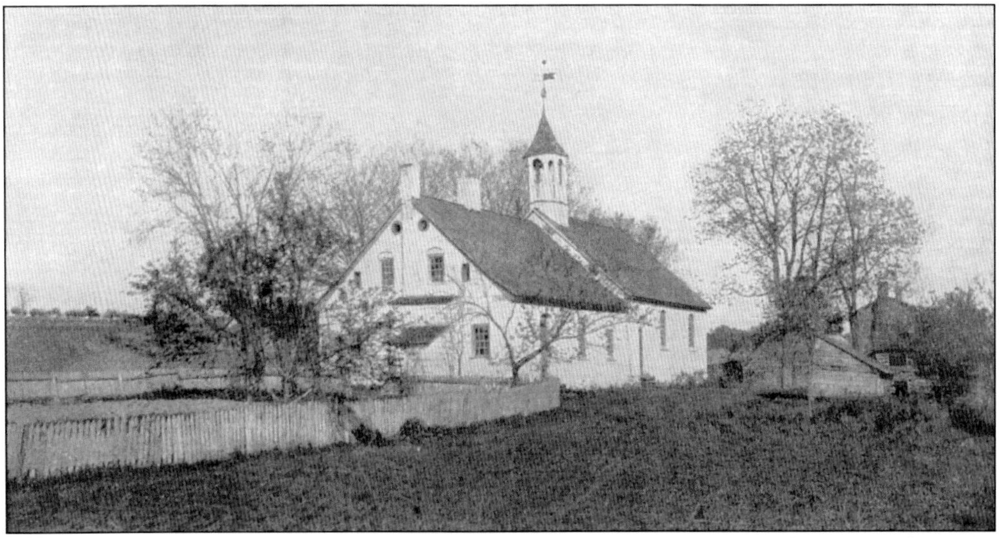

Bethabara, the first settlement of the Moravians in North Carolina, saw the first push by the brethren to identify a town in part of "a total governed parish." A total governed parish was the understanding of the Moravian people with their relationship with the Colonial government as well as the American government after the Revoluntionary War. The Church of England was the established church of Wachovia. Arthur Dobbs, then governor, was forthright in his understanding of the importance of Wachovia and privileges with ecclesiastical government: "It would be almost impossible to entice more of the brethren to move here without it." Bethabara Church, built about 1788, is pictured here. (Courtesy WSHA.)

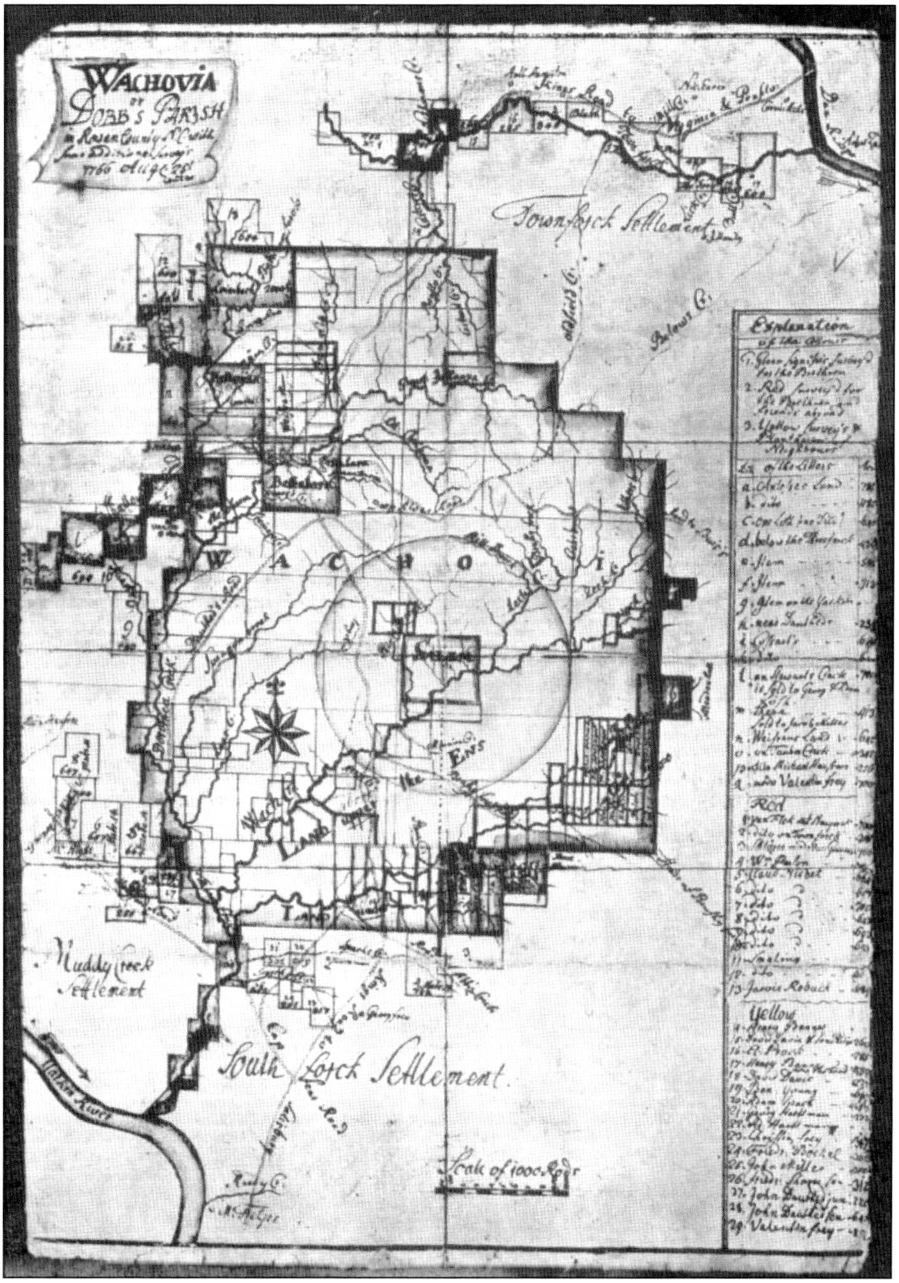

Dobbs Parish and Wachovia are depicted in this early 1766 map drawn from the Moravian Archives. The central town, Salem, is the bullseye of the map. Encircling Salem are the planned out-lot farms: Bethabara, founded about 1753; Bethania, about 1759, to the north; Rural Hall, about 1760, to the north; Town Fork settlement, including Salem Chapel, about 1865; Walkertown, about 1790; South Fork settlement, about 1754, to the south; Hope, about 1760; Friedberg, about 1754; Friedland, about 1770; and Waughtown, about 1806. The Muddy Creek settlement, founded about 1759 to the west of Salem, includes Clemmons, about 1757; Lewisville, about 1777; and Pfafftown, about 1786. Further west toward the Yadkin River is Old Richmond, about 1774; Vienna, about 1760; and Brookestown, about 1790. (Courtesy Moravian Archives.)

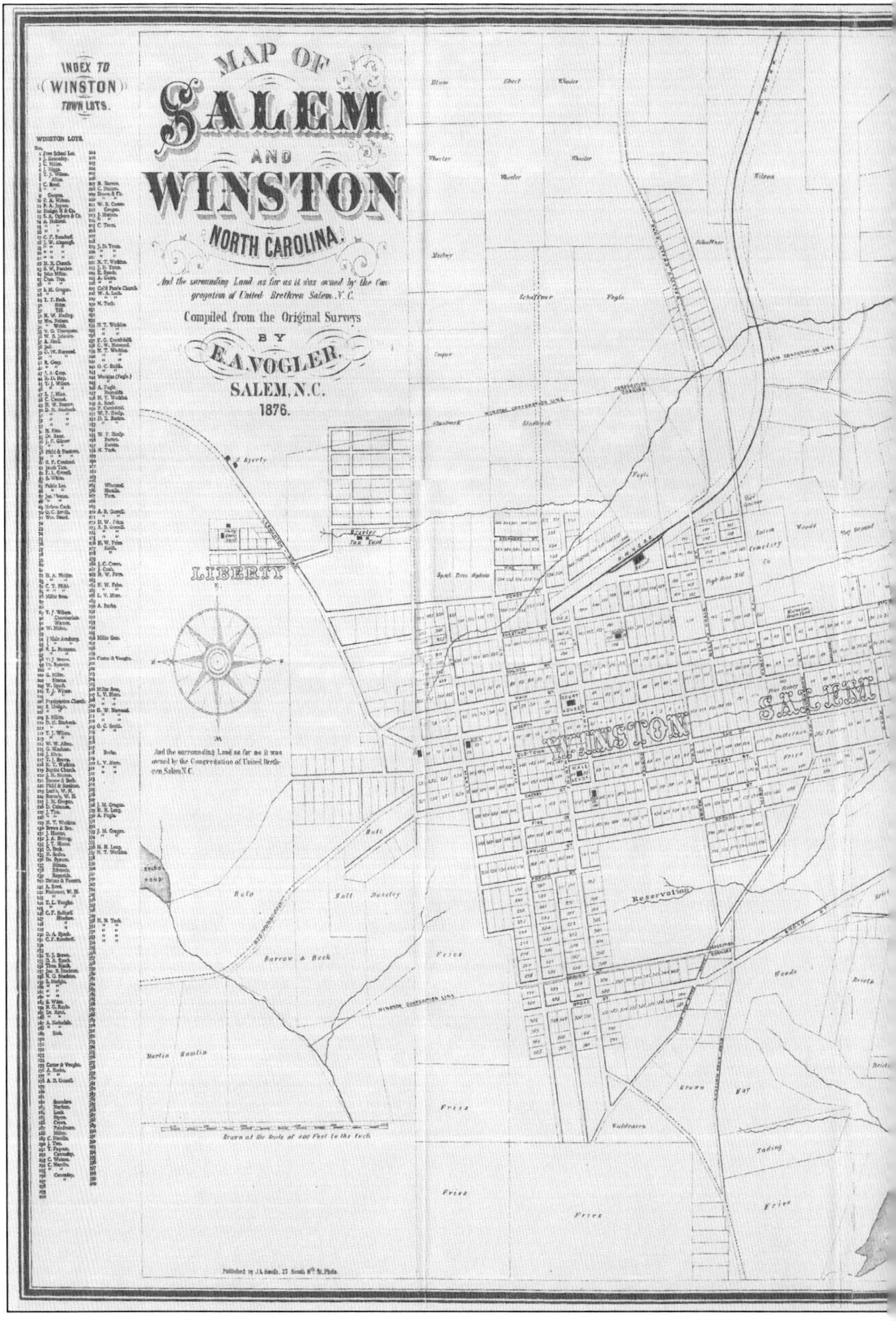

INDEX TO WINSTON TOWN LOTS.
MAP OF
SALEM
AND
WINSTON
NORTH CAROLINA.
And the surrounding Land as far as it was owned by the Congregation of United Brethren Salem N.C.
Compiled from the Original Surveys
BY
E.A.VOGLER.
SALEM, N.C.
1876.
LIBERTY
WINSTON
SALEM
Reservation
Published by J.L. Smith, 27 South 6th St. Phila.

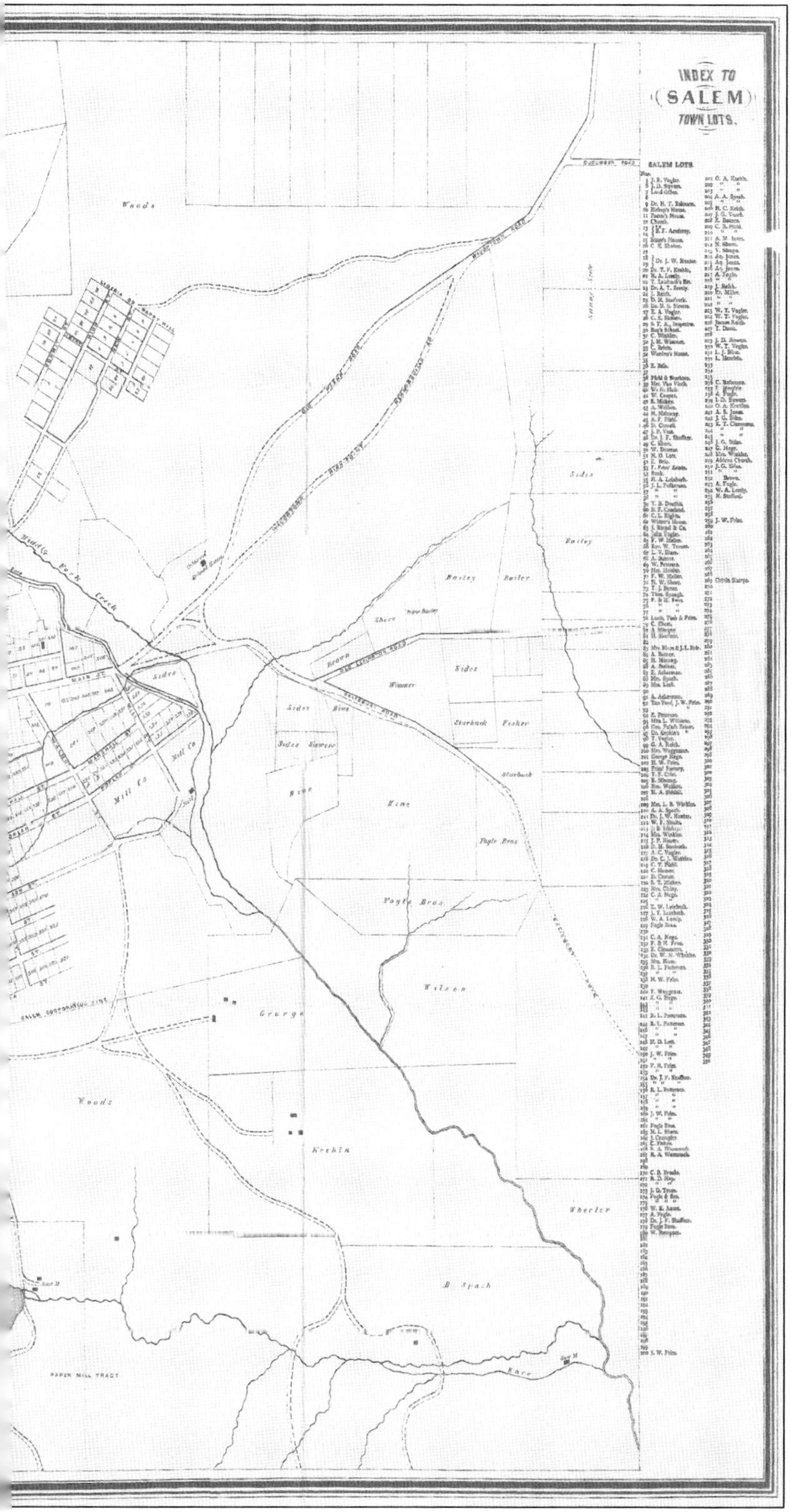

Dobbs Parish had evolved into Forsyth County by 1851. The central town of Winston and Salem had taken over much of the commerce, government, and business interests of the county by the time this c. 1876 map by E.A. Vogler was drawn. In the outskirts of the two towns, The Paper Mill settlement tract to the south, located in the West Salem Historic District today, was coming to a close; to the west, the town of Liberty had not been annexed into Winston; farm outlots surrounding the town were numerous. (Courtesy Moravian Archives/WSHA.)

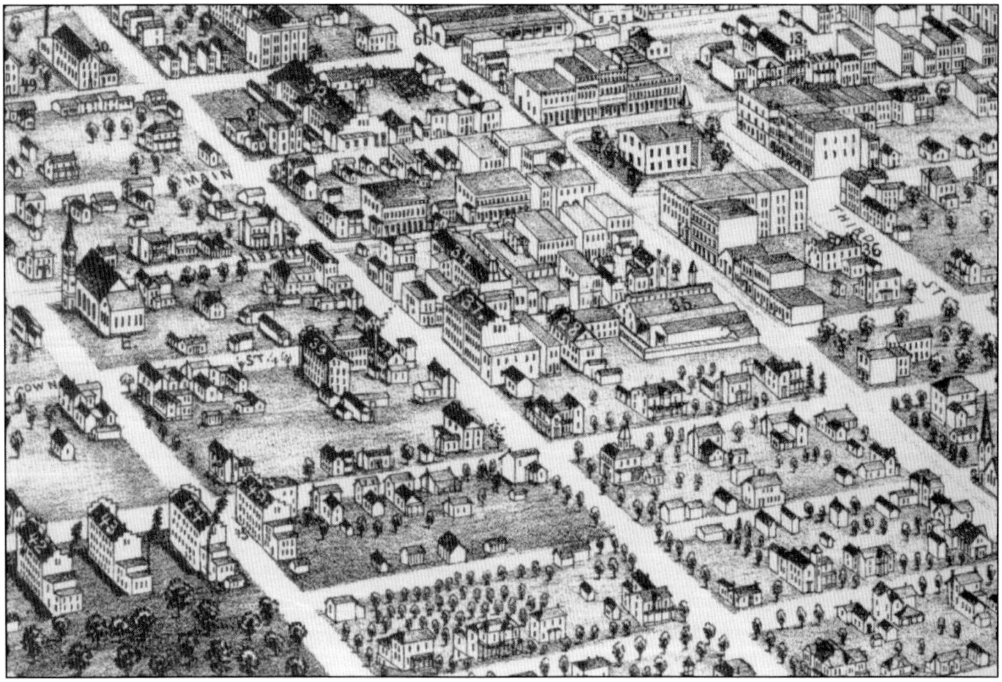

This c. 1891 Bird's Eye Map of Winston-Salem was published by Ruger and Stoner of Wisconsin. The 1850s Centenary Methodist Church is pictured to the right at Sixth and Liberty Streets and the c. 1849 Court House Square is at Main and Liberty Streets. The Brown and Carter Tobacco Warehouse, built about 1850, was the location of the first Forsyth County Fair. (Courtesy Bird's Eye Map/WSHA.)

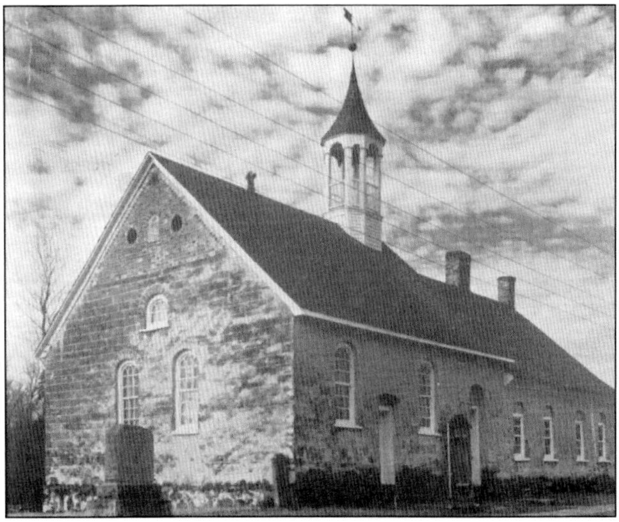

Bethabara was located in the current "Old Town" community of Winston. The town survived an Indian War, a Regulator War, and the American Revolution. From the surrounding out-lot farms of Forsyth to the central town of Salem, the parish would survive intact thanks to Moravian peacemakers. Doctor Fries, archivist, explained: "The brethren's friends were generally among the better educated classes, their representation in the Continental Congress of the General Assembly were many, both Continental and Royalist." (Courtesy M. Bricker.)

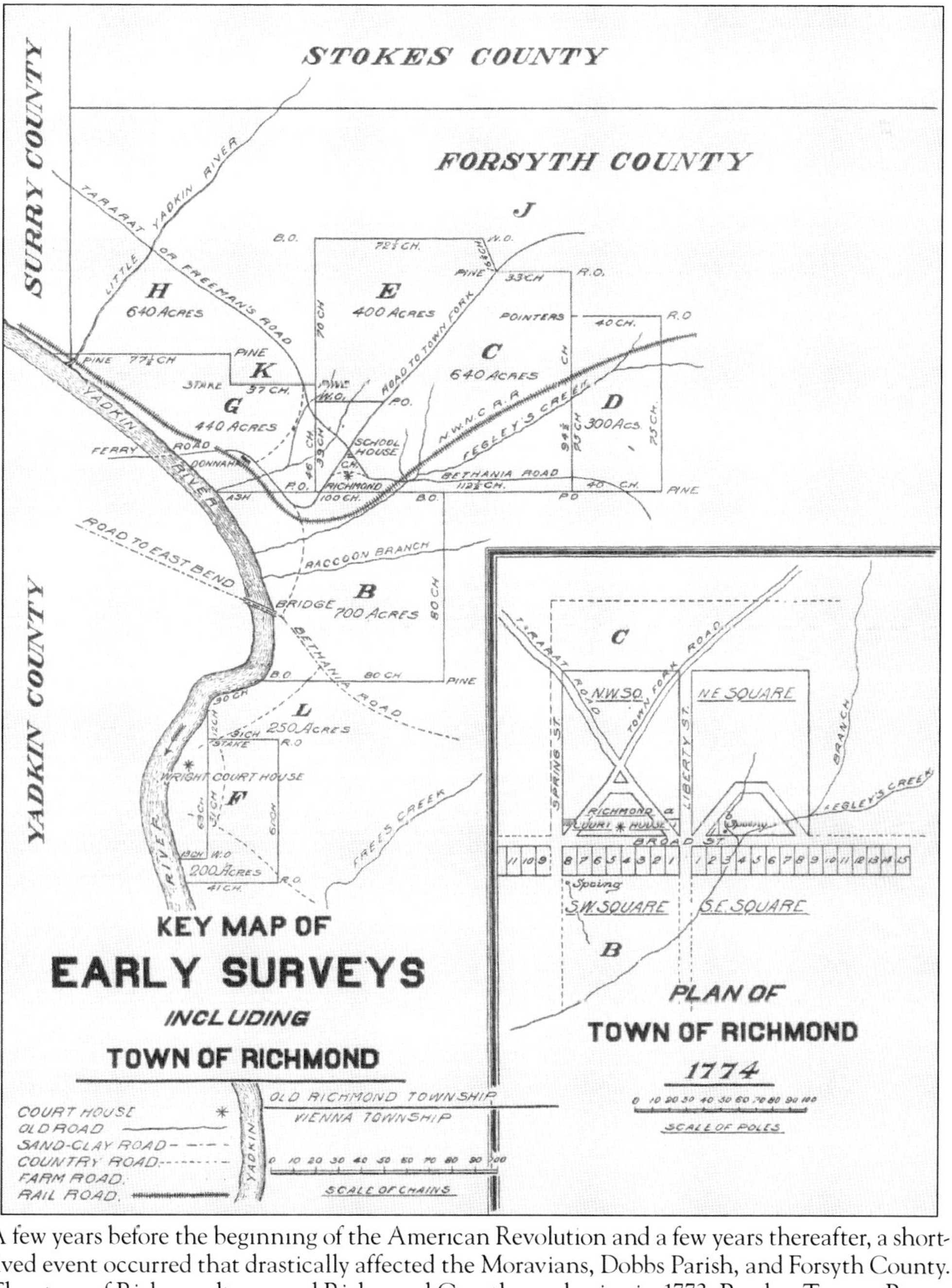

A few years before the beginning of the American Revolution and a few years thereafter, a short-lived event occurred that drastically affected the Moravians, Dobbs Parish, and Forsyth County. The story of Richmondtown and Richmond Courthouse begins in 1773. Brother Taggott Bagge, a spokesperson and merchant of the early Moravians, had agreed to buy the land where the town of Richmondtown would be built. Locals in the area, led by a sheriff, slighted the Moravians and purchased the land. If this had not occurred, Dobbs Parish would have expanded, and this section of Surry County to the north would have been controlled by the Moravians. A rare, c. 1774 summary is pictured here. This plat shows early survey details along the Yadkin River. Roadways are noted by their purpose and material: sand/clay road, country road, farm road, and rail road. (Courtesy WSHA.)

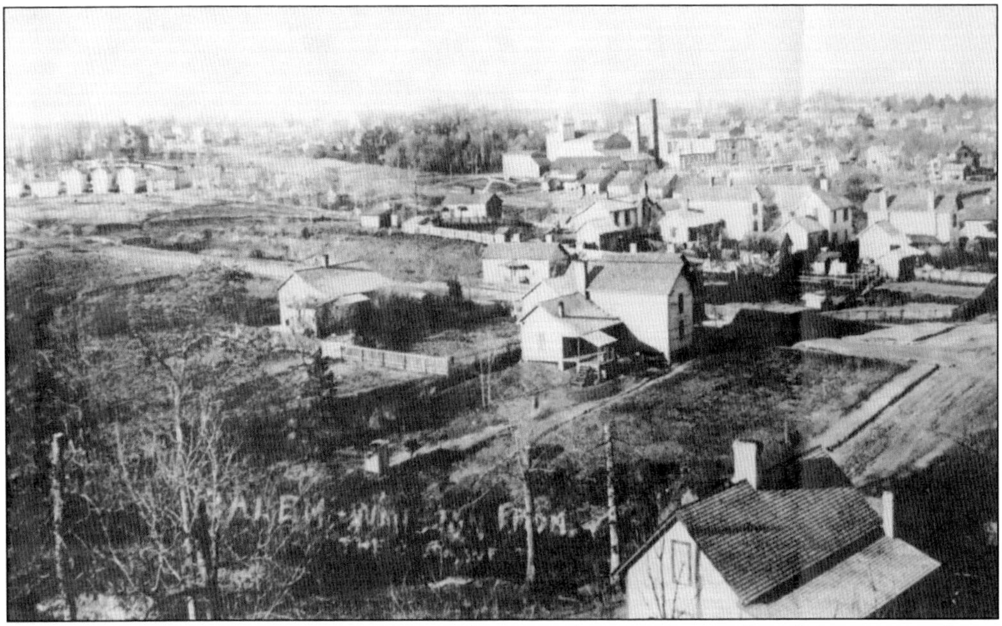

The "City of Peace" (Salem) led Dobbs Parish into embracing the newfound American culture. The town lot of early Salem is shown here about 1882, with Old West Salem indicated by farms and industry in the foreground, and Old East Salem, the religious and craftsman center of the town, in the background. (Courtesy M. Bricker.)

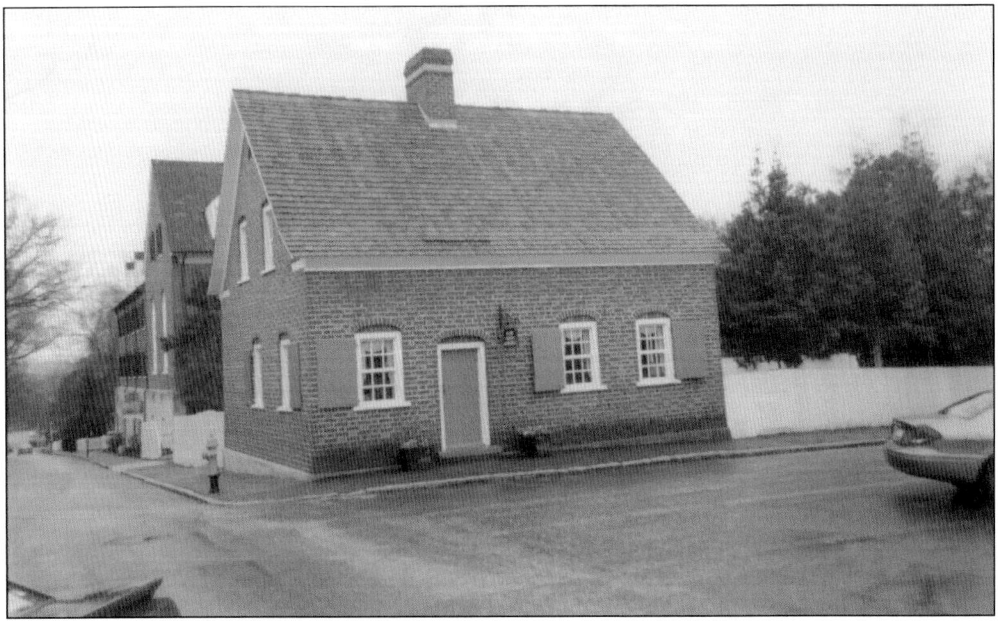

By 1820, Dobbs Parish inhabitants were true Americans. Both German and English languages were used throughout the town. Progressive business, religion, and government practices expanded from 1789 to the 1830s. One of several movers and shakers was Brother Gottlieb Schober, a statesman, paper mill owner, postmaster, and landowner who helped the area transition to the 19th century. His reconstructed house at West and Church Streets in the Old Salem district, built about 1785, is pictured here. (Courtesy WSHA.)

Two

THE MAKING OF A COUNTY

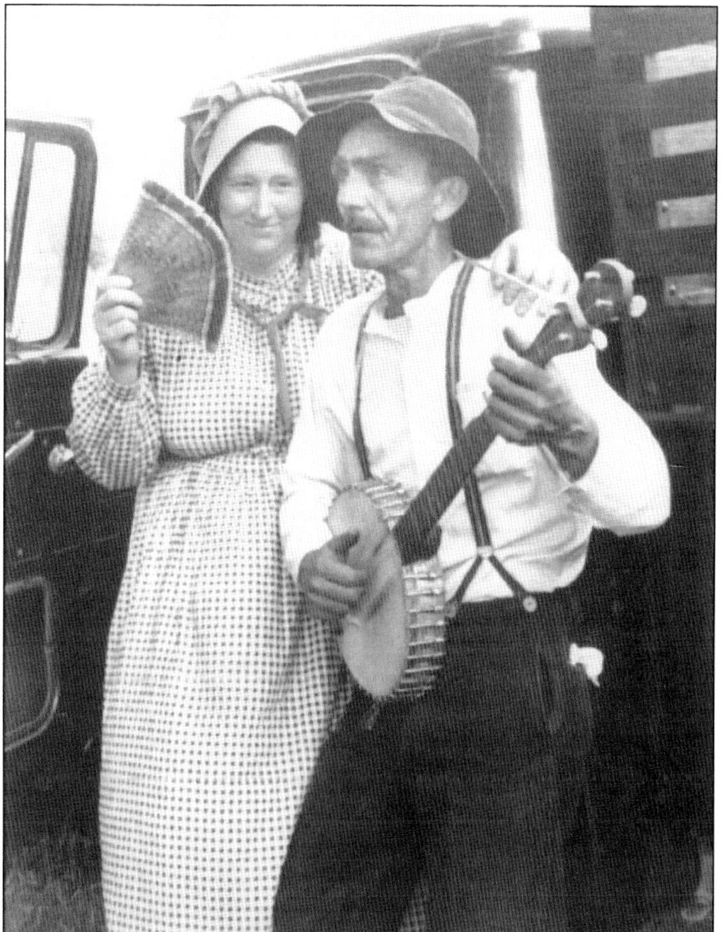

English, Scots-Irish, African American, and other nationalities call the county home. Farming, tobacco and textile industry, and manufacturing enveloped the land and its people. According to Forsyth historian Gwyene Taylor, "Tobacco fields and urban sprawl, country folks and city 'slickers,' wood stoves, and microwave ovens, log cabins . . . and interstate highway represent old and new that characterized the county." This c. 1949 photograph was taken during the county's centennial celebration. (Courtesy FJ/WSHA.)

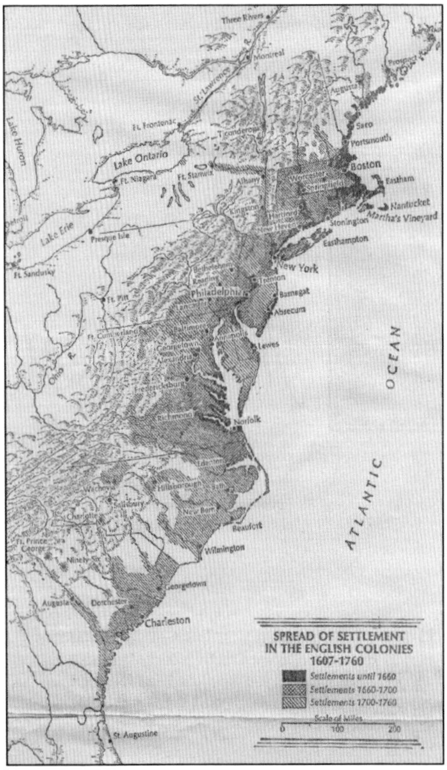

Wachovia contained the deepest backwoods settlement of the Moravians. Salem became the furthest inland town of the 13 colonies in 1776. This historic map of the United States shows the isolation of Wachovia from other population centers. Not to be stopped, the Moravians believed God destined the Salem Tract for them alone, since the land remained unoccupied until their arrival in the piedmont. (Courtesy WSHA.)

In the words of the Moravian leaders, "The tract had the best location of water sources and quality of rich farm land to be found in all of North Carolina." Other settlements existed before their arrival. Indian tribes established trails and passes throughout the piedmont. Many of the early roads were built over these Indian trails. This c. 1940s photograph shows the isolation of Dobbs Parish and the surrounding landscape beyond the Moravian Tract. (Courtesy FJ/WSHA.)

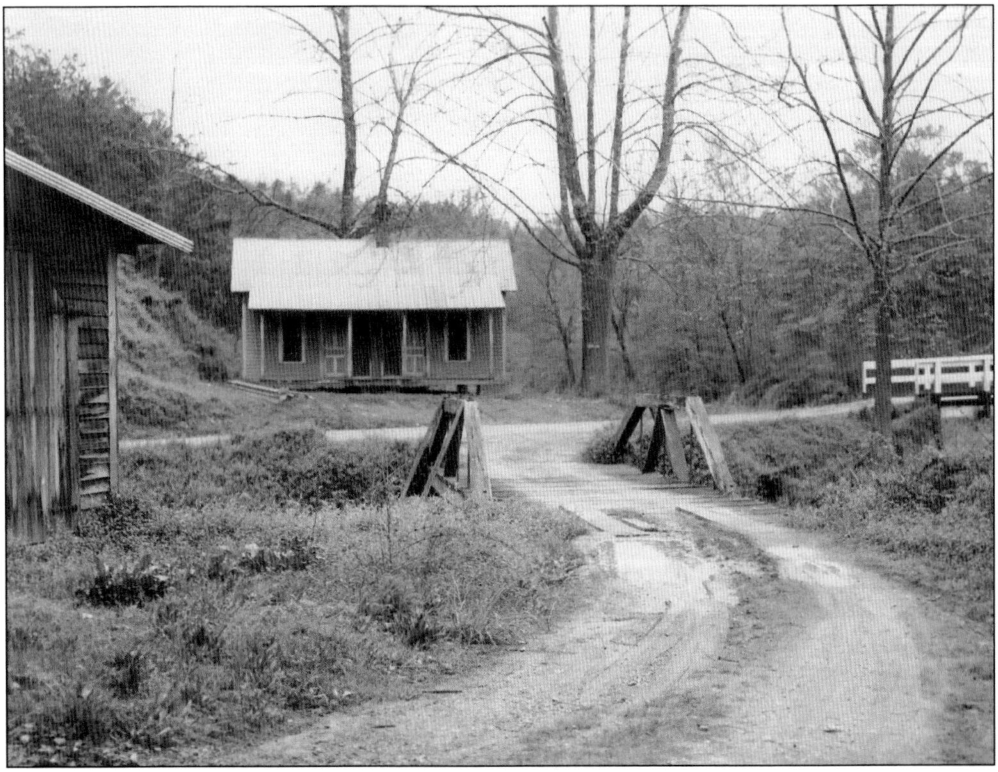

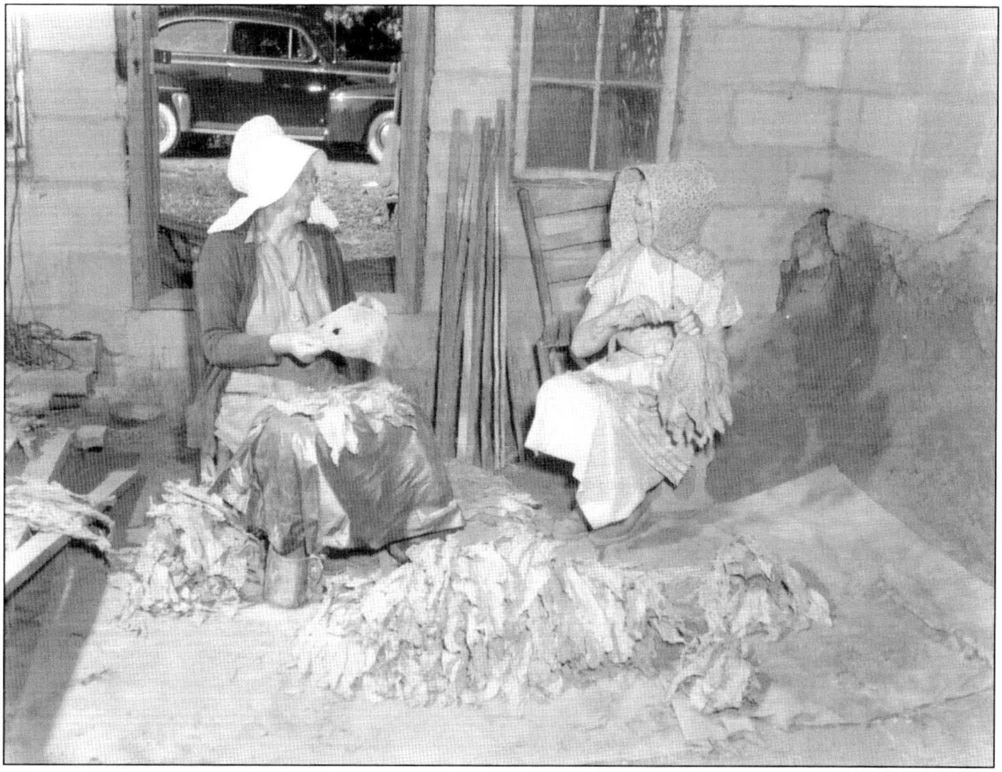

The roots of the early pioneers of the Colonial period allowed future citizens to produce tobacco, textiles, and agricultural products. Whether they were Scots-Irish or German, the bulk of Carolina backcountry settlers did not move inland from existing British colonial settlements. These ladies illustrate the pioneer spirit in a 1950s reenactment showing the preparation of the county's cash crop—tobacco. (Courtesy FJ/WSHA.)

Located in the West Salem part of the original c. 1766 Salem town lot, the home pictured in this 1960 photograph was dismantled, to be used in reconstruction work for the 1950s Old Salem Village. The home was one of several in the area dating from the mid- to late 18th century, originally known as part of the c. 1740s Langenauer Settlement. (Courtesy FJ/WSHA.)

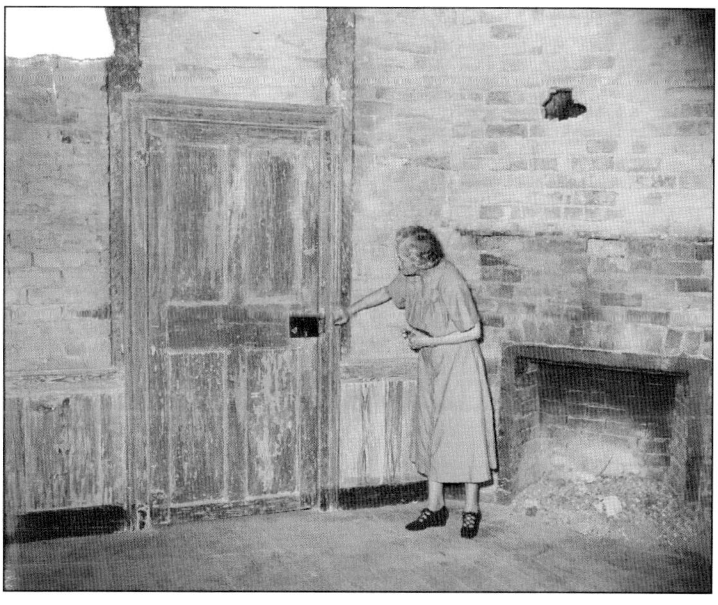

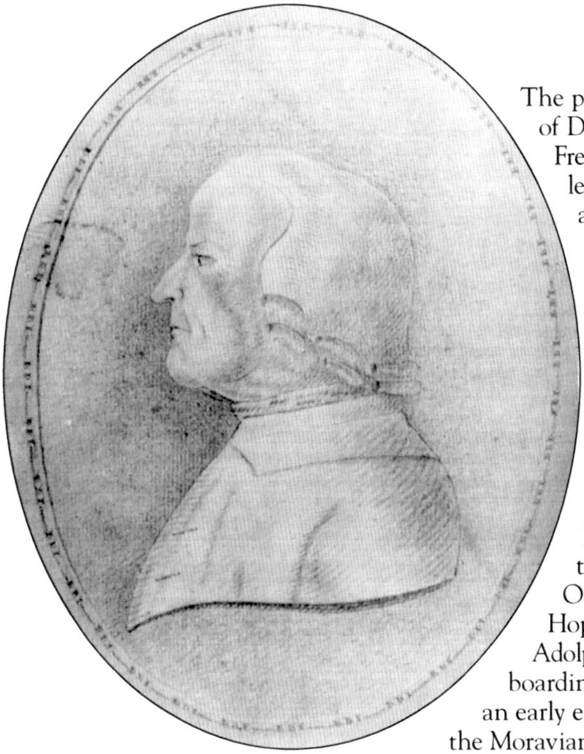

The planning of Salem as the central town of Dobbs Parish began with the arrival of Fredrick William Marshall in 1764 (shown at left in an 18th-century painting). Serving as the financial director and business administrator of the Moravian Church, Brother Marshall oversaw the building of Salem. In 1773, Dobbs Parish was threatened with division, and Brother Marshall delivered a petition to the General Assembly of North Carolina. It stated, "To do their upmost that Wachovia remain one Parish, and belongs to one count." He succeeded, and Dobbs Parish continued intact. His words established the surrounding towns of Dobbs Parish, Bethabara, Old Town, Friedberg, Friedland, and Hope. The photograph below shows Emil Adolphis De Schweinitz, the head of the girls' boarding school Salem Female Academy and an early educator in Dobbs Parish. (Courtesy to the Moravian Archives/WSHA.)

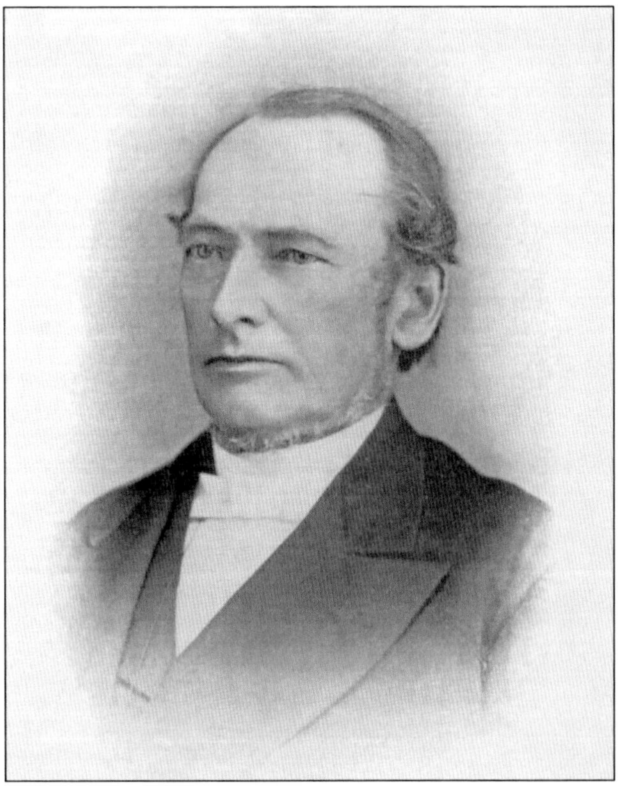

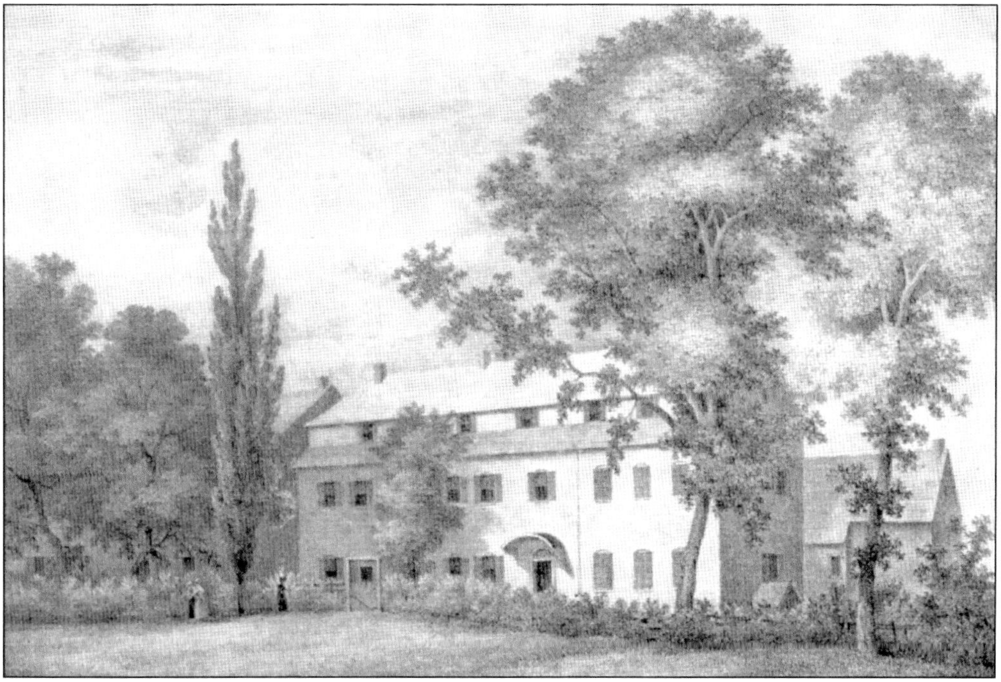

This 1840s lithograph shows the first building of the c. 1805 Salem Female Academy, designated the oldest practicing school for women in the United States. Through these academy doors passed some of the most influential and gifted women in the county. Their presence has been felt in government, business, the arts, and beyond. (Courtesy Moravian Archives/WSHA.)

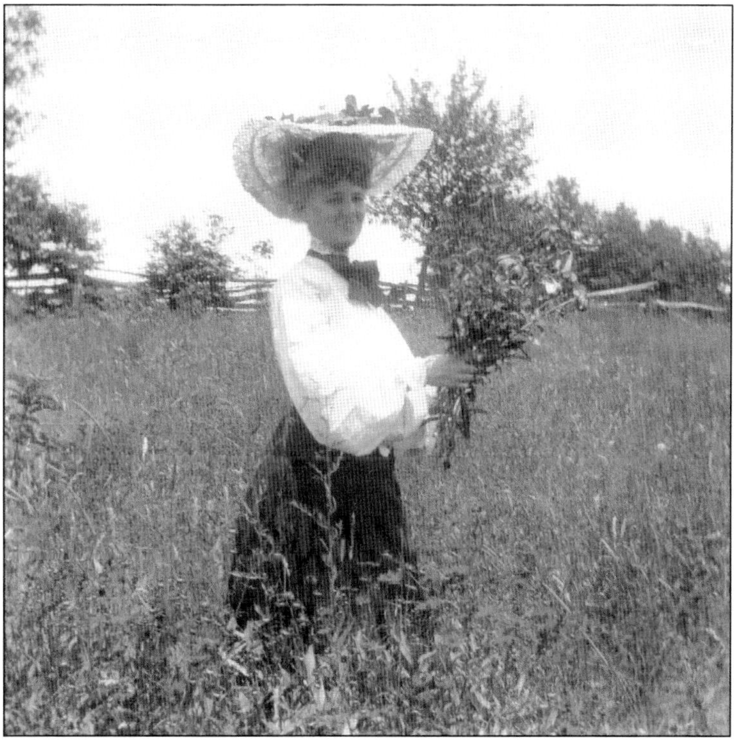

Students of Salem Female Academy and College hailed from Dobbs Parish, Forsyth County, and across the nation. Cherokee girls also attended. During the Civil War, Southern families sent girls to the institution believing it was a safer environment. A young lady picks flowers in a field in this c. 1890s photograph. Early classes at the academy included writing, syntax, history, geography, drawing, and needlework. (Courtesy FJ/WSHA.)

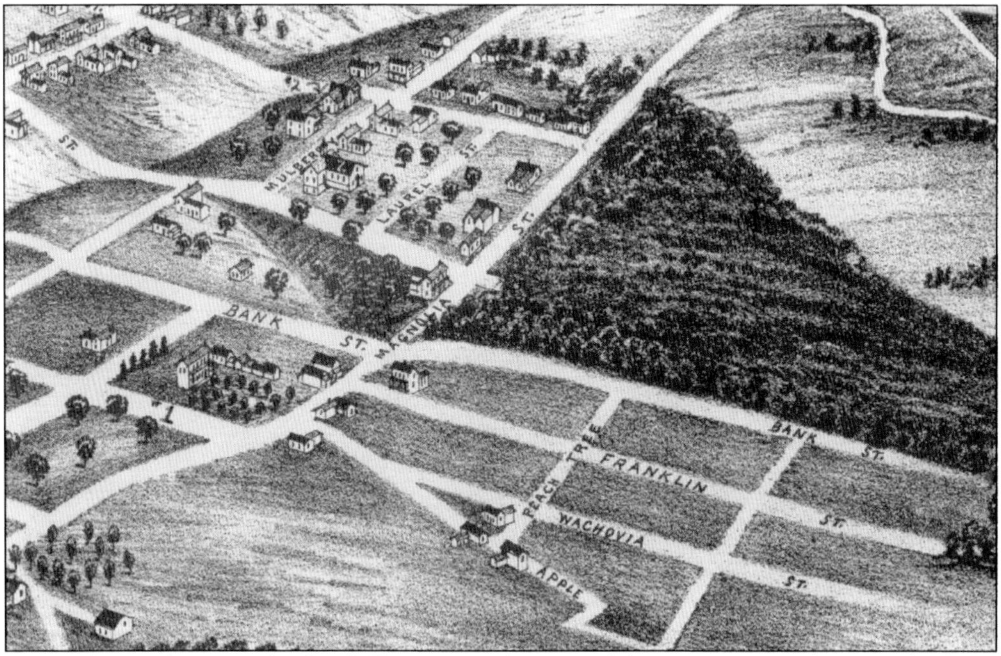

West Salem is shown in this Bird's Eye Map to the west of the congregational town. The farms and industries of West Salem completed the town lot of Salem. East Salem and West Salem were the central parts of Salem about 1766 during the rise of Dobb's Parish. Broad, Bank, and Magnolia Streets were home to West Salem's largest plantation, the Kreuser-Levering-Brietz homeplace, built about 1818. (Courtesy Bird Eyes Map/WSHA.)

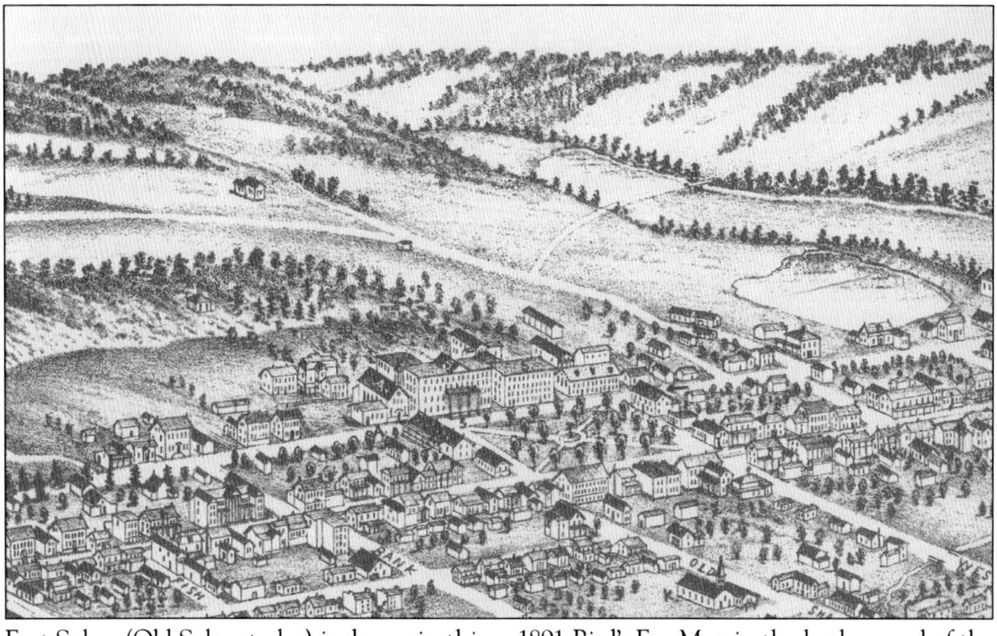

East Salem (Old Salem today) is shown in this c. 1891 Bird's Eye Map in the background of the central town of Forsyth, Winston. The congregational town, its craftsmen, and their workshops were located here. Home Moravian Church (A) and Salem College and Academy (no. 5 and no. 6) are pictured on Main Street. (Courtesy Bird's Eye Map/WSHA.)

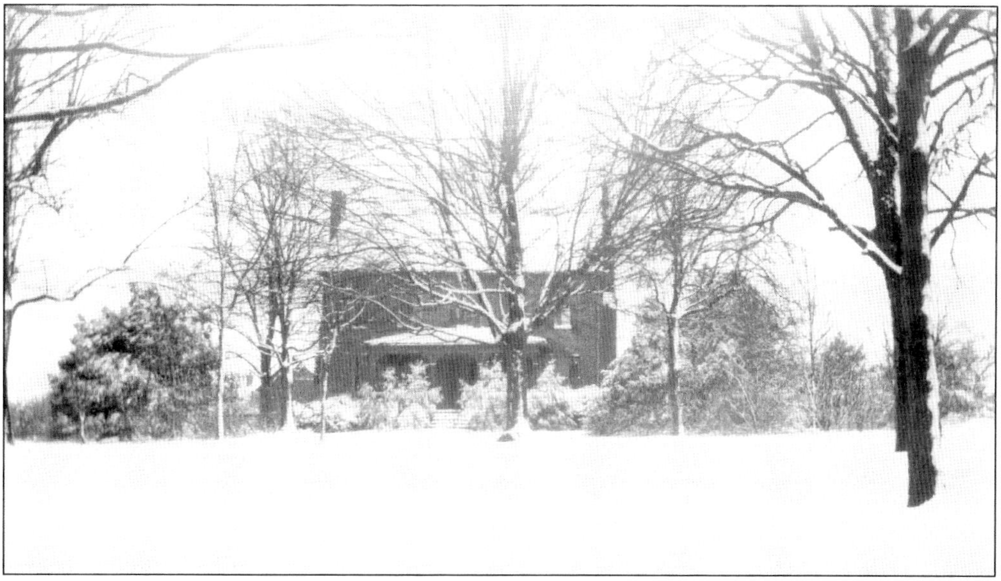

The Kreuser-Levering-Brietz homeplace is shown in the 1960s photograph above. In 1820, Brother Steiner from the Home Moravian Church held a meeting for the outlying families of the area; he also ministered to the African Americans in the community that year. An African American church and school was planned for construction. St. Phillips Church was built on Church Street below Home Moravians. In 1840, black freedmen met to discuss an African American school to be built near the brick farmhouse of the Brietz Farm. The parcel in today's landscape was located at the intersection of Broad and Bank Streets. The freedmens' offer was turned down, and later, the school was built in the area known today as Happy Hill. The Red Tannery (below) was worked by whites and blacks in West Salem as well. (Courtesy WSHA.)

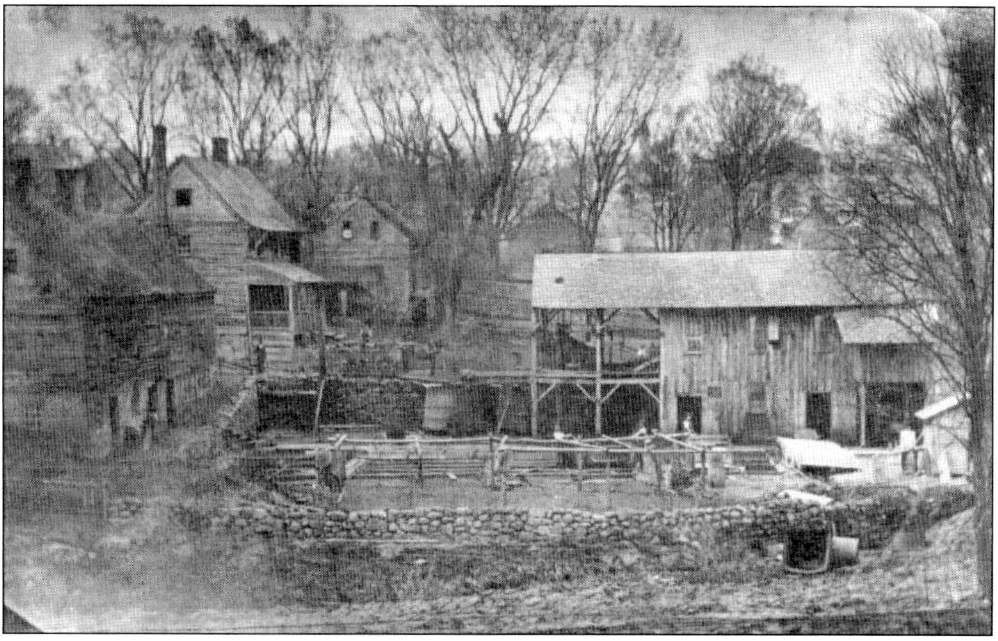

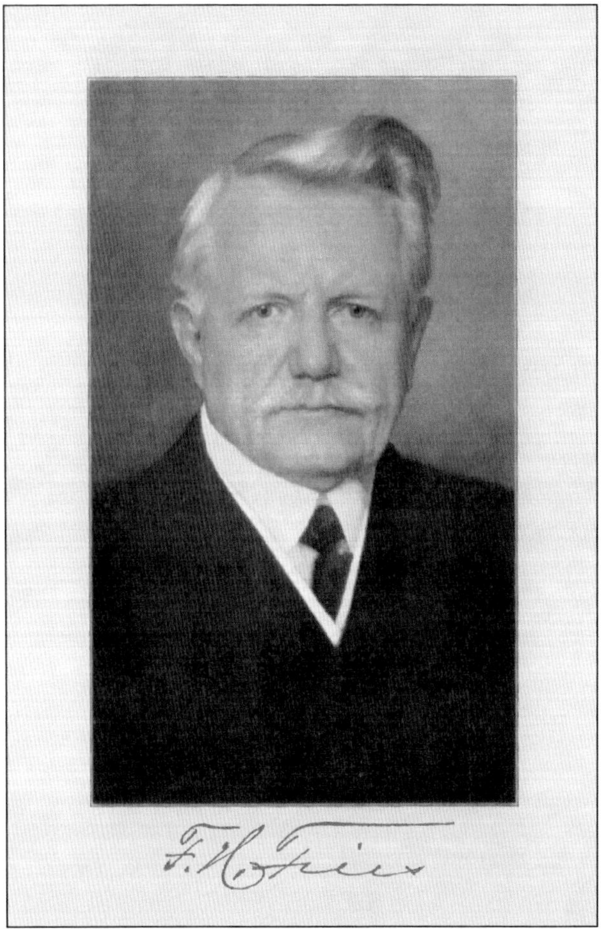

The Fries family was instrumental in providing leadership and employment in Forsyth County. With Col. Henry E. Fries at the helm, the family created mill, bank, financial, and railroad interests. (Courtesy WSHA.)

The Colonel Fries residences on New Shallowford Road (Brookstown Avenue), Salt Street, and Liberty Street were home to many meetings that decided the fate and future of Salem during the late 19th and early 20th centuries. (Courtesy WSHA.)

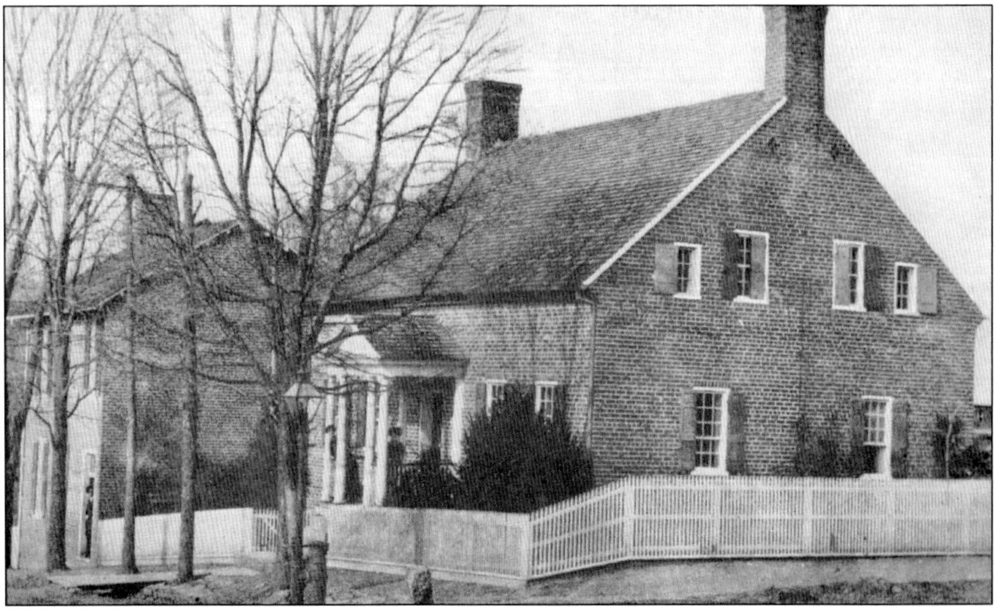

This 1849 map shows Winston comprised of only a couple of streets. Fast forward 30 years, and it encompasses an area larger than its mother city, Salem. Clemmons, located in southwest Forsyth County, is another example of growth. It began as a settlement by William Johnson Welshman about 1757. Edwins Clemmons started a stagecoach line there in 1840, and by the time the Village of Clemmons incorporated in 1986, it had over 1,600 residents. (Courtesy WSHA.)

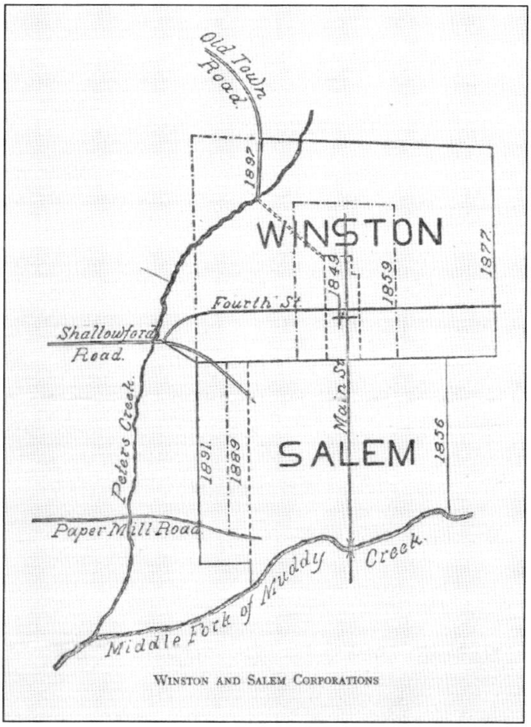

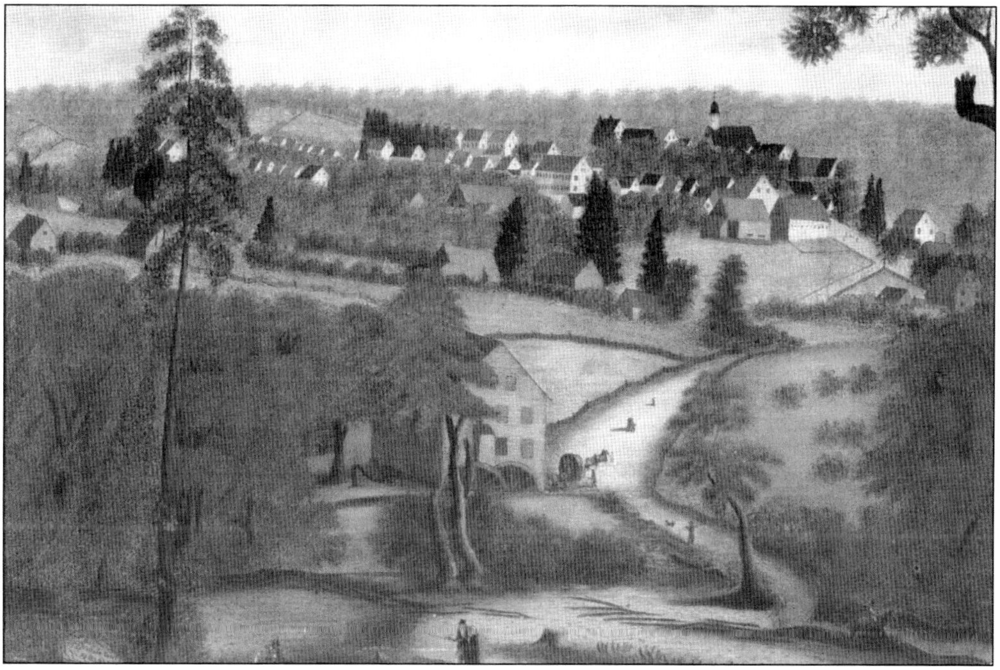

One of the first mills in the area was the c. 1750s Langenauer Mill in West Salem on Salem Creek. In 1820, the mill was replaced by the Salem Flour Mill (pictured as it appeared around 1820), located in West Salem near Salem Avenue and Broad Street at Salem Creek. The mill owner bought grain and manufactured flour for sale to the public. For 81 years, the mill was considered one of the most successful ventures in the town of Salem. (Courtesy WSHA.)

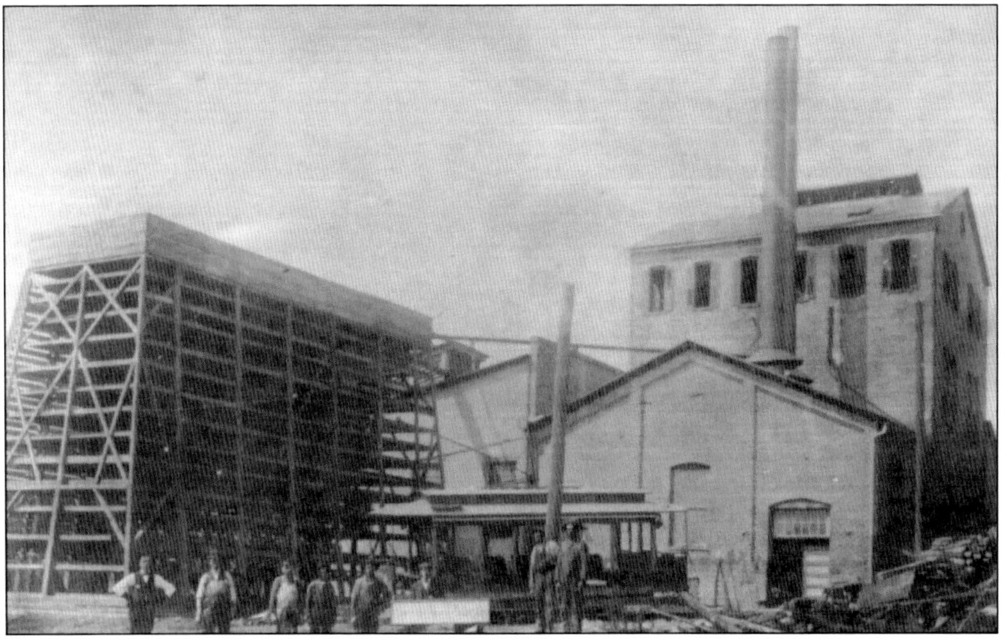

In 1830, a controversial opportunity was brought to Dobbs Parish. Textile mills were profitable in the Northern states, bringing in a return of 15 to 20 percent on their investments. At that time, the Moravian craftsmen's trades had taken a downturn in profit. The Moravians began the first textile mill of Salem about 1830. Hiring workers from surrounding Forsyth and Guilford Counties, against tradition, the future domination of the textile industry in Winston-Salem and Forsyth Counties had begun. The Fries complex in Salem, pictured above in the 1890s on Brookstown Avenue, was one such textile giant. This complex had its own electric power plant—the first in the South. The photograph below of artillery training in Hawaii shows that Forsyth County citizens fought heavily in World War I and World War II. (Courtesy Tommie Howell/Bricker collection.)

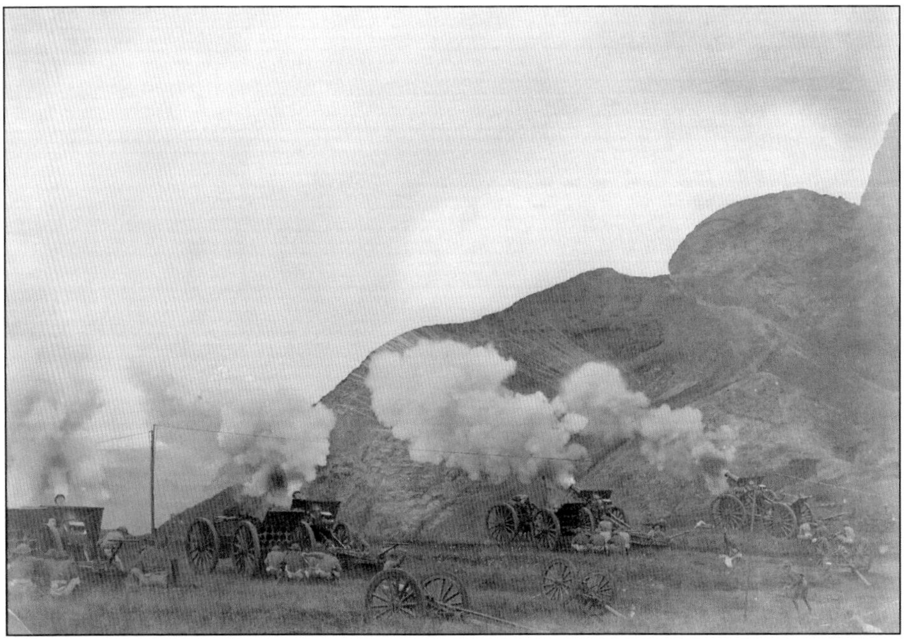

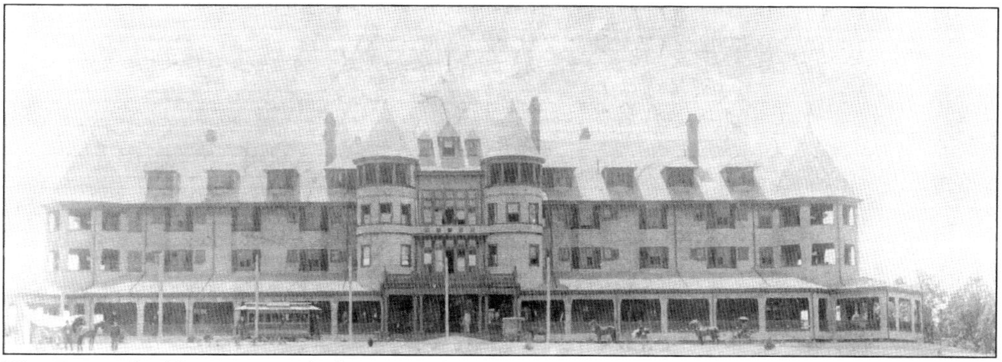

The Zinzendorf Resort Hotel, shown in this c. 1892 photograph, was another venture by the industrialist of Forsyth County, William Fries. "A playground of the rich and powerful," the hotel was located in northwest West Salem, outside the town limits of Winston. The land had been the farm and plantation of the Fries family patriarch, William Fries, about 1800. The resort hotel, with an abundance of land for hunting and camping, was to become the premier resort of piedmont North Carolina. (Courtesy FJ/WSHA.)

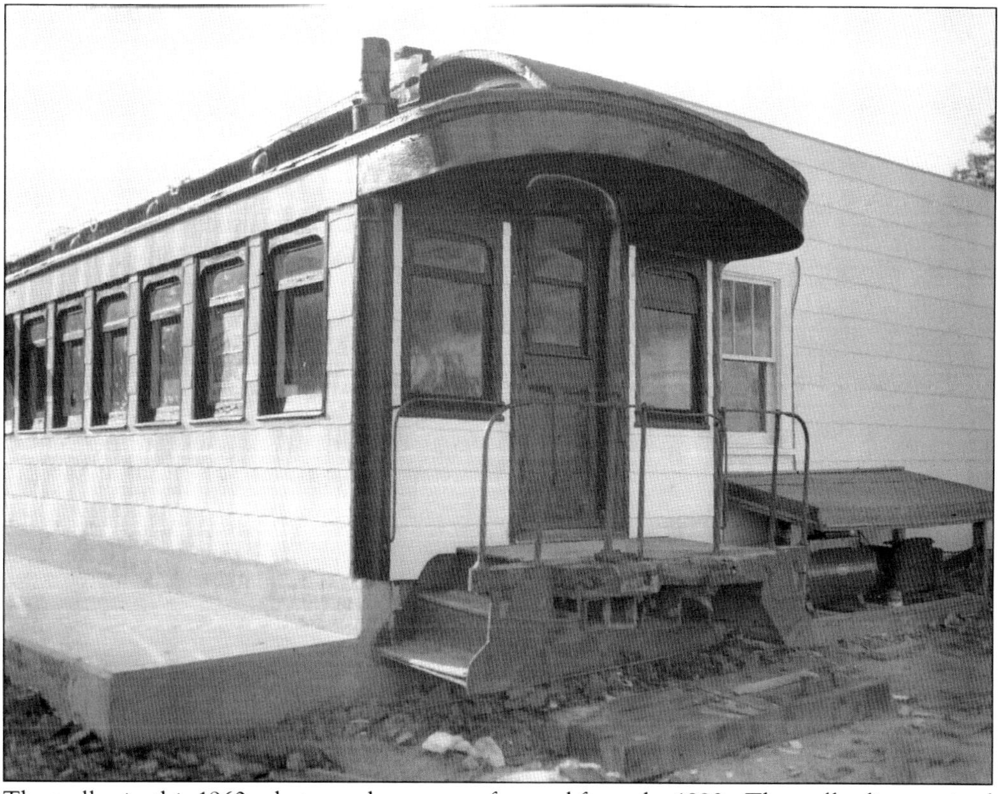

The trolley in this 1960s photograph was one of several from the 1890s. The trolley lines arrived to Forsyth County with big fanfare from the likes of Thomas Edison and Frank Sprague, who founded the trolley lines of Winston and Salem. This streetcar was the last in Winston-Salem and was converted into a restaurant called Ollie's Trolley. (Courtesy FJ/WSHA.)

The story of Forsyth County would not be complete without showcasing "The Salem Teapot." It started out as an advertising gimmick to showcase the talents of two tinsmiths, brothers Julius and Samuel Mickey, but became an icon of Southern culture. (Courtesy FJ/WSHA.)

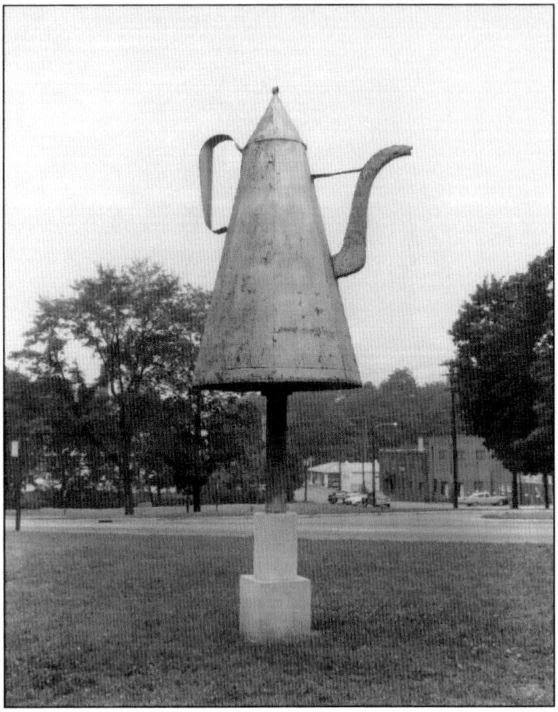

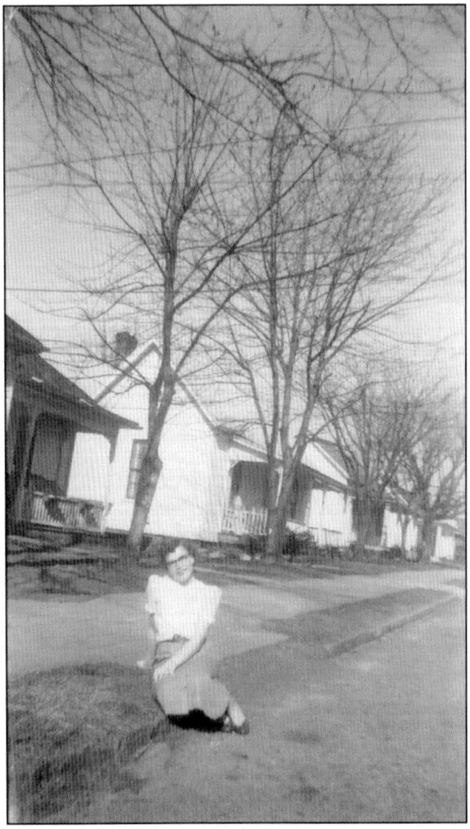

The tinsmith trade has been practiced for as long as Dobbs Parish and Forsyth County have existed, and many apprentices have trained in Salem. Nearly all the houses in this photograph were built by Salem tinners. Samuel Mickey, builder of the Salem Teapot and veteran of the Civil War, helped train them. In Mickey's later years, he moved to Old West Salem and resided on Mulberry Street. The woman pictured is Franklin Street resident LaNelle Hunter Church. (Courtesy LaNelle Hunter Church.)

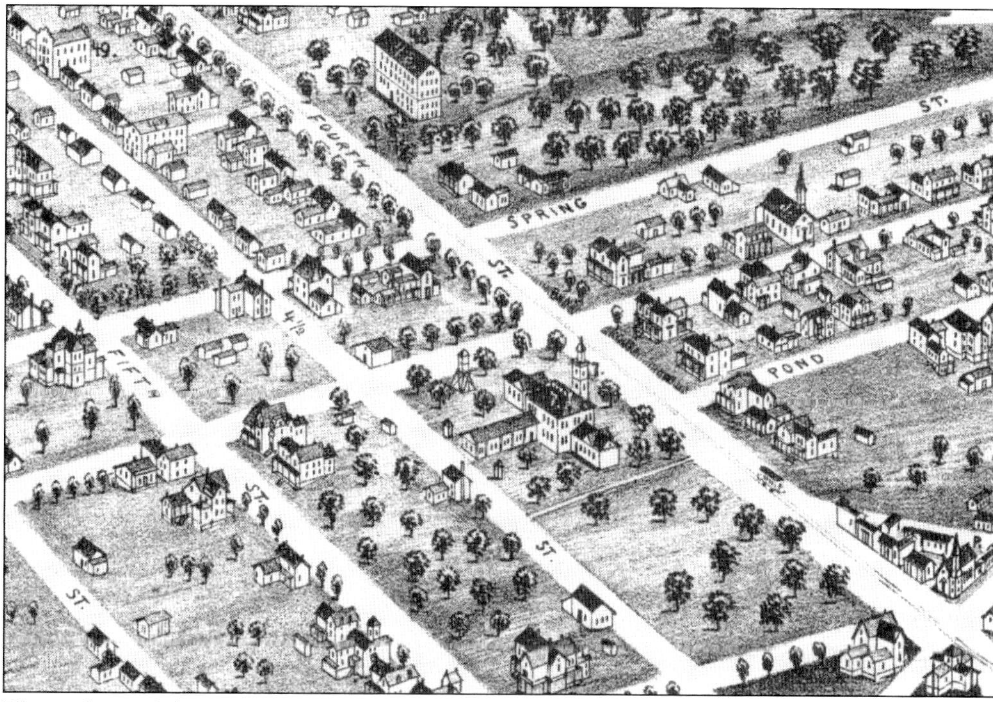

The making of the county continued with the involvement of church and state. This Bird's Eye Map shows two examples: Winston Graded School (West End School) on Fourth Street and the first Baptist church in town, The Primitive Baptist Church on Broad Street. All locations were in the original West End neighborhood. (Courtesy Bird's Eye Map/WSHA.)

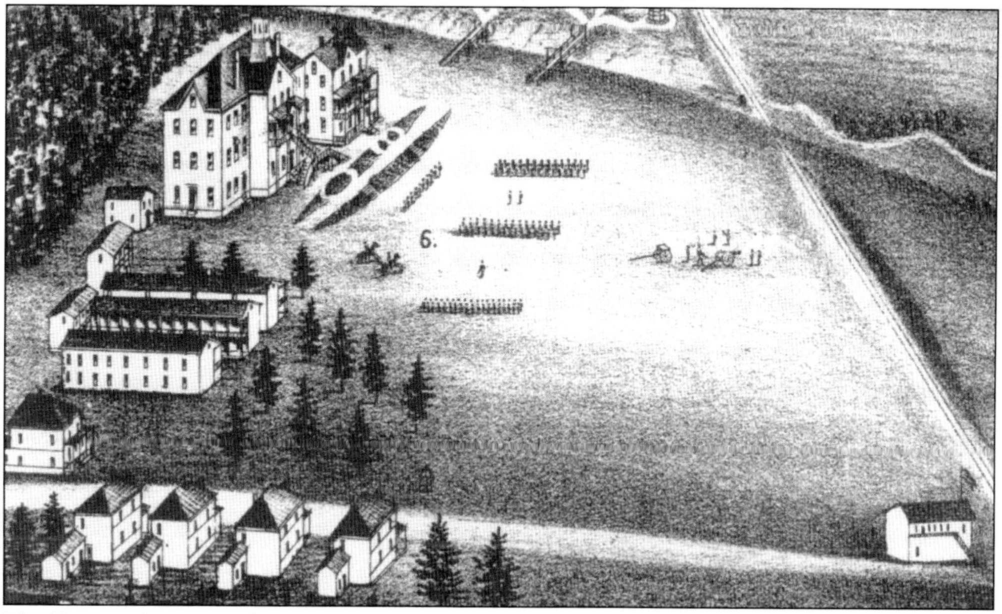

The Davis Military Academy is shown in another Bird's Eye Map of the county. Located in the Old Mulberry Society District (which was formed in the 1830s), a division of the Methodist Church, Old Jerusalem Church, and the Children's Home reside here today. The academy was brand new when this map was produced. (Courtesy Bird's Eye Map/WSHA.)

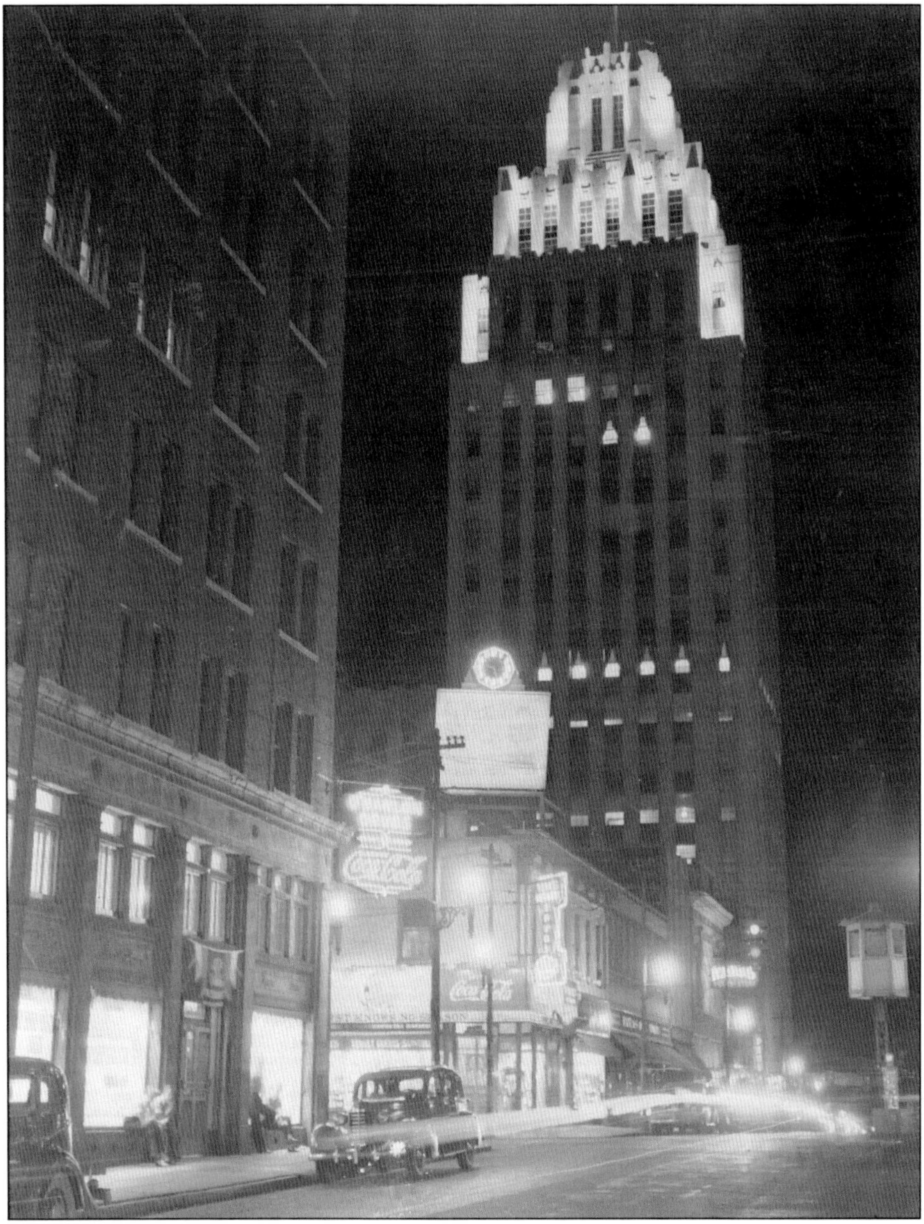

By the 1920s, the central town of Dobbs Parish (Forsyth County) was not called Salem anymore, but rather Winston-Salem, since 1913. The making of a county was almost complete with the rise of power of the Richard J. Reynolds Tobacco Company, pictured here in the 1940s. Without the early tobacco and textile pioneers, none of this success would have been possible. Industrialists like Nat D. Sullivan began the manufacture of tobacco products in 1850. He started out in a log building in Sullivantown, two miles from Walkertown. James Ogburn became one of the first tobacco farmers in North Carolina. Ogburn Station, located north of Winston, is named for him. Ogburn's son Charles would work as a salesman for Nat D. Sullivan. In 1873, W.H. "Bill" Leak began W.H. Leak and Company Plug and Twist Tobacco in Kernersville. The Reynolds Building has towered over Forsyth County since the 1920s. It may soon have a new incarnation as a luxury hotel. (Courtesy FJ/WSHA.)

Across Forsyth County, business and industry, like Reynolds Tobacco and Hanes Hosiery, pictured in Salem in the 1930s, helped create the towns we know today. The surrounding towns and hamlets had their own creators. In Kernersville, in about 1756, Irishman Caleb Story bought 400 acres 12 miles east of Salem. In 1754, Adam Spach started the Friedberg community three miles south of the Wachovia Tract. (Courtesy FJ/WSHA.)

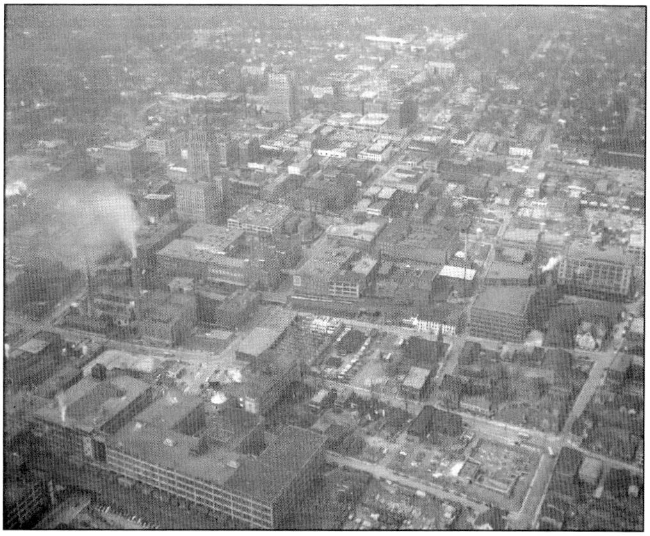

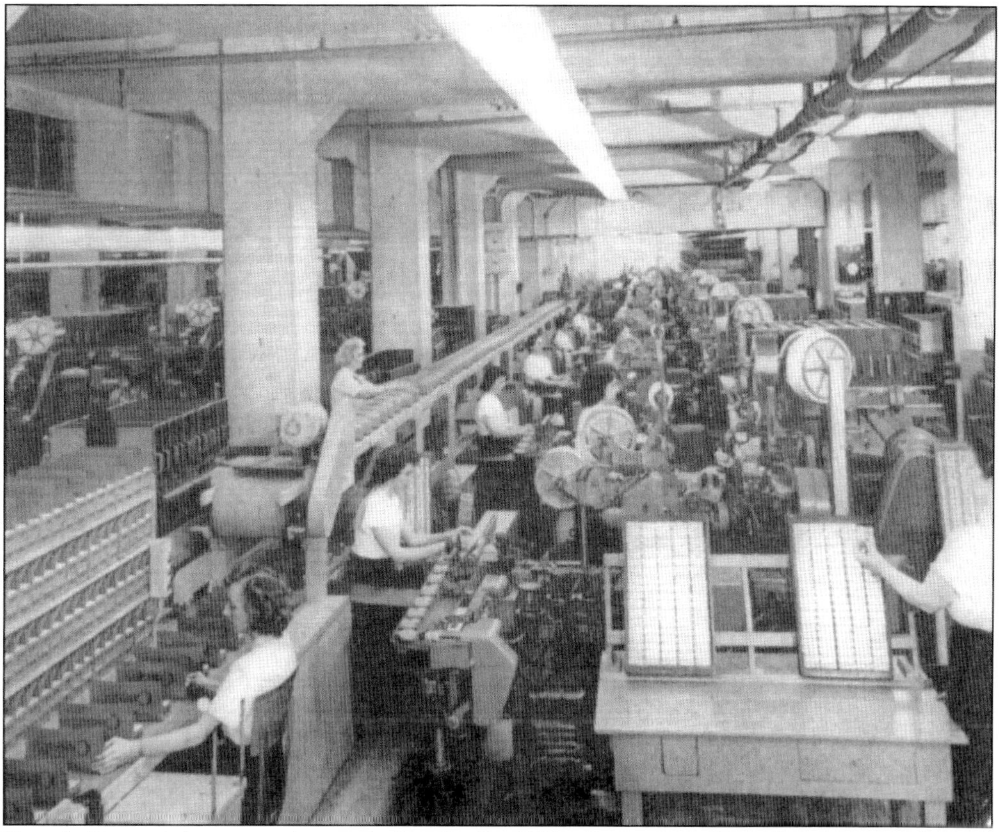

Forsyth County's businesses boomed after the Civil War. Factories and warehouses were relocated from surrounding communities to Winston. Tobacco pioneers arrived here, including Sullivan Factory (Walkertown), T.F. Leak (Kernersville), S.A. Ogburn (Ogburn Station), and Mr. Bitting (Rural Hall). Women, however, became the backbone of cigarette processing. In the early 1900s, the "Baby Line" brought young ladies from rural Forsyth County to work, and helped make R.J.R Tobacco king. (Courtesy M. Bricker.)

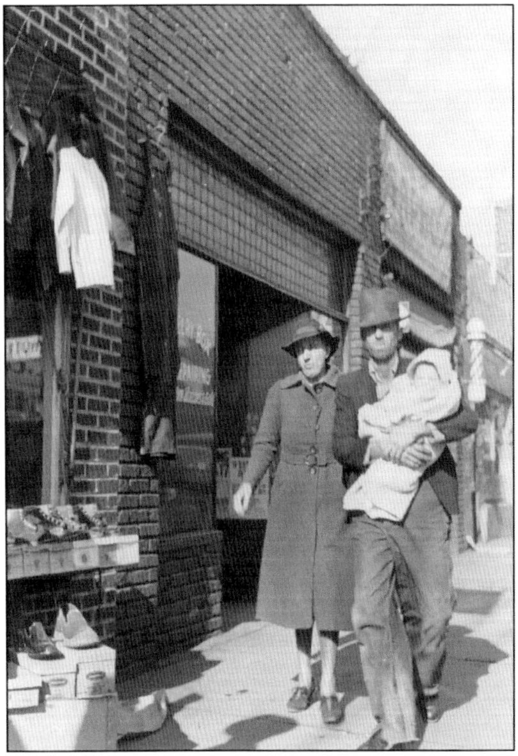

The Great Depression affected Forsyth County. The hustle and bustle of Trade Street, where most Forsyth County tobacco farmers brought their wares to sell since the 1880s, began to dwindle for the merchants and retail establishments in the 1930s. This 1930s photograph speaks for most of the residents of the county, illustrating a quote of the time: "Brother, can you spare a dime?" Below, the Great Depression, World War II, and the Korean War may have been behind them, but the county residents in this c. 1960 photograph still knew very well the meaning of the expression "hard times." Isolation and poverty had slowly crept into the county throughout the booming 1950s. "Urban renewal," the federal government's attempt to clean up slums and downtrodden areas, arrived in 1968, none too soon for this Forsyth family. (Courtesy FJ/WSHA.)

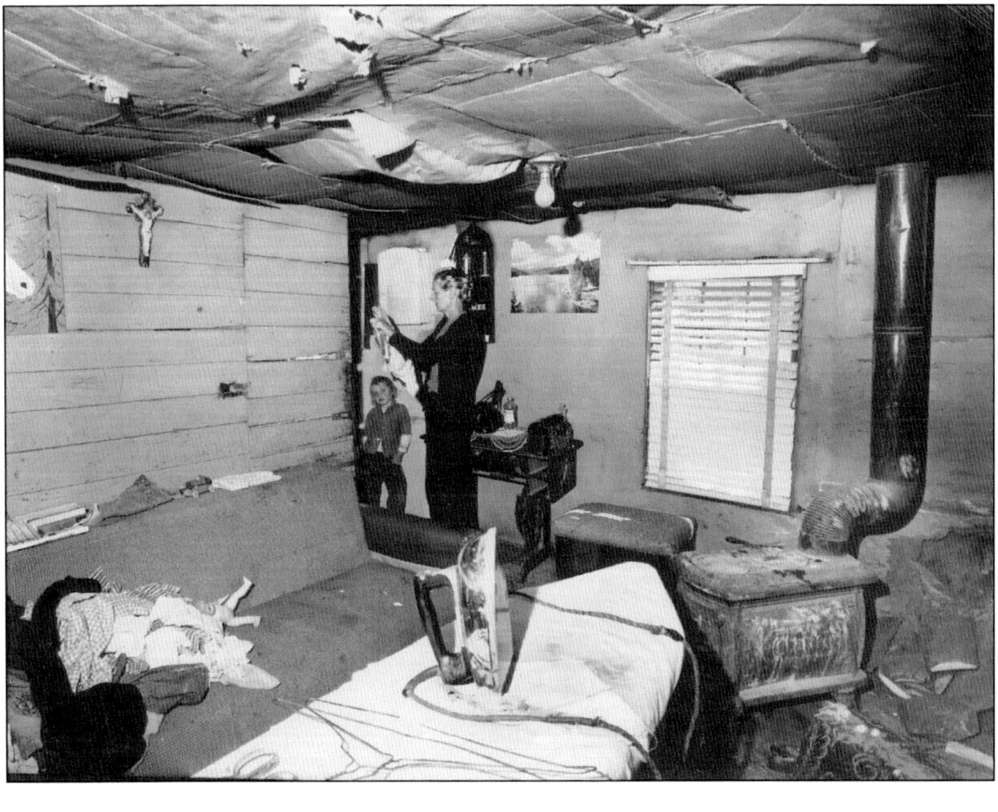

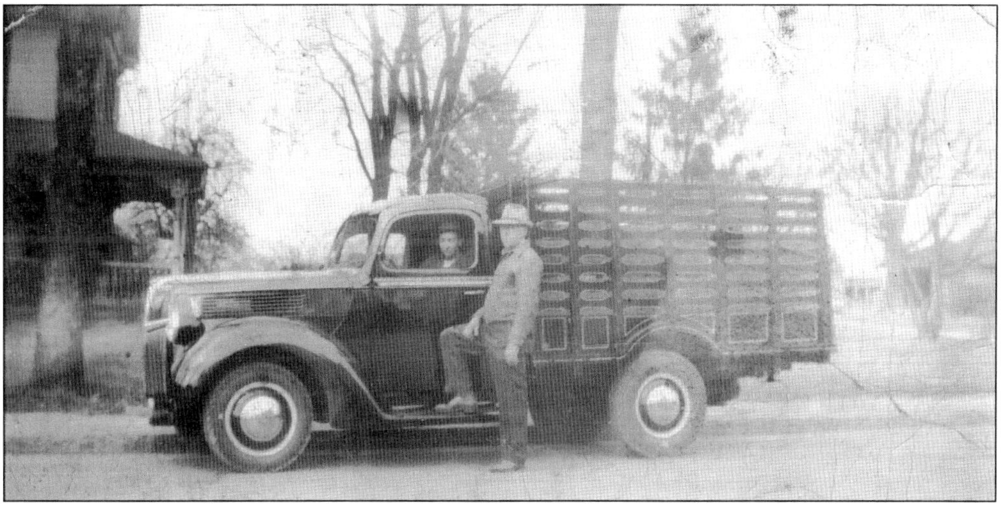

The tobacco and textile empire's backbone proved to be its merchants and workers. The Joyce Grocery Store in West Salem was led by Mr. Joyce (standing). The driver, Mr. Gruenant, was headed to his next delivery. Joyce often drove his Model T Ford around Forsyth County. Gruenant ran the West Salem Greenhouses in the 1880s. The Joyce residence was on Green Street at Academy Street in Winston Salem. (Courtesy WSHA.)

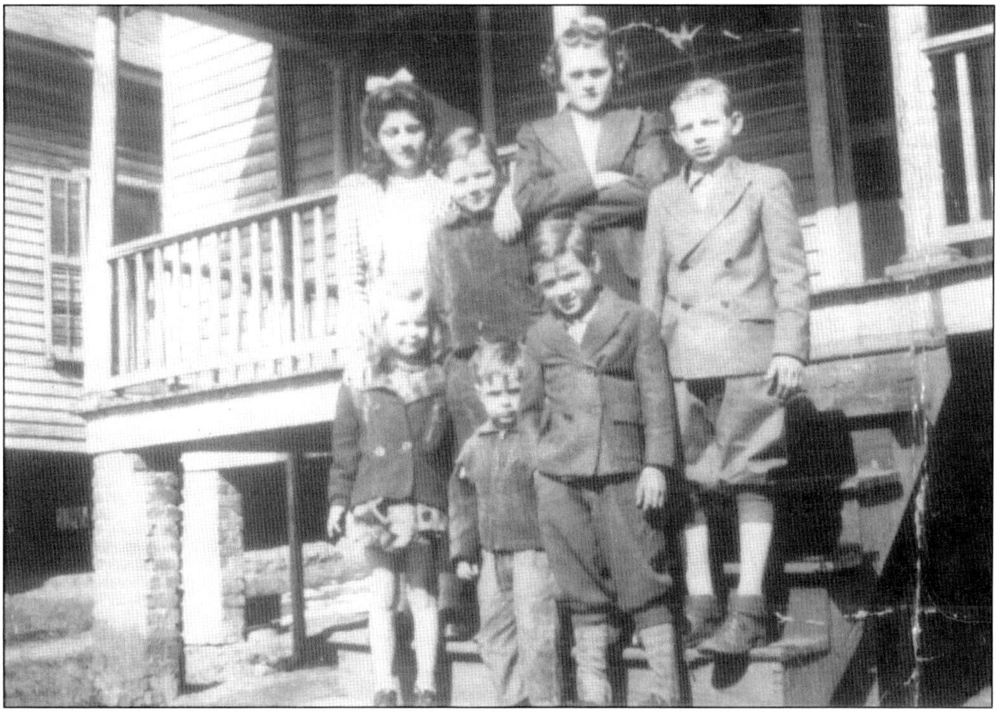

Reynolds Tobacco and Hanes Textiles became the principal employers of Forsyth County throughout most of the 20th century. Pictured here are Thomas and Lily Howell. The family resided at 712 South Broad Street in West Salem. Thomas was a mechanic at Reynolds Tobacco. The boys were eventually employed as carpenters, merchants, truck drivers, and military men. They attended Salem Baptist Church. This was 20th-century Americana in Forsyth County. (Courtesy Tommie Howell Bricker.)

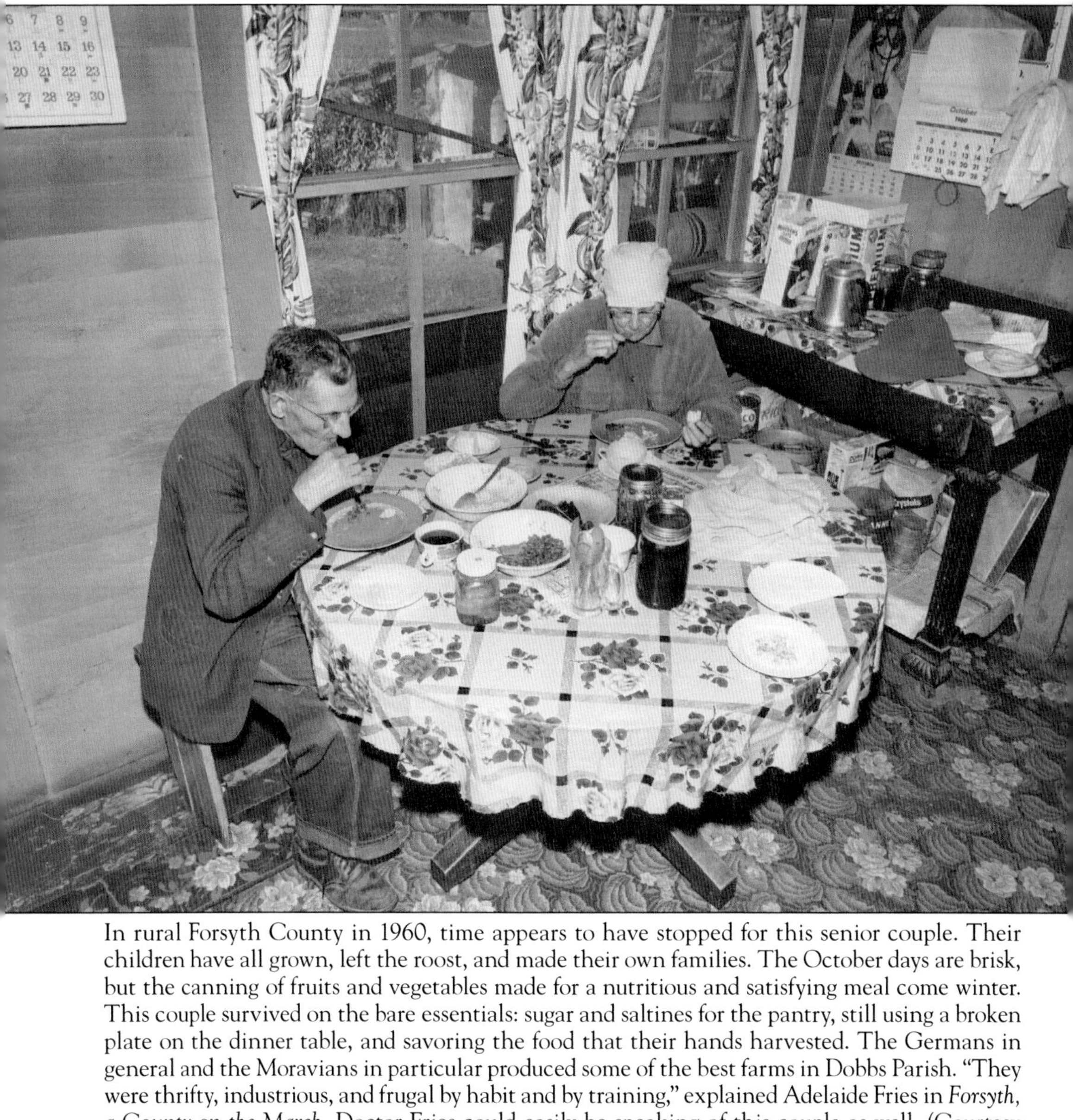

In rural Forsyth County in 1960, time appears to have stopped for this senior couple. Their children have all grown, left the roost, and made their own families. The October days are brisk, but the canning of fruits and vegetables made for a nutritious and satisfying meal come winter. This couple survived on the bare essentials: sugar and saltines for the pantry, still using a broken plate on the dinner table, and savoring the food that their hands harvested. The Germans in general and the Moravians in particular produced some of the best farms in Dobbs Parish. "They were thrifty, industrious, and frugal by habit and by training," explained Adelaide Fries in *Forsyth, a County on the March*. Doctor Fries could easily be speaking of this couple as well. (Courtesy FJ/WSHA.)

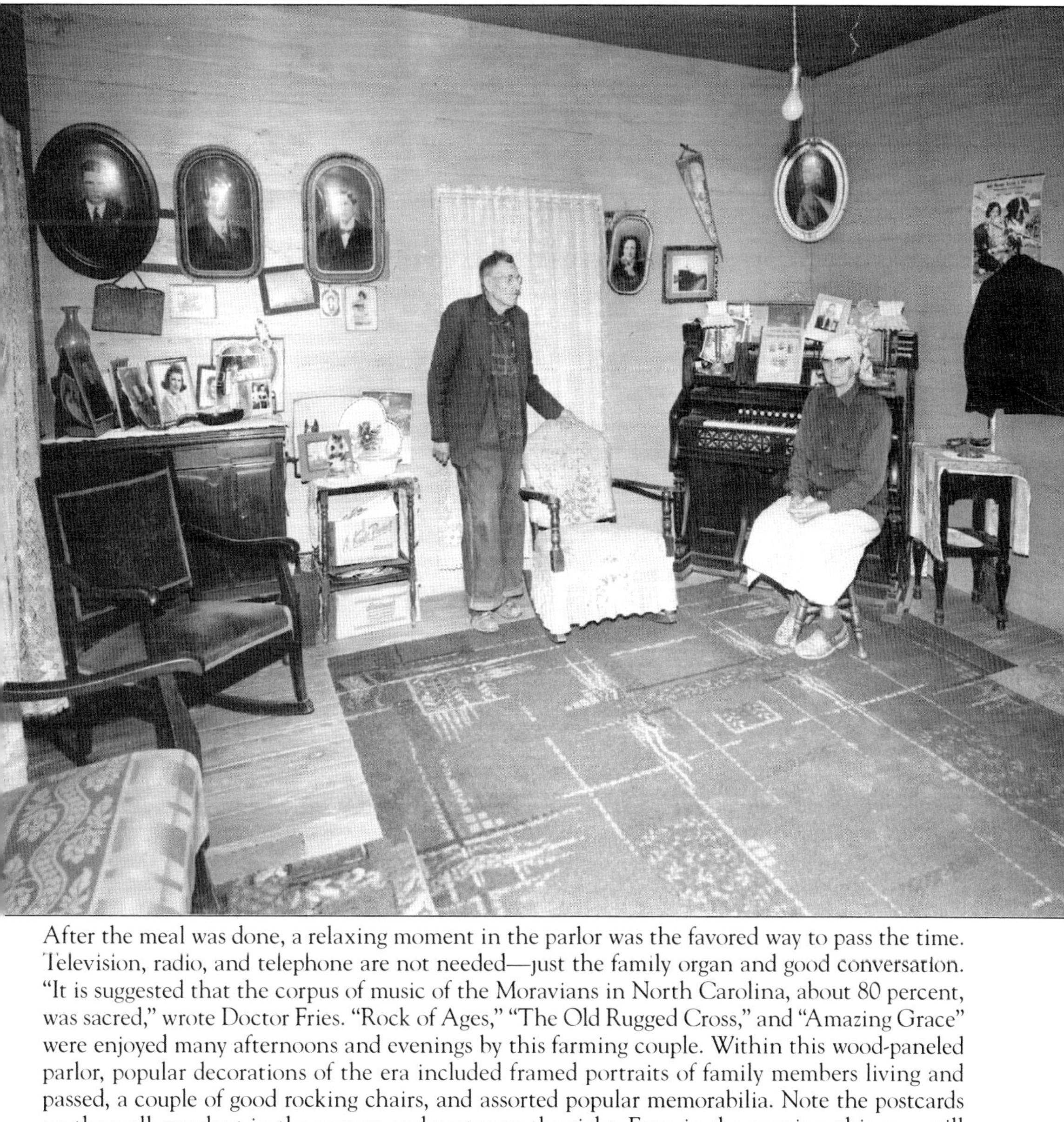

After the meal was done, a relaxing moment in the parlor was the favored way to pass the time. Television, radio, and telephone are not needed—just the family organ and good conversation. "It is suggested that the corpus of music of the Moravians in North Carolina, about 80 percent, was sacred," wrote Doctor Fries. "Rock of Ages," "The Old Rugged Cross," and "Amazing Grace" were enjoyed many afternoons and evenings by this farming couple. Within this wood-paneled parlor, popular decorations of the era included framed portraits of family members living and passed, a couple of good rocking chairs, and assorted popular memorabilia. Note the postcards on the wall, pendant in the corner, and poster on the right. Even in the evening, this man still wears his overalls, perhaps to do some evening chores after a short rest. (Courtesy WSHA.)

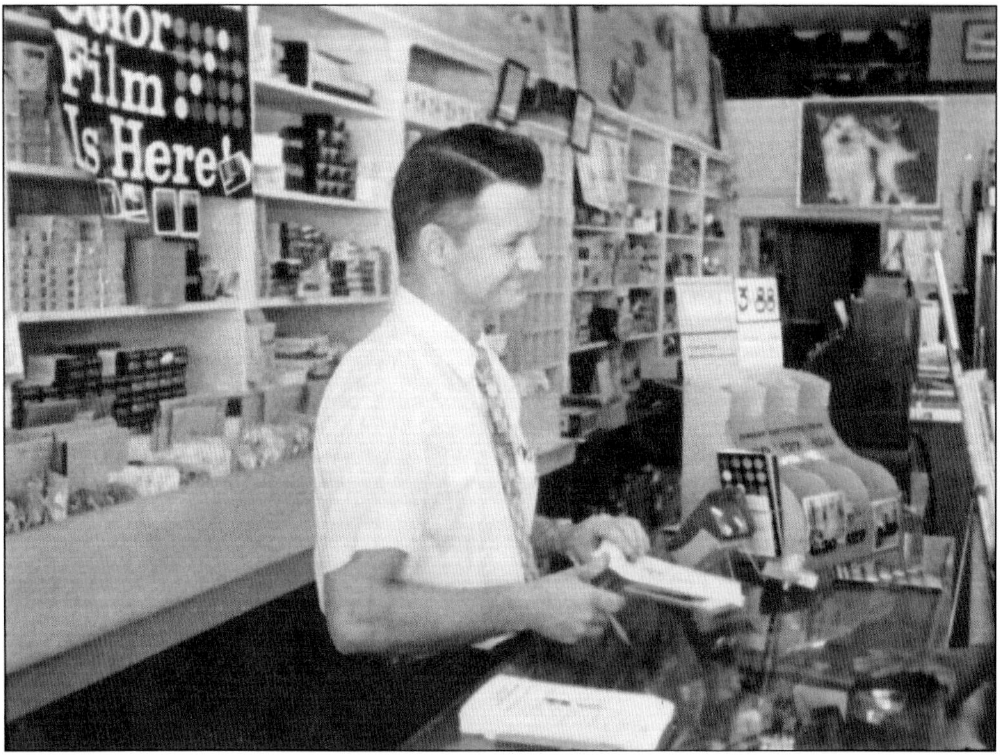

Photography began in Salem with the practice of Moravian Henry Linebach. As the first homegrown photographer of Forsyth, he is responsible for the oldest photographs in this book as well as most of the history books documenting the piedmont area. Mr. Lindley, pictured in the 1960s, ran a second-generation photography shop, Lindley Photograph Company, on Fifth Street across from the post office in Winston. (Courtesy FJ/WSHA.)

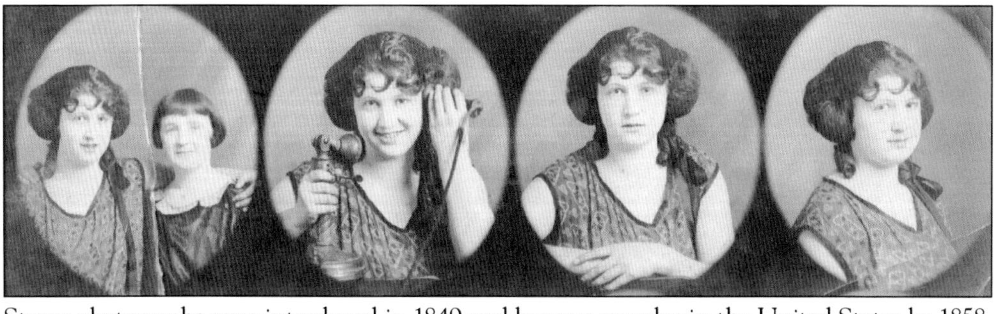

Stereo photographs were introduced in 1849 and became popular in the United States by 1858. Stereo photography was popular into the 20th century. Forsyth County resident Sarah Shoaf is pictured here. Sarah experienced photography at the 1893 Chicago Worlds Fair. (Courtesy Tommie Howell Bricker.)

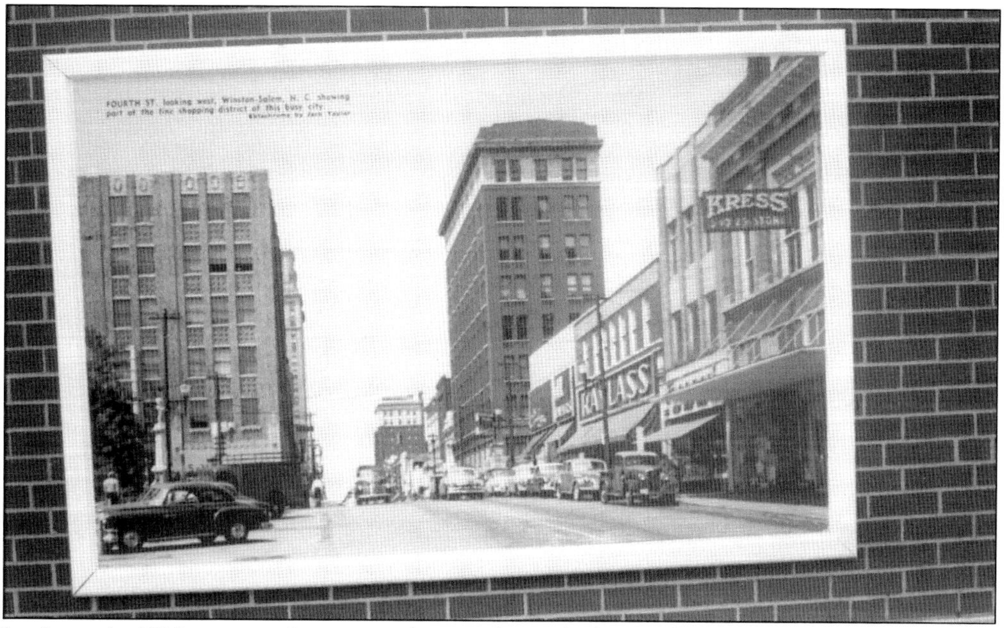

In the early 1900s, postcards were used more than telephones for communication. Shown is a rare photograph postcard of the downtown business area of Fourth Street in the central town of Winston. Unfortunately, the buildings on the right side up to the tall brick building were all lost to the wrecking ball. (Courtesy M. Bricker.)

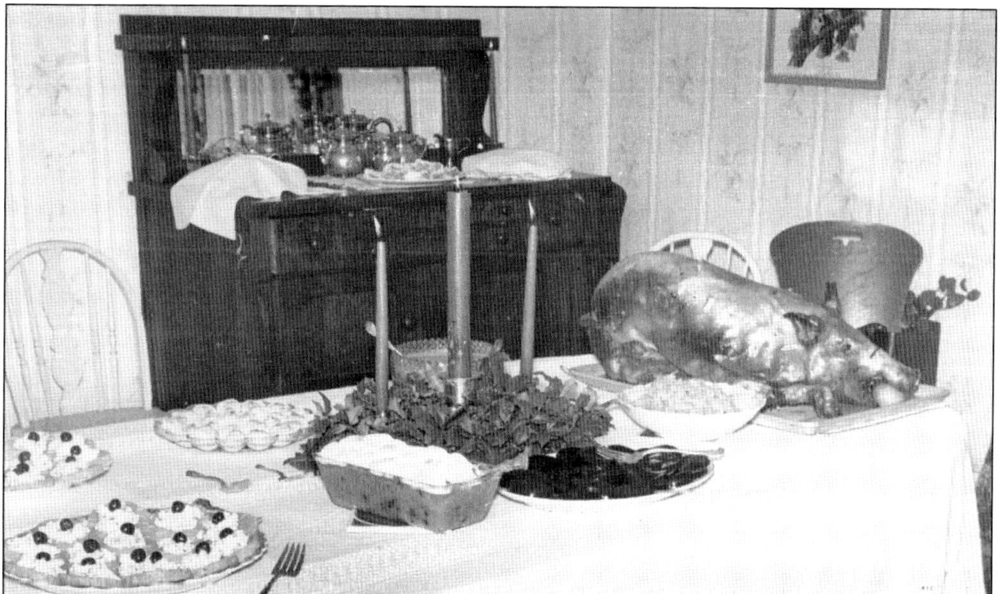

The Colonial days of Dobbs Parish were celebrated with banquets, reunions, weddings, and simple family get-togethers. The spacious complex of the 1786 Single Brothers House, with its spit, cook pots, and oversized oven, allowed the Moravians of Wachovia to feed more than 60 Single Brothers at a sitting. This festive table of goodies, pictured in the 1950s, would have made the Single Brothers proud. (Courtesy FJ/WSHA.)

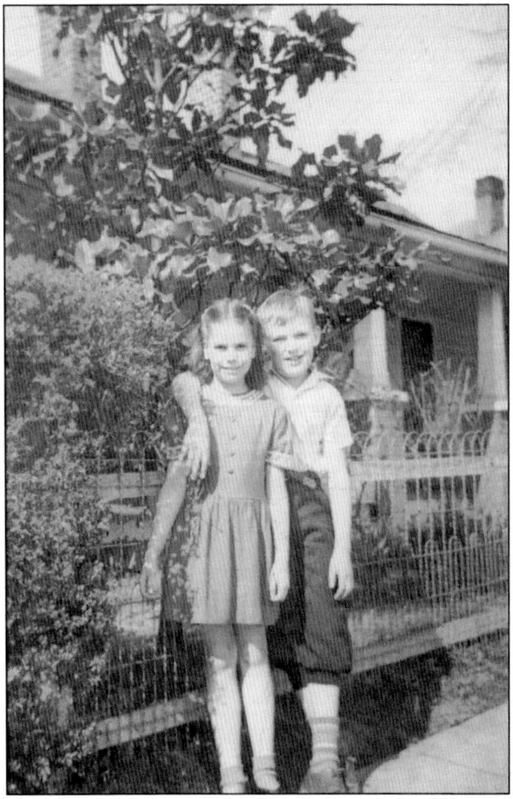

Children from Colonial times to the present show similar interests. The caption printed on these photographs reads, "Friends." The image at left shows the friends in front of a wire gate, with a young magnolia and porch in the background. They wear the fashions of the day—the girl in a lace-collared dress and the boy in knee-length knickers. The image below shows three brothers on Christmas Eve, all dressed in matching pajamas. These boys live a comfortable life, surrounded by simple yet classic window dressings, holiday window frosting, and Colonial Revival wallpaper. (Left, courtesy LaNelle Church; below, courtesy FJ/WSHA.)

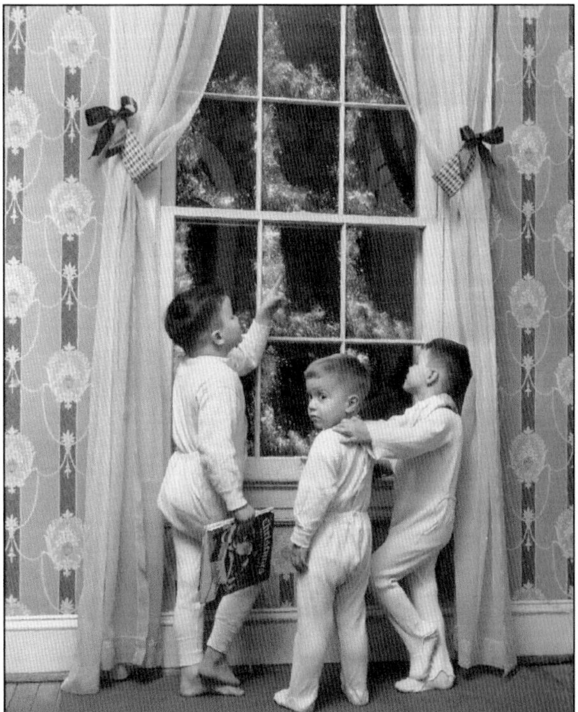

Three

Lost Towns and Neighborhoods

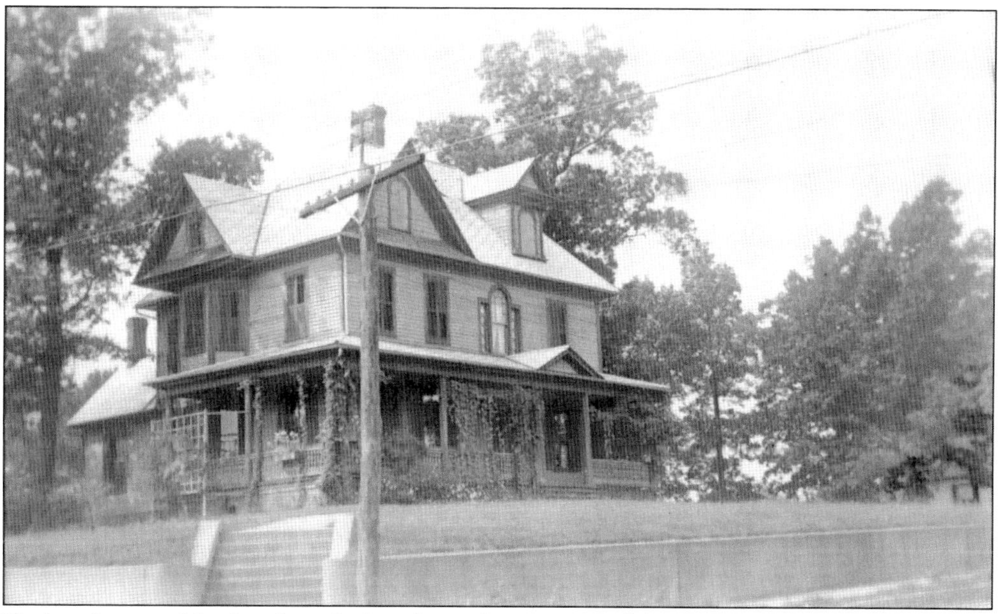

Finding lost neighborhoods and identifying them is crucial for preservation in rich historical areas. Such is the case with Old West Salem shown on this c. 1920 postcard. Christ Moravian Church has survived, but unfortunately, the pastor's residence has not. This is the case with many historical landmarks throughout the county. (Courtesy WSHA.)

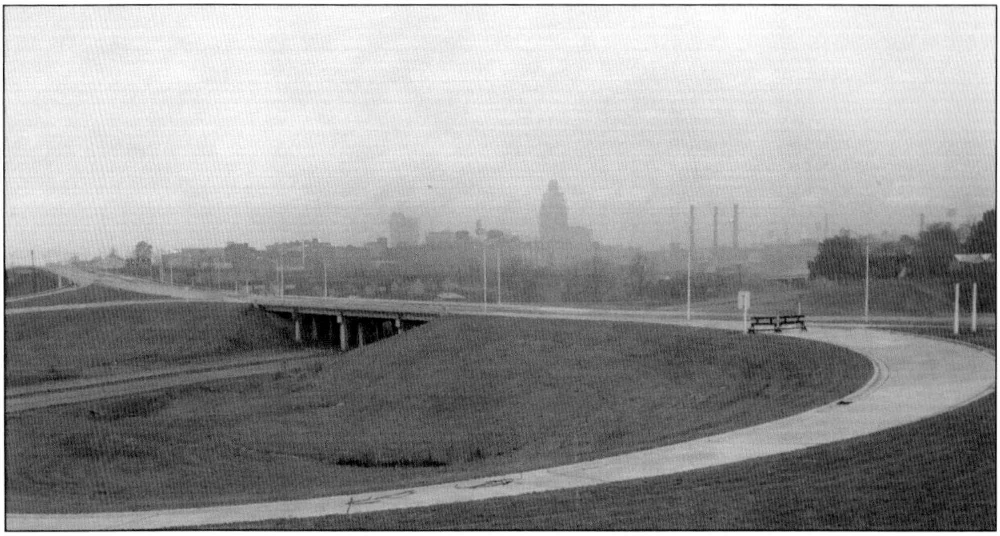

Many neighborhoods, including businesses and private residences, were either lost or relocated in preparation for Interstate 40. This c. 1960 photograph shows an extension of the roadway near the present intersection of Business 40 and Highway 52. The streets connecting Linden, East Third, and Belews Streets, between the central downtown city and East Winston, were divided and lost. (Courtesy FJ/WSHA.)

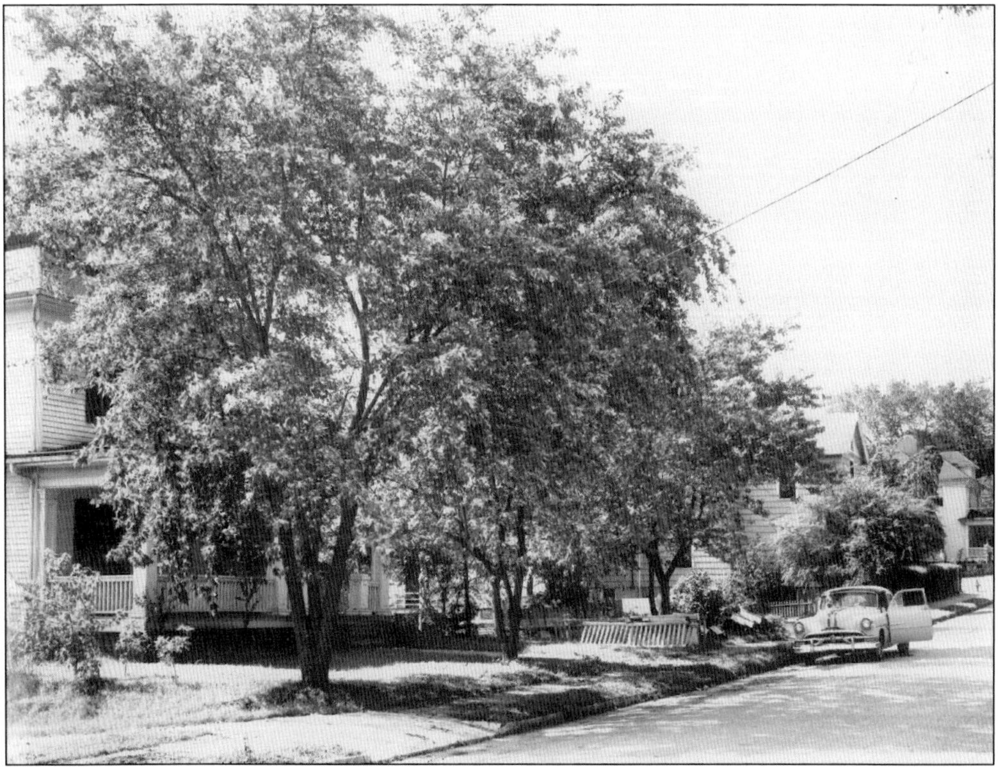

This c. 1950s photograph shows an area before it was destroyed by another expansion of Interstate 40. Located between Salem and Winston, Poplar Street connected First Street in Winston to High Street in Salem. (Courtesy WSHA.)

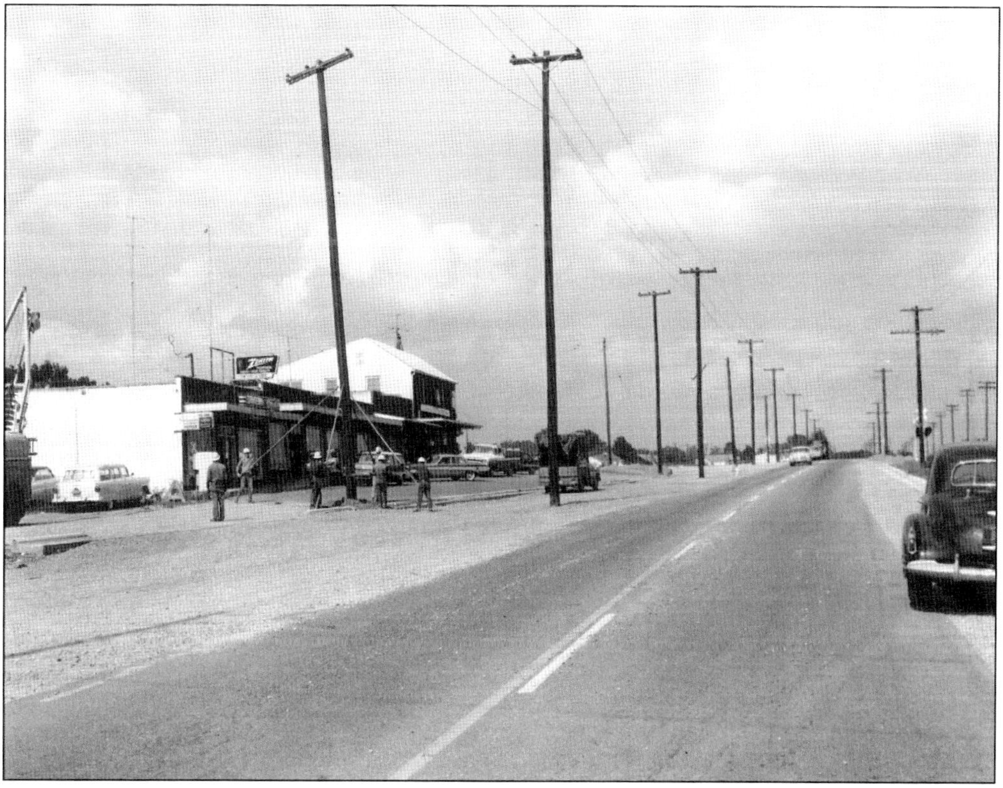

Rural Forsyth County was much larger when this c. 1960 photograph was taken along Highway 158 between Winston and Clemmons. Now called Stratford Road, it has been transformed from a very sparse and rural road into the major retail and business section of Winston-Salem. The downtown of Winston-Salem, the heart of business and retail of Forsyth County, has been replaced by Stratford Road, the new downtown. (Courtesy FJ/WSHA.)

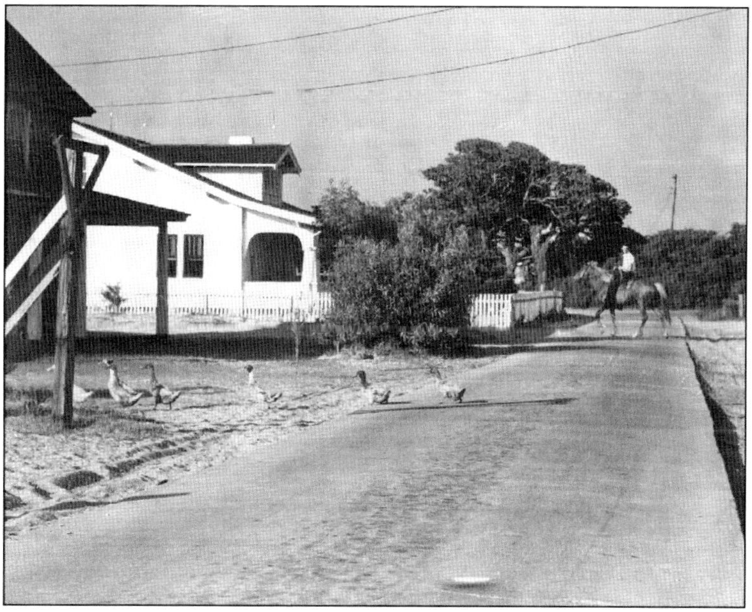

A simpler time is shown in this 1950s photograph of Rural Stratford Road between Winston and Clemmons. This two-lane road has been transformed into a four lane, 55-mile-per-hour racetrack between the two cities. (Courtesy FJ/WSHA.)

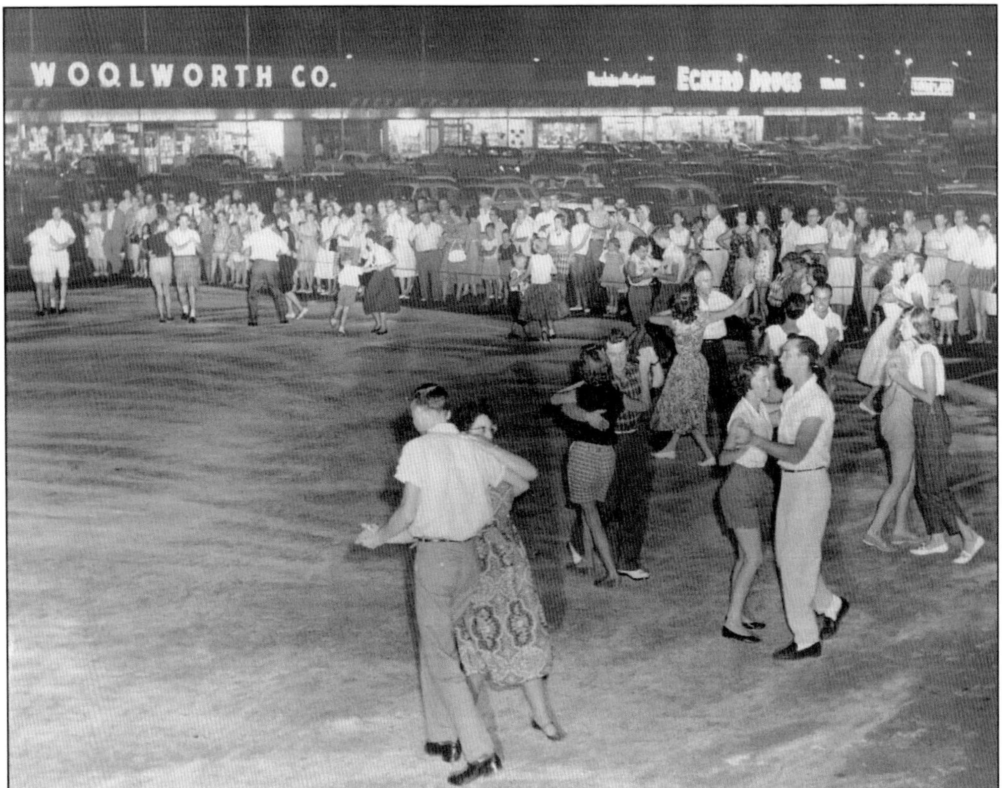

The original farm of P.H. Hanes was in this area of Stratford Road. It was developed in the 1950s; the first modern-day shopping center, located here, led to the demise of downtown shopping in many Forsyth County towns and hamlets. The 1950s photograph above shows a mixture of entertainment and shopping at the grand opening of the center. In the 1950s photograph below, a hootenanny provides entertainment for another group of Forsyth County citizens in this transformed High School gymnasium. No, this horse is not Roy Rogers's horse, Trigger, but a wooden horse, which was often used as a prop for local events and parties. (Courtesy FJ/WSHA.)

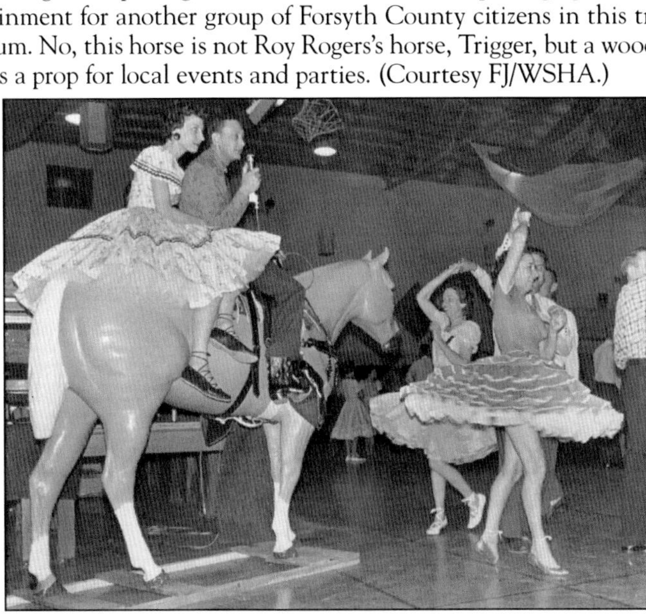

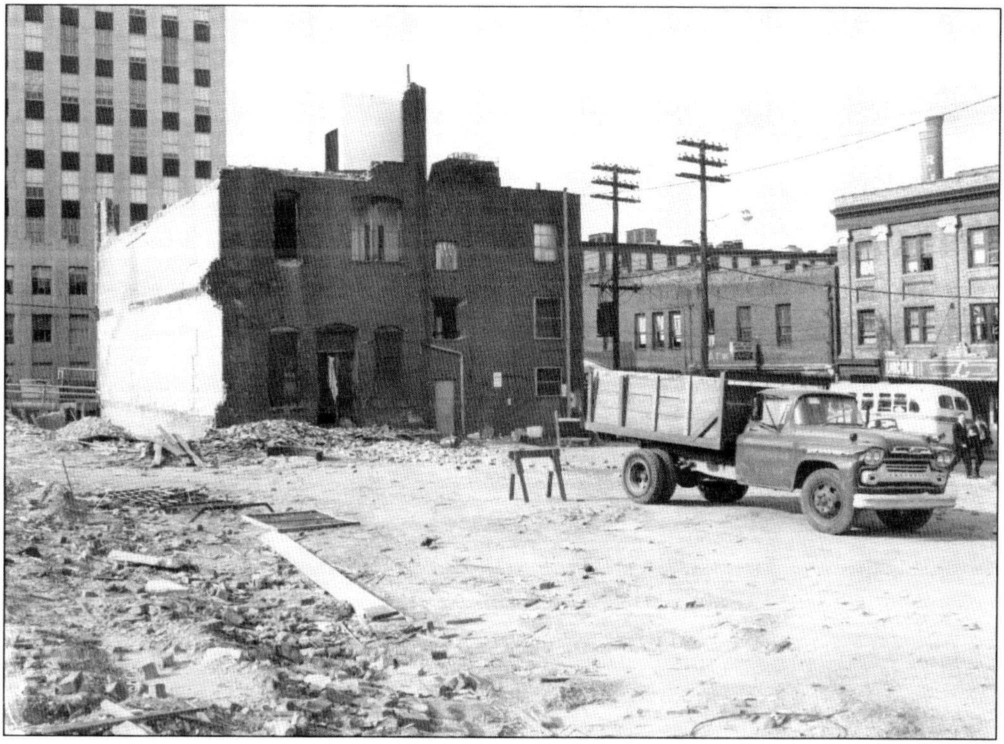

Lost neighborhoods of African Americans were as prevalent as those of whites, as shown in the 1960s photograph above. The area of East Third, East Fourth, and East Chestnut Streets is in the process of being razed as part of the urban renewal of the late 1960s, which has been called "urban removal" by several historians. This is because city blocks throughout the area were totally destroyed. Many parts of these blocks contained valuable and salvageable historic properties. The 1960s photograph below shows another example of an area that experienced urban renewal near the Cherry-Marshall interchange and Fifteenth through Twentieth Streets. Unfortunately, this all happened before historic preservation was recognized throughout Forsyth County with the coming of the bicentennial of 1976. (Courtesy WSHA.)

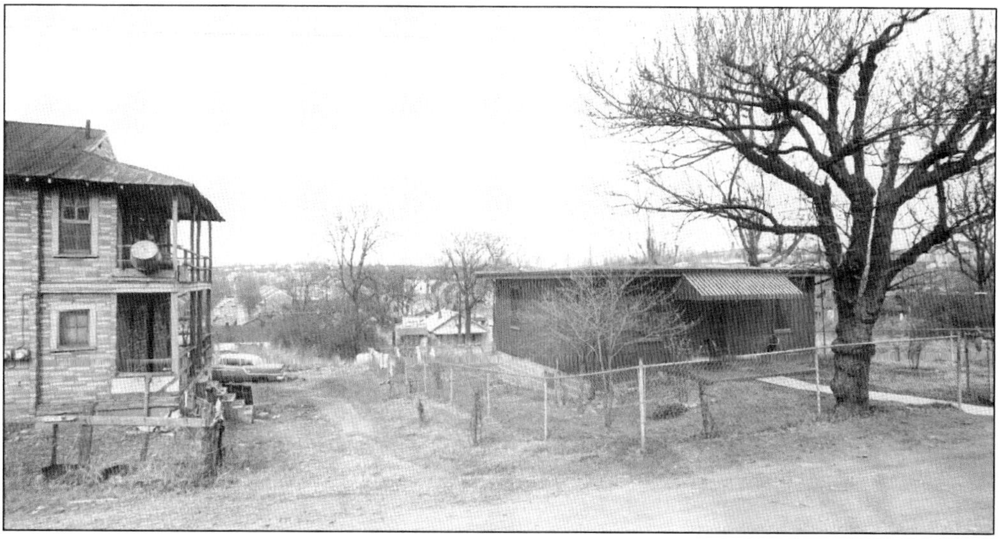

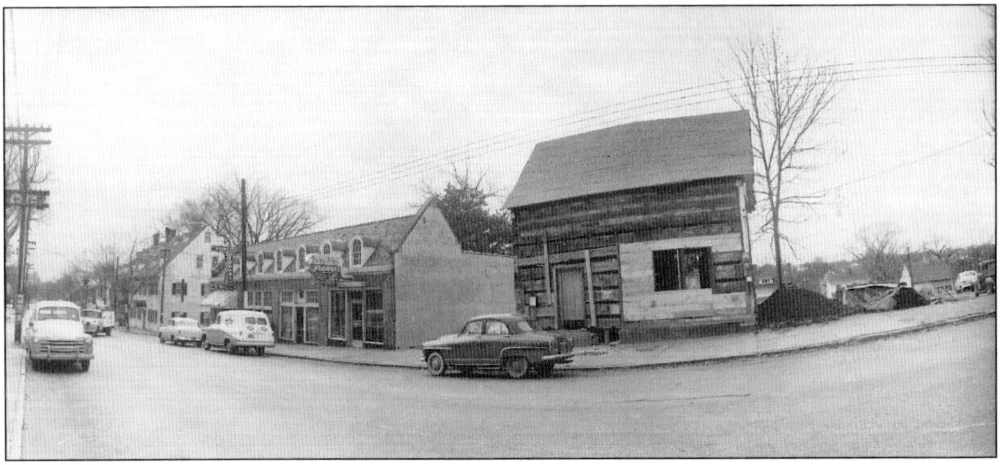

Historical preservation is well underway in this c. 1950s photograph showing the restoration of the central township of Salem. The historic landmark Miksch Tobacco Shop, built by Brother Miksch in the 1770s, appears to have been raised mysteriously from the ashes, much like a phoenix. The old and the new are presented here, with the Tobacco House on the right and the Krispy Kreme doughnut shop, built in the 1930s, on the left. (Courtesy FJ/WSHA.)

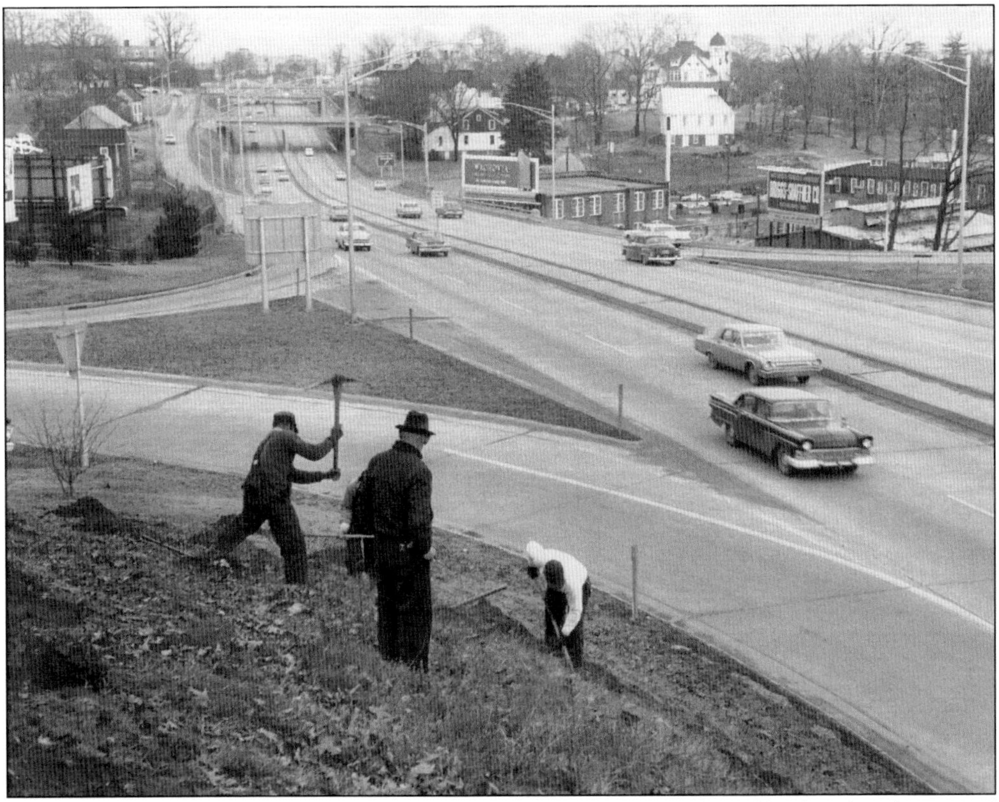

Traveling through the heart of Winston, Interstate 40 is a divider of neighborhoods. The c. 1766 West Salem neighborhood is pictured here in two parts. Most of the buildings in the upper right, including the 19th century Briggs-Shaffner Company, the large white church, and the mansion on the hill, have all been destroyed through urban renewal or neglect. (Courtesy FJ/WSHA.)

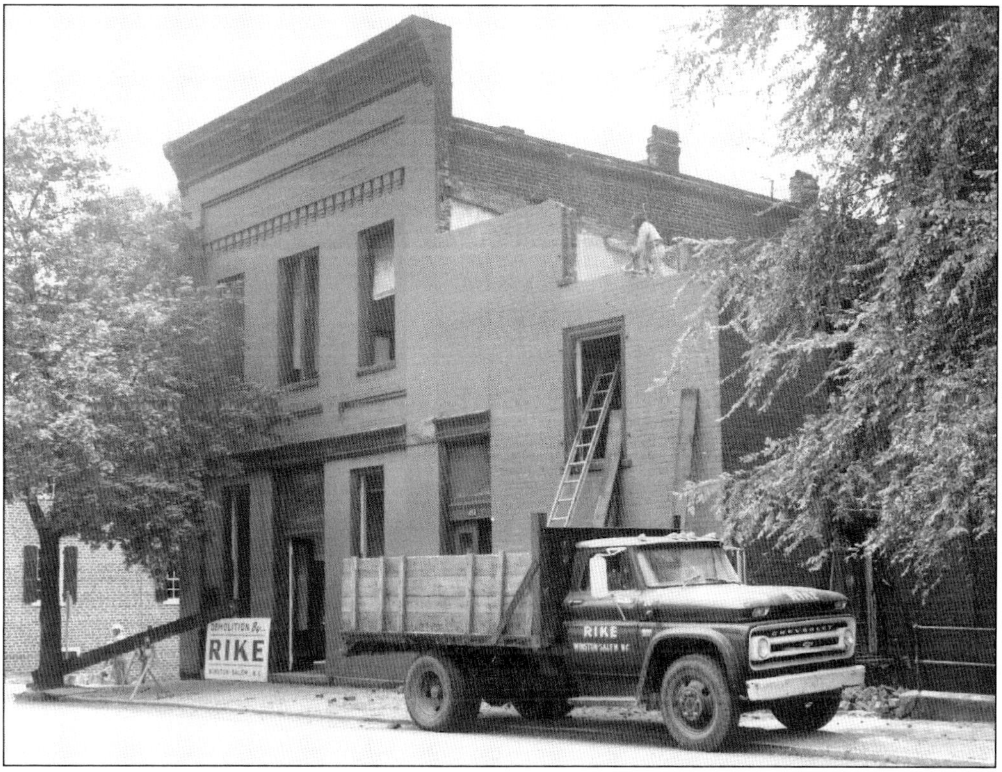

Here are two examples of lost architecture on Main Street in Old Salem. When Old Salem was being reconstructed, a huge 1870s neighborhood was lost. The photograph above shows a building being razed by the Rike Demolition Company in the 1960s. This building sat on the original property of the second house built in Salem, known as the "Two Story House." The house was used during the Revolutionary War as a makeshift hospital. The early-20th-century building below was used by Graham Plumbing Company. The building was razed and replaced by the reconstructed third house in Salem. Historical preservationists in Forsyth County are now beginning to look at buildings such as these for preservation. (Courtesy FJ/WSHA.)

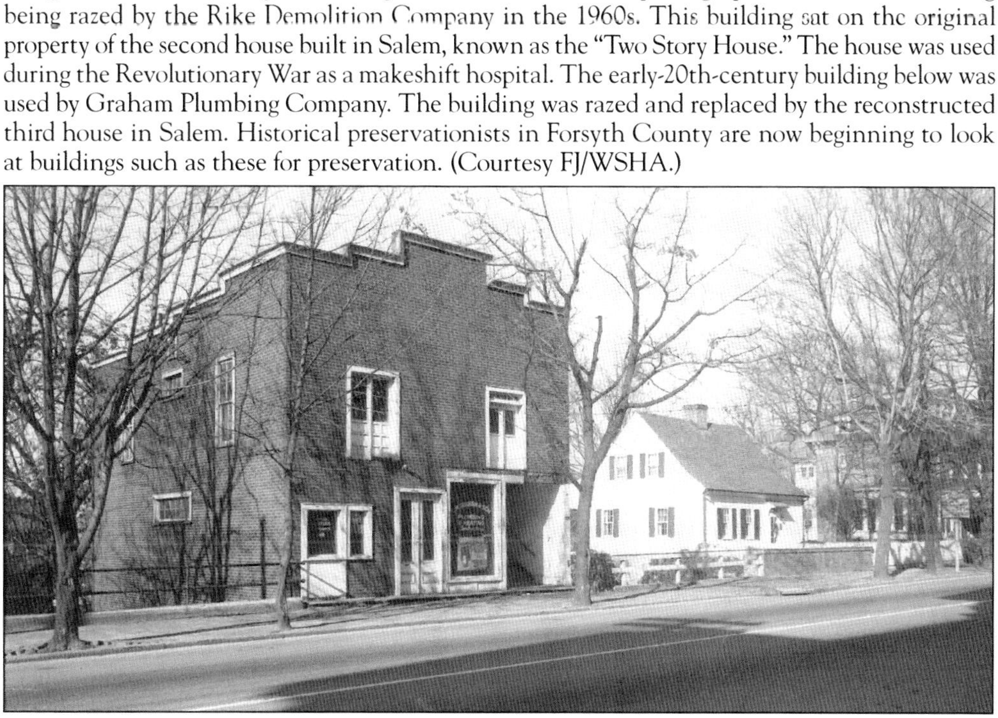

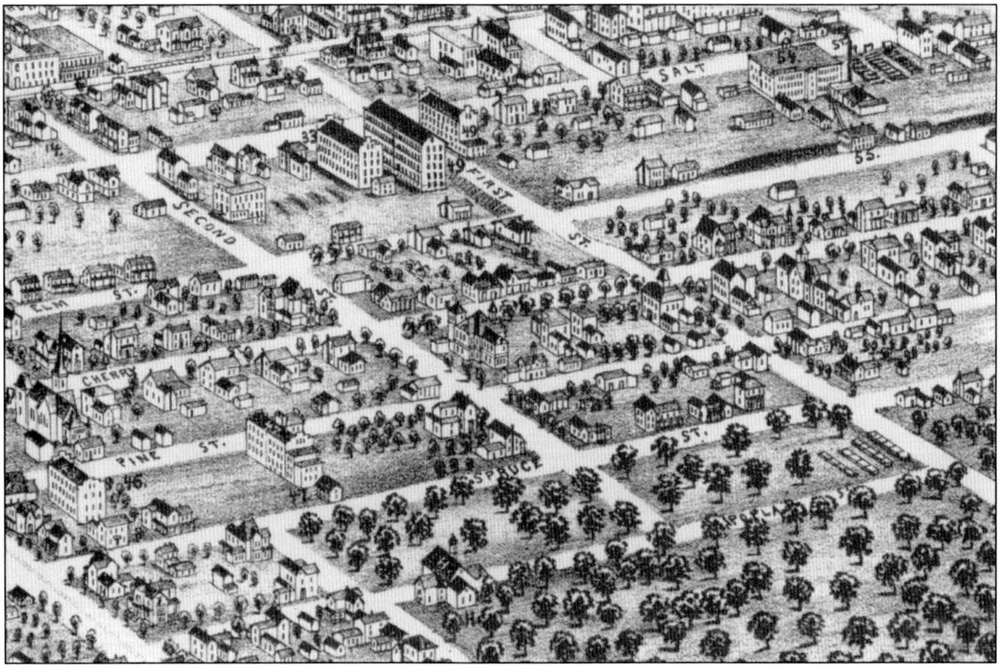

The first suburb of Winston, begun about 1870, is shown 20 years later in the c. 1891 Bird's Eye Map above. This lost neighborhood was very rural in 1870, existing outside the city limits. Trees are plentiful on the bottom right but have been cleared for recent development toward the center and top. One of the residents whose husband had just built a house on Cherry Street remarked, "I am scared for myself and the children since wolves are often spotted in this area." In the 1891 photograph below, the First Presbyterian Church (built about 1870), Saint Paul's Church, and the Episcopal Church are shown. (Courtesy Bird's Eye Map/WSHA.)

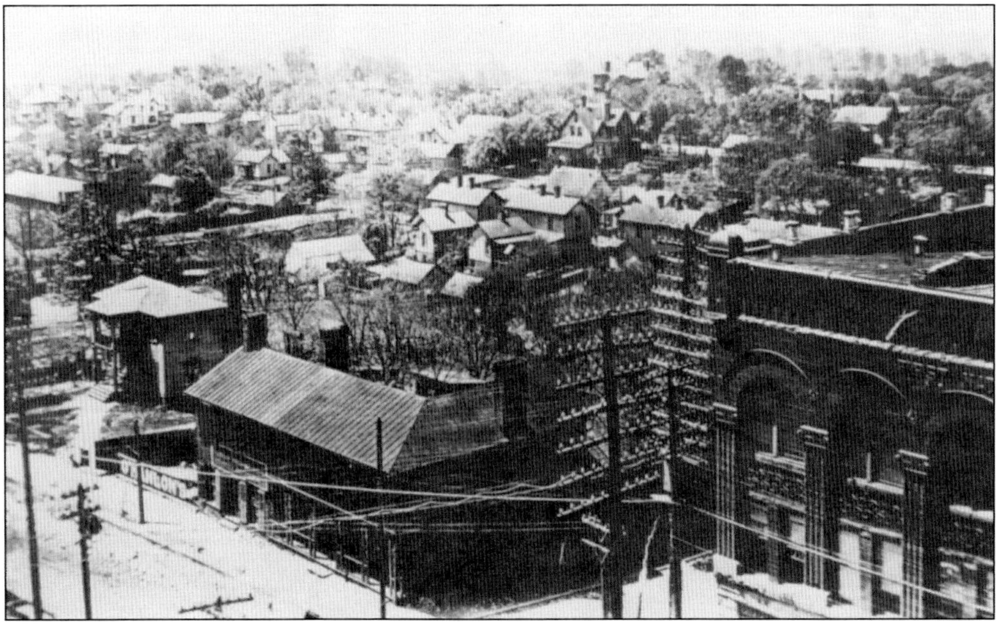

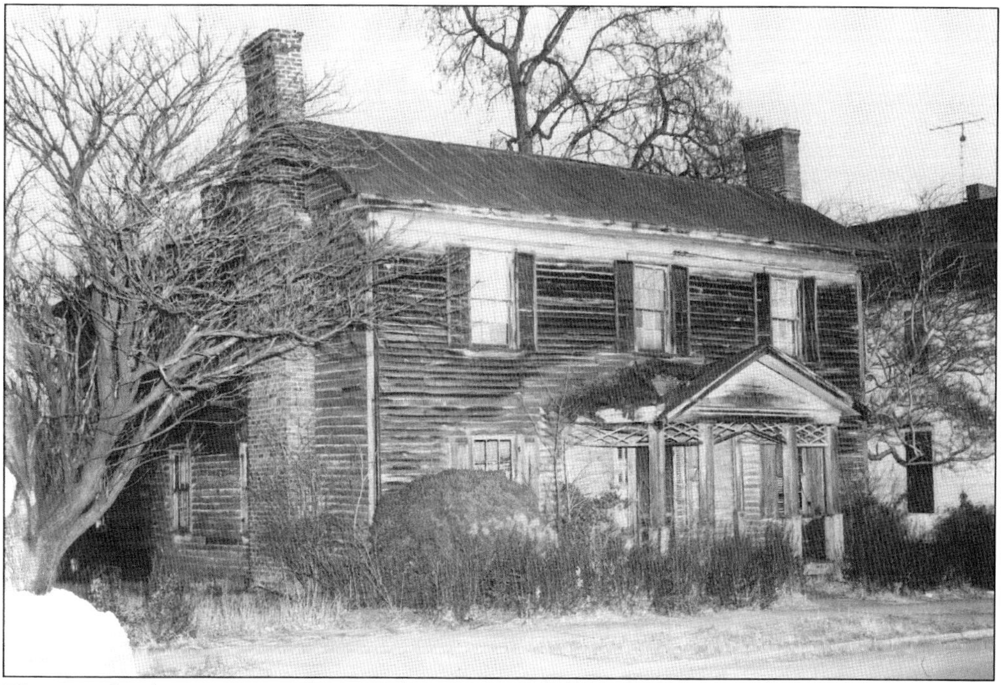

These two lost historic properties are examples of early rural Forsyth County. The 1950s photograph above shows an 18th-century wooden structure that unfortunately did not make it until the historic preservation years of the 1970s. This is an example of a homestead typical in the early neighborhoods of Bethania, Pfafftown, and Clemmons. The 19th-century building below was a rural homestead with a store and gas station. It is an example of the many establishments found at the crossroads of Forsyth County. These stores provided a meeting place for locals as well as needed products. (Courtesy WSHA.)

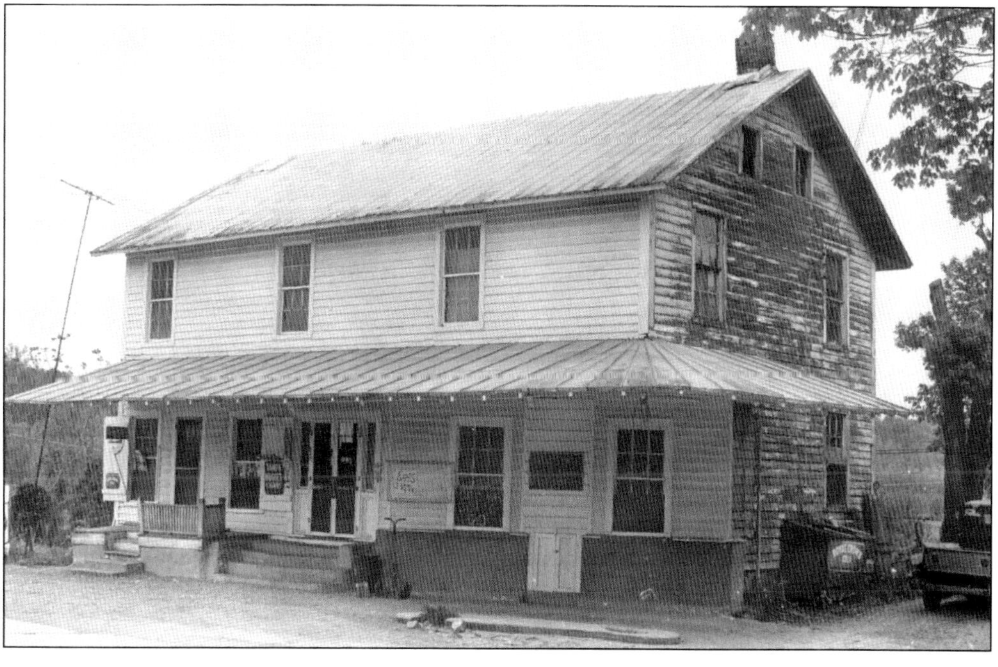

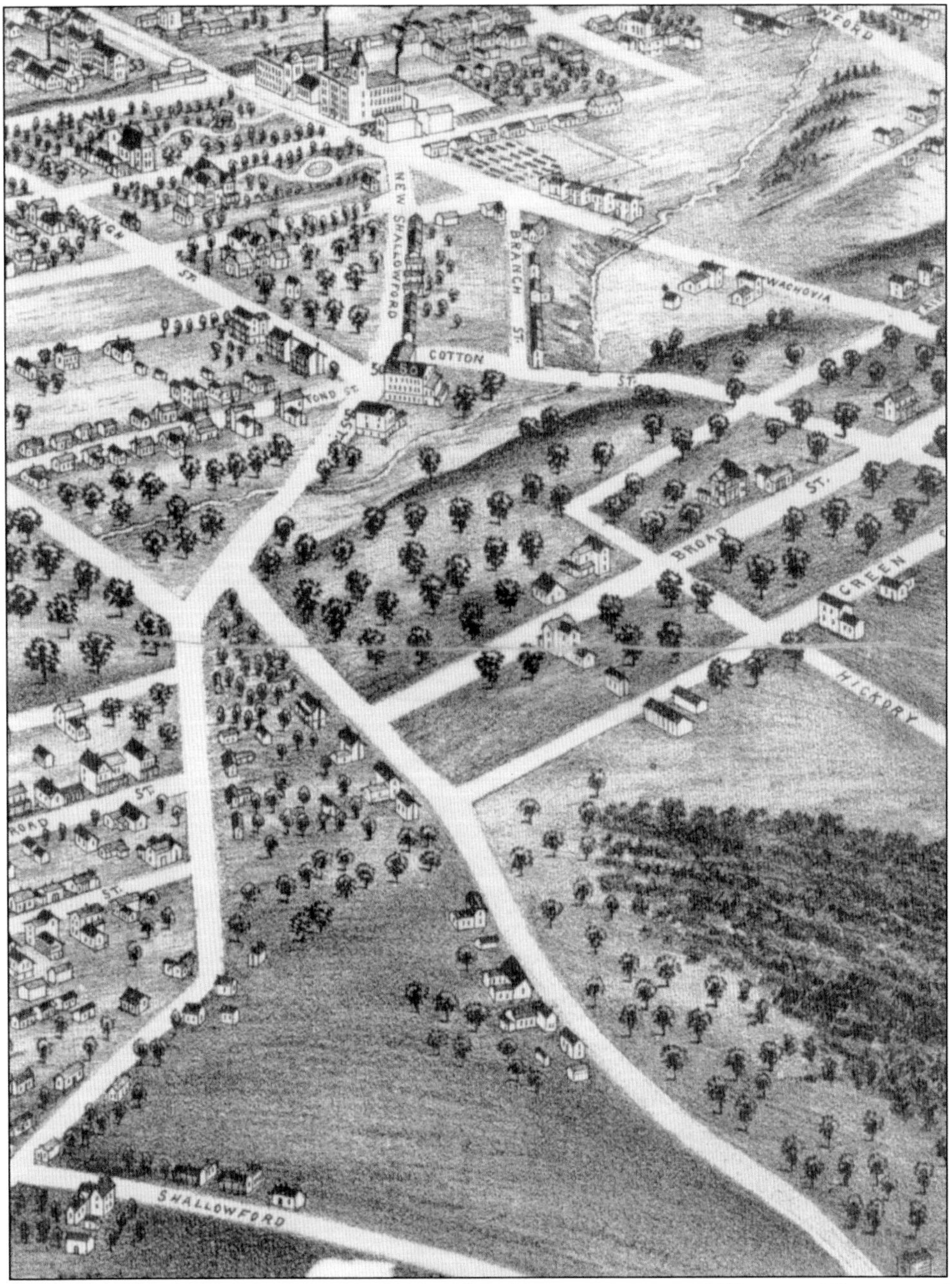

This is a section of a map showing the dividing line between Salem and Winston. The triangular section in the foreground is bordered by the dividing roadways that were part of the early Colonial roads into Salem. The middle road intersecting with Green and Broad Streets is the Old Shallowford Road, which was the first road built to Salem in 1766. The original Old Plank Road between Salisbury and Bethania intersected with what was called the New Shallowford Road. Other road names include Hickory, Wachovia, High, and Cotton Streets. At the top of the map is the Salem Textile Mill Complex, complete with smokestacks. The neighborhoods that were associated with this section were West End, West Salem, and the outskirts of the central town of Salem. (Courtesy Bird's Eye Map/WSHA.)

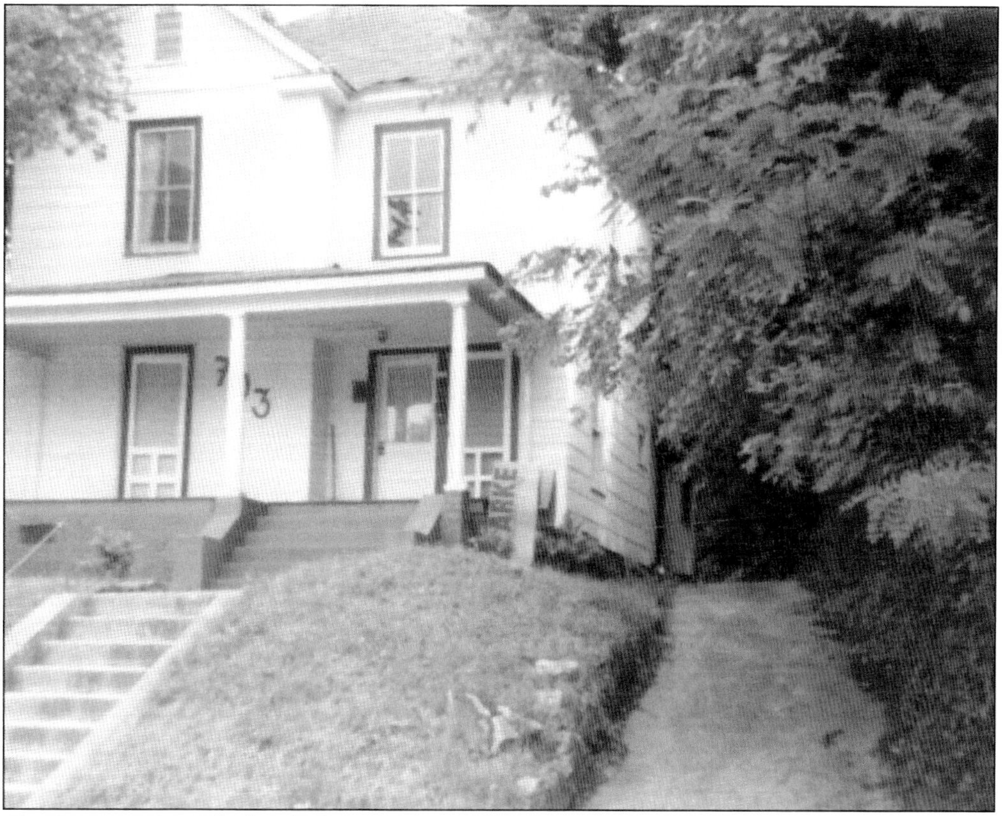

This house, at 703 Shallowford Street, sits next to one of the older houses along the Old Plank Road. Spring Street was originally one street that connected Salem to Winston. This neighborhood was demolished for Interstate 40. Spring Street became Fairview Street in Salem. This 1970s photograph shows one of the few houses that were left; today, there is nothing but a set of cement steps leading to nowhere. (Courtesy M. Bricker.)

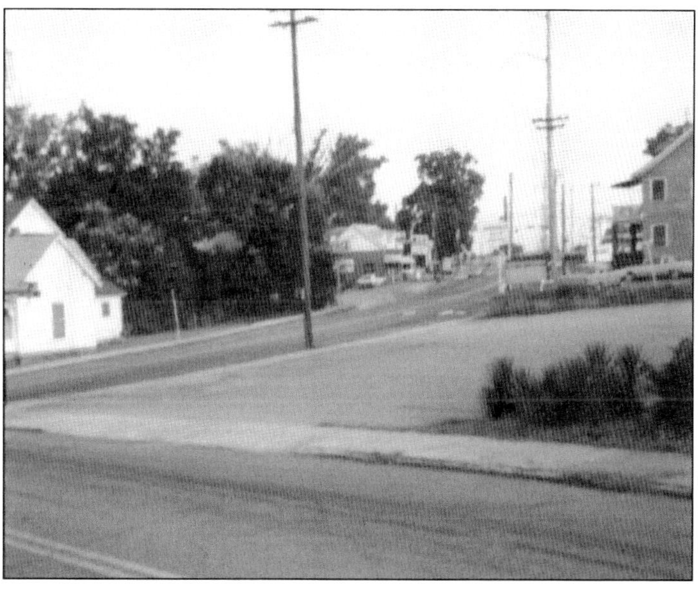

Here is another lost part of the central neighborhood of West Salem and West End. The empty lot was once home to the second incarnation of the Pentecostal Holiness Church, built in the 1930s. The neighborhood, which grew up around it, has been depleted. In the background is the 1920s-style Green Front Store, used today as a retail store. Of these buildings, it is the only one that still exists. (Courtesy M. Bricker.)

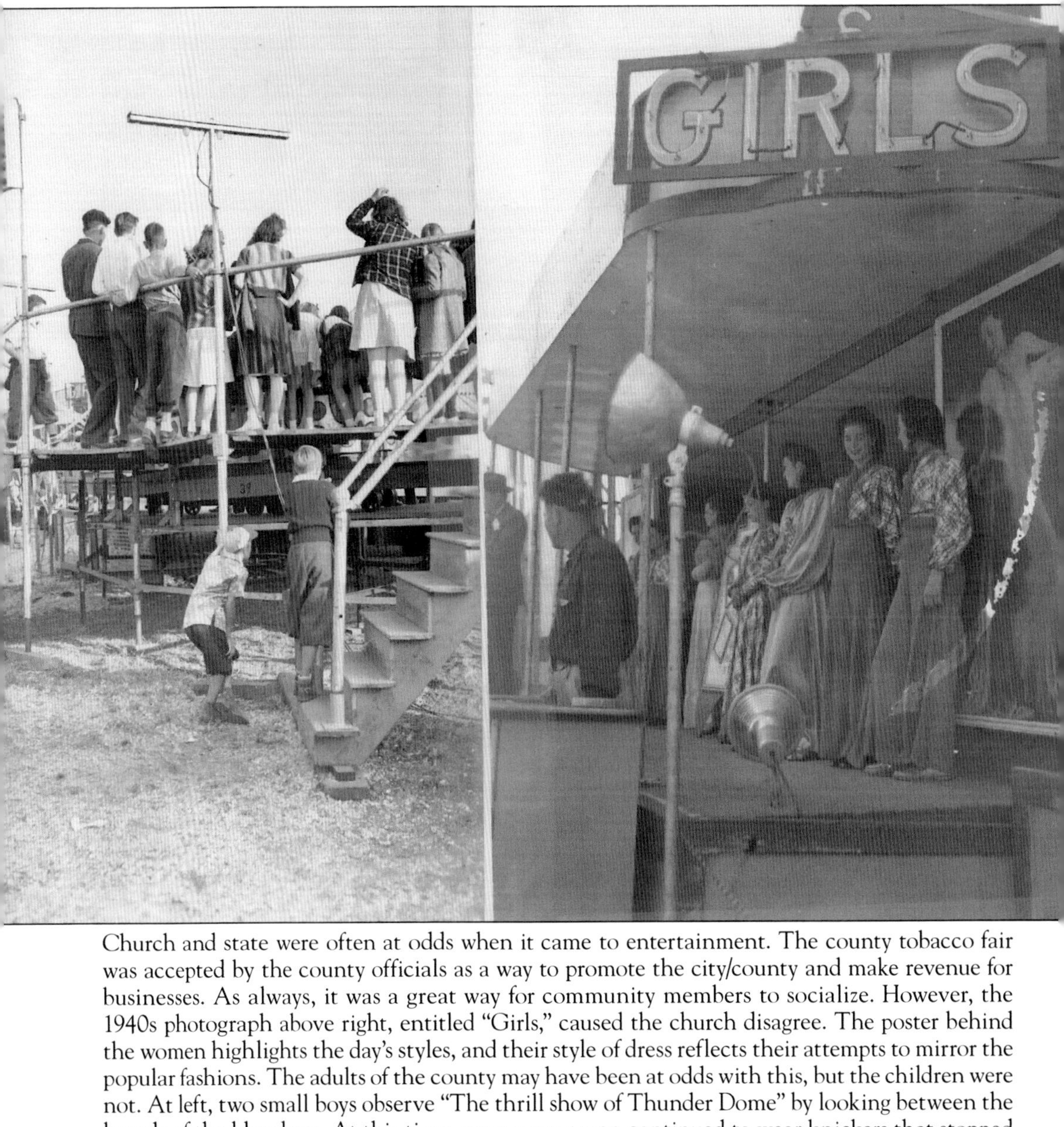

Church and state were often at odds when it came to entertainment. The county tobacco fair was accepted by the county officials as a way to promote the city/county and make revenue for businesses. As always, it was a great way for community members to socialize. However, the 1940s photograph above right, entitled "Girls," caused the church disagree. The poster behind the women highlights the day's styles, and their style of dress reflects their attempts to mirror the popular fashions. The adults of the county may have been at odds with this, but the children were not. At left, two small boys observe "The thrill show of Thunder Dome" by looking between the boards of the bleachers. At this time, some young men continued to wear knickers that stopped below their knees. (Courtesy WSHA.)

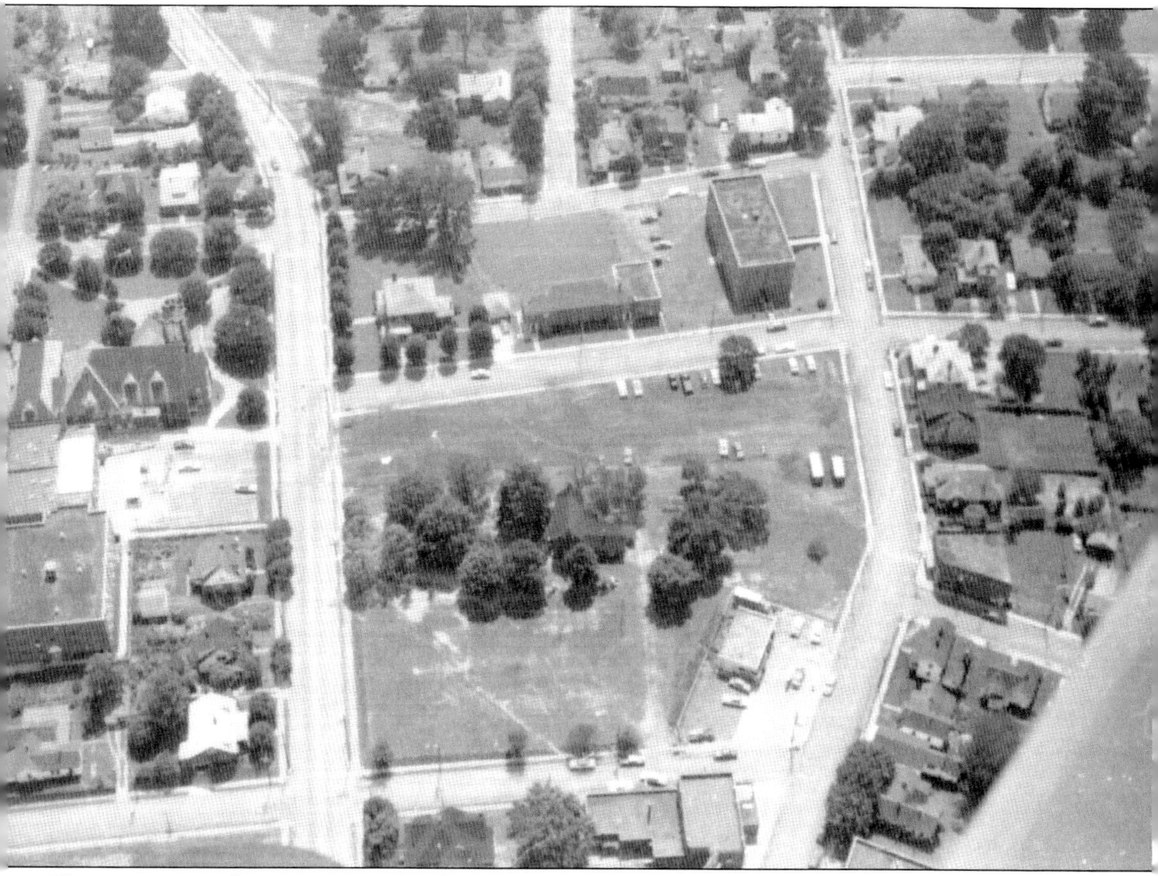

Plantations existed in many parts of early Forsyth County. This 1950s photograph shows the remains of the Kreuser-Levering-Brietz farmhouse in the center. The complete area of the photograph was part of the c. 1818 farm until becoming a plantation in 1838 owned by the Brietz family until the 1960s. Historic trees surround and shade the large farmhouse. The large lawn around the lot is occupied by buses and cars. Across the street to the top, trees are planted in clear rows and manicured, which differentiates this more modern home from its historic neighbor. Currently, the site is part of the campus of Piedmont International University. To the left is the first complex of the Salem Baptist Church. On the right is a lost neighborhood—part of the Brietz farm that was an extension of Christ Moravian Church. (Courtesy Piedmont International University.)

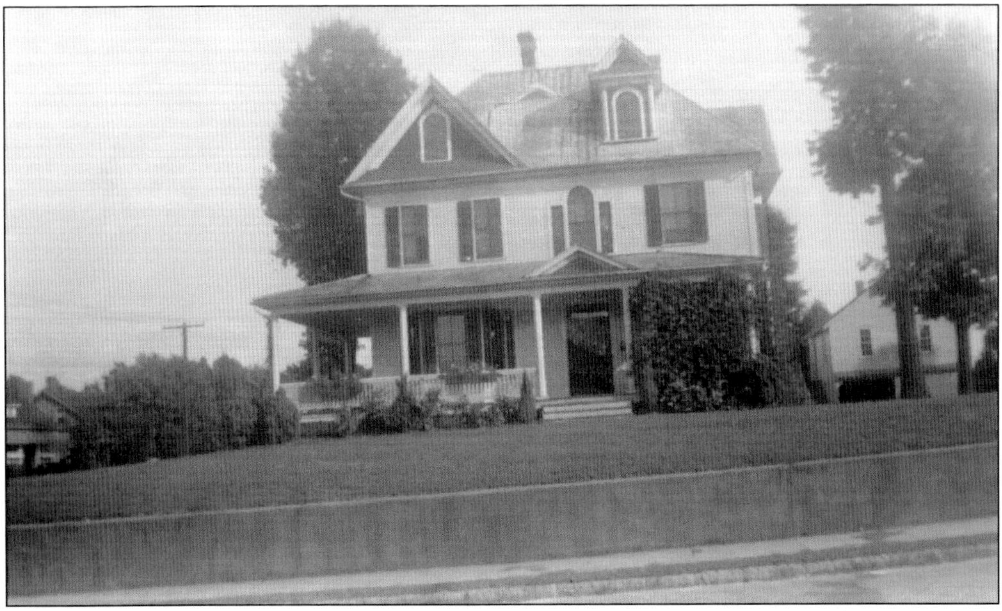

This Victorian home was used as the parsonage for Christ Moravian Church and operated from 1900 until 1960. It was located at the corner of Academy and Green Streets. The loss of the home in the 1960s was due to a minister who arrived at Christ Moravian with the stipulation that he could not live in an older house. This house was replaced with little fanfare by a 1960s brick ranch. (Courtesy M. Bricker.)

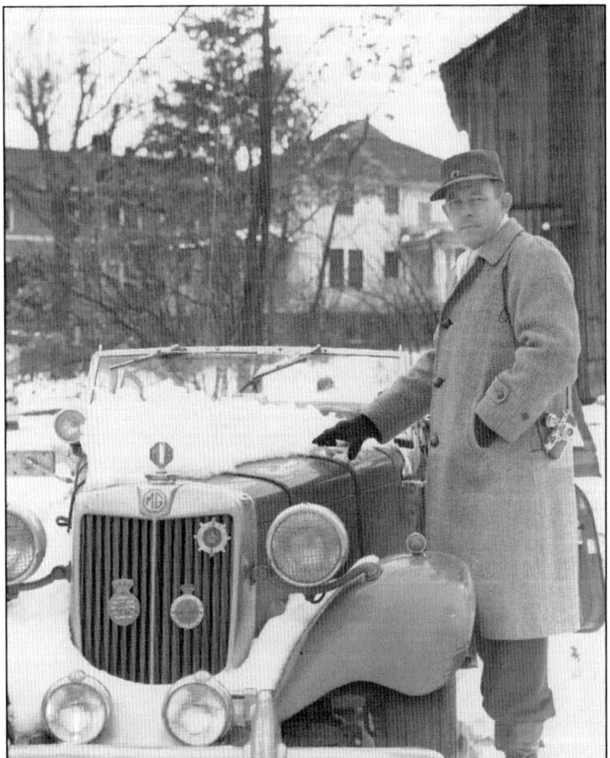

Frank Jones poses with one of his prized automobiles. The large white house behind him was the home of Dr. Charles Street, pediatrician of Forsyth County. The larger house was home to the physician for the Tuberculosis Clinic in northern Forsyth. The Broad Street mansions were connected between West End and West Salem. Unfortunately, all of the original mansions in this corridor have been razed. (Courtesy FJ/WSHA.)

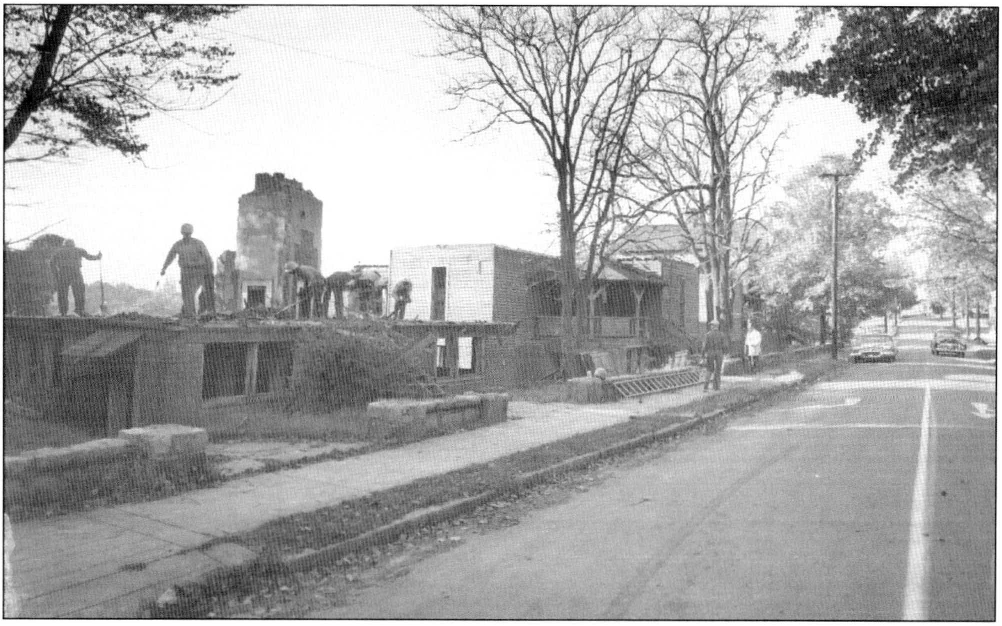

Urban renewal found more victims along Old West Salem and Old West End. The photograph above shows the last remnants of the neighborhoods that existed around the Old Winston Graded School (West End Graded School), built about 1882. As shown in the c. 1960s photograph below, just visible on the right of the street was one house that was saved on Green Street. The house was to be torn down in the 1980s, but a longtime resident believed it was originally a log cabin. Before the resident moved, after mistakenly knocking a hole in the wall while taking down a picture, he discovered a wooden log underneath the plaster. The house was researched by Old Salem Inc. and found to be the first "Free School House" of West Salem, Winston's first school, which had been moved from the corner of First and Liberty Streets in the 1890s. The log cabin was restored and is now at the old-time village in the Dixie Classic Fairgrounds. (Courtesy FJ/WSHA.)

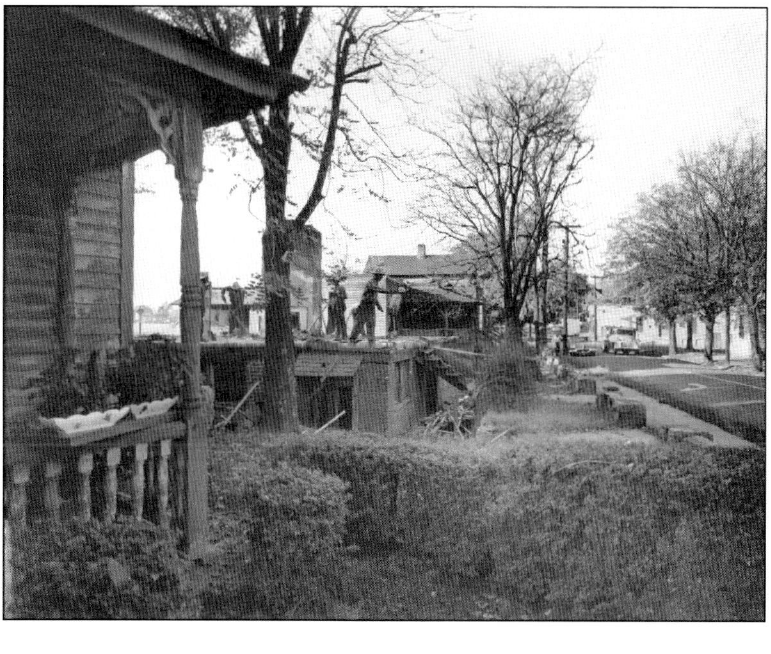

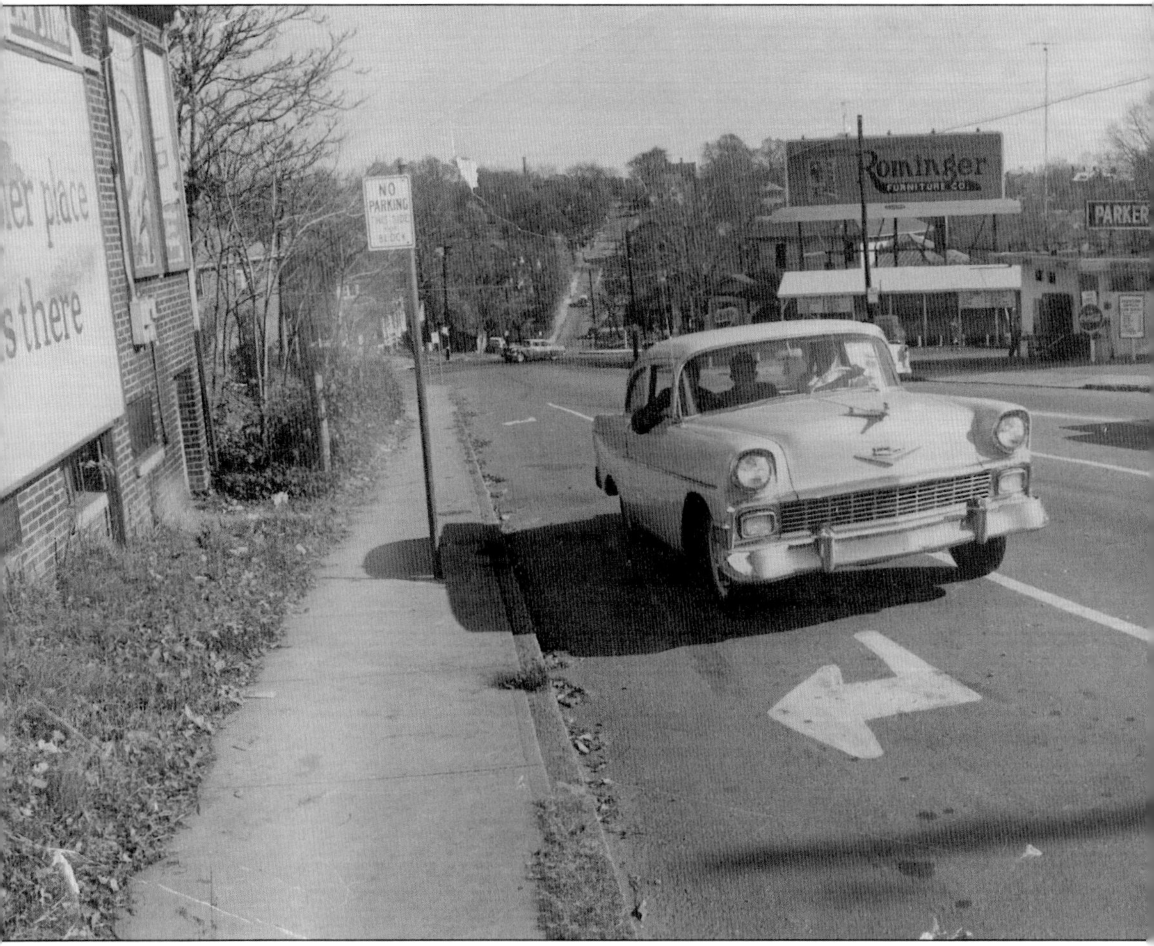

The lost neighborhood between Winston and Salem was bordered by First Street (Old Shallowford Road), Shallowford Street (between Old Shallowford and Old Plank Roads), Broad Street (Old Shallowford Road), and Brookstown Avenue (Old Plank Road). This image from the mid-20th century shows two classic cars passing, a telephone booth to the right, and a nice view down the

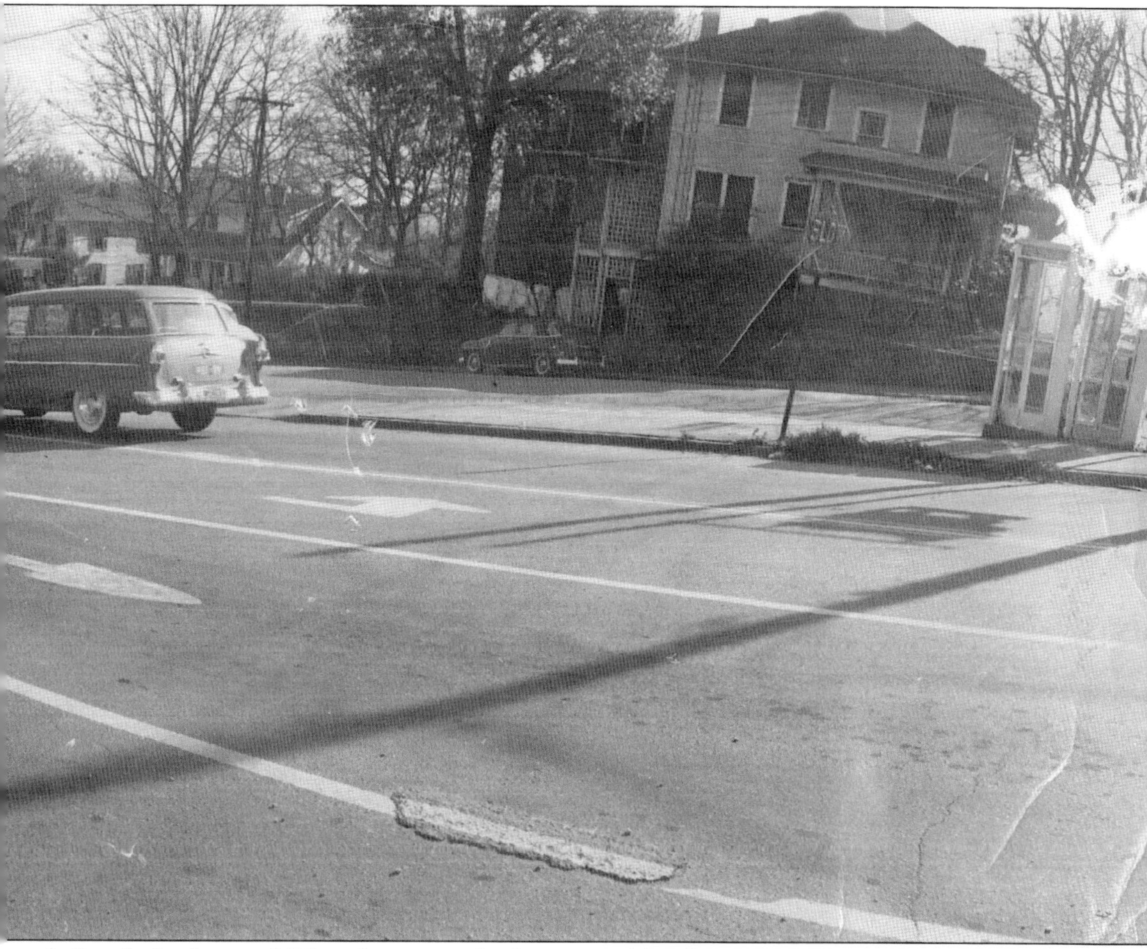

hill in the background. Three boys sit in the front seat of the closest car enjoying their newfound freedom. Various advertisements can be seen in this image: Coca-Cola, Rominger Furniture Company, and Parker's Drive-In. David and John Ferriaolo were residents in this piece of lost history at the dividing line between Salem and Winston. (Courtesy M. Bricker.)

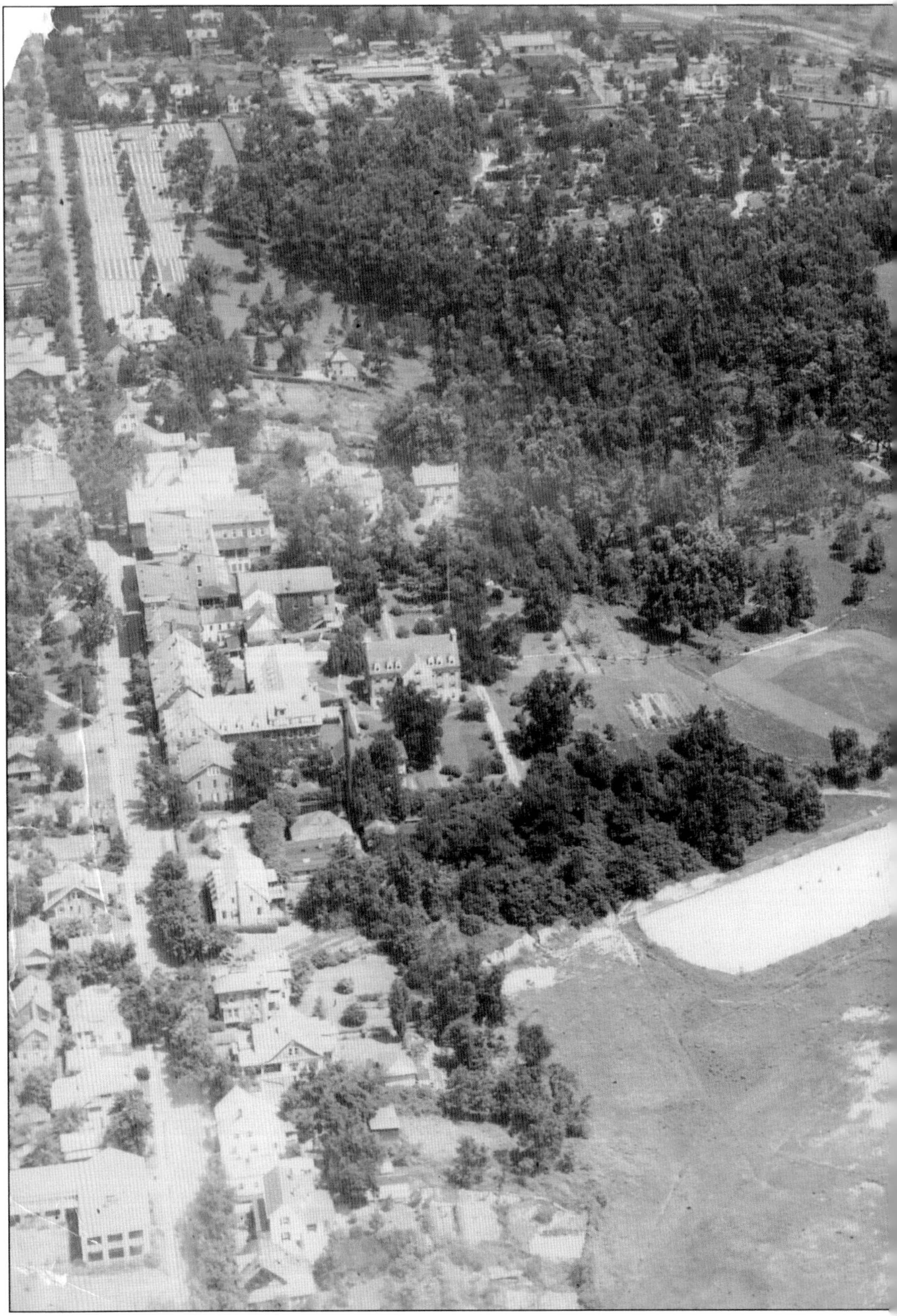

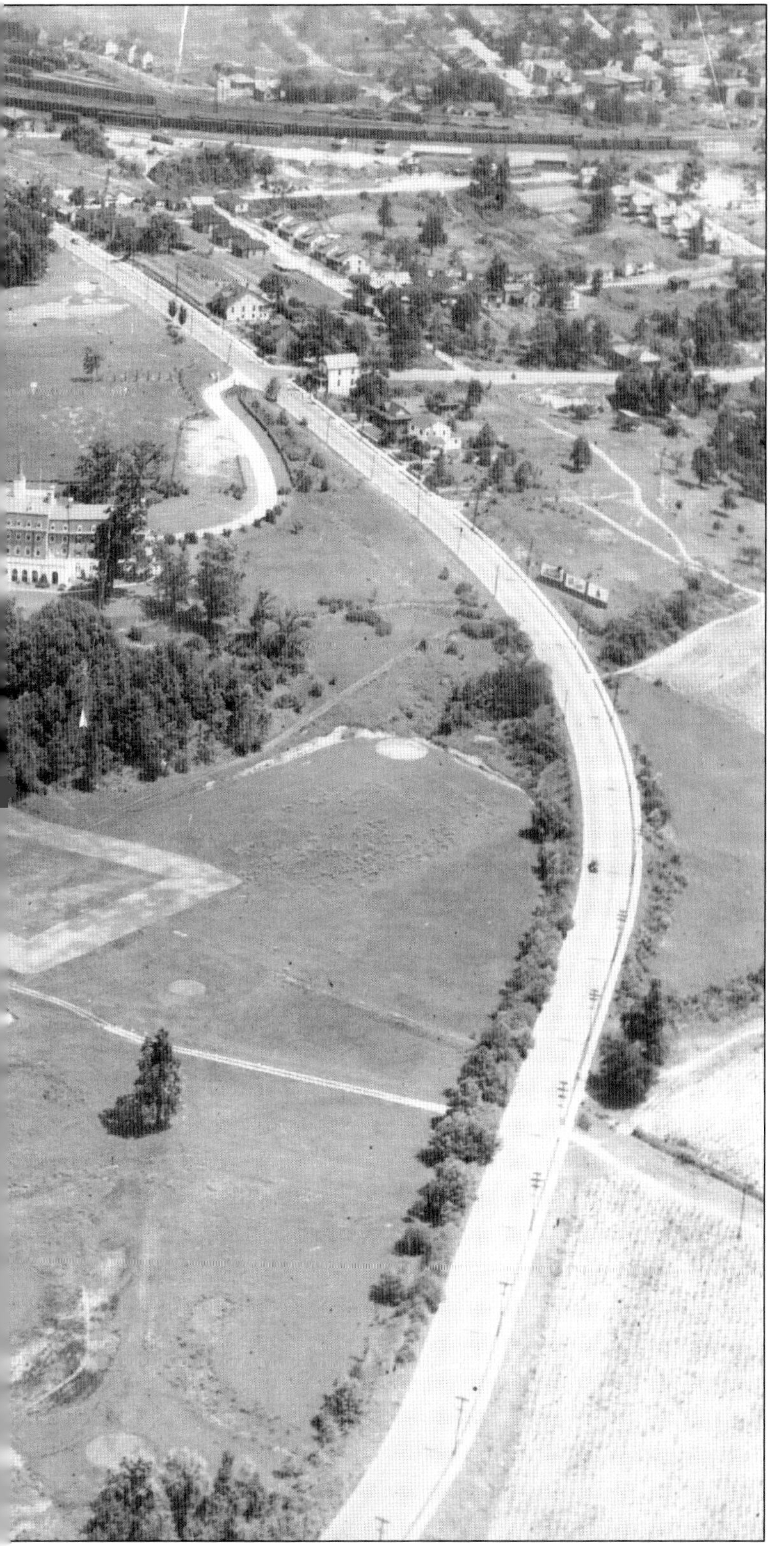

This c. 1950s photograph is part of a larger aerial image showing the Old Salem District, including Salem College, the northern perimeters of Cemetery Street, and Old Belews Creek Road. The surrounding area includes the c. 1771 Moravian graveyard and the c. 1850 Salem Cemetery. Most homes along Church Street (top left) were razed or changed drastically to conform to the specifications of Old Salem Inc. The upper right part of the larger aerial photograph shows vividly the span of the Old Belews Creek Road. The industrial complex of the Fogle Brothers Lumber Company, plus Water Street, included the grounds of many older establishments that processed mineral water, along with sarsaparilla factories. The Old Belews Creek Road continued to the outer Forsyth County towns of Walkertown and Belews Creek. (Courtesy M. Bricker.)

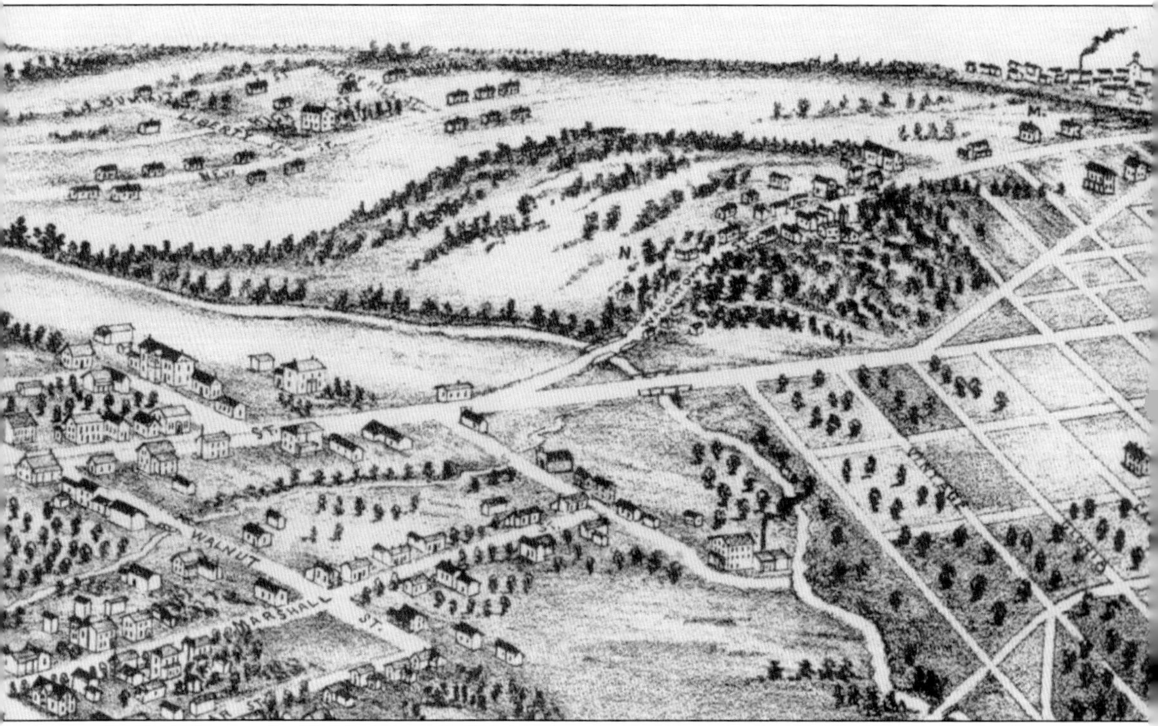

This c. 1891 Bird's Eye Map shows a section of Salem Mill before Salem Avenue was extended through the neighborhood. The intersection of Main and Mill Streets shows the mill homes of West Salem. To the north is Waughtown Street. This Colonial street would lead to "Centerville" before ending at the large Nissen Wagon Works. The right side of this street was heavily forested and on a hill. Two church steeples can be seen in this area. The Happy Hill area, home to African Americans in the 19th century, is visible in the upper part. (Courtesy Bird's Eye Map/WSHA.)

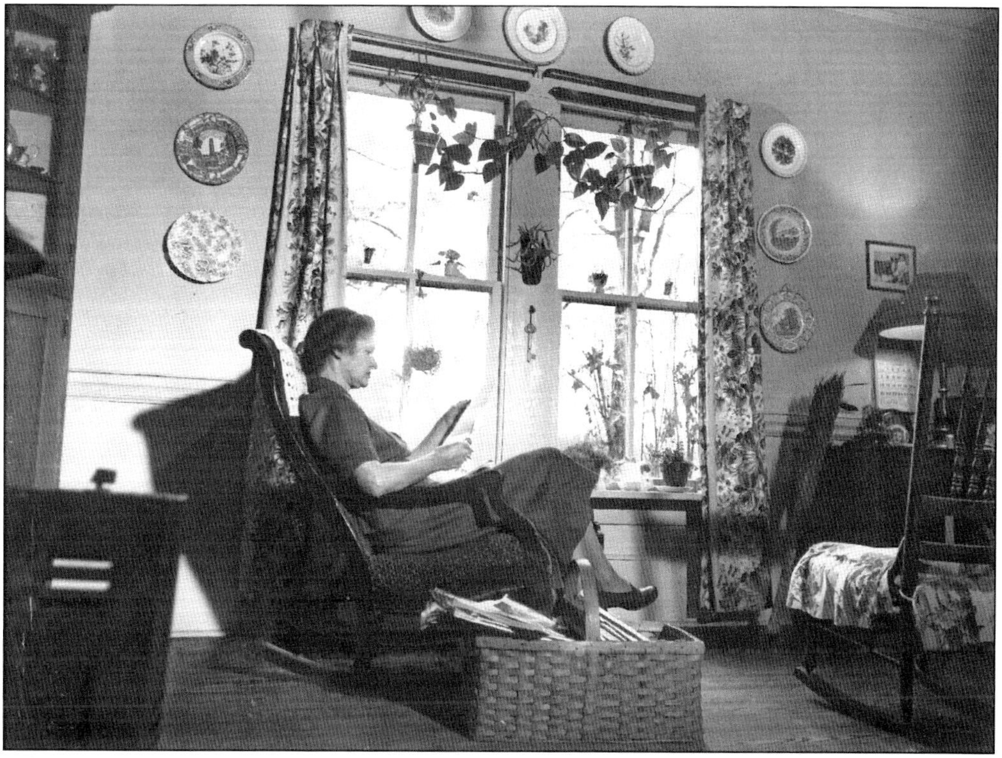

Life in the early to mid-20th century in Forsyth County continued to reflect the simpler times of the 19th century. The c. 1950s photograph above shows a time of reflection and study. Below, a friendly get-together among friends without electronic equipment such as television, radios, or telephones was commonplace in the early 20th century. The styles may change, but camaraderie and communication between human beings, especially in Forsyth County, has remained the same. (Courtesy M. Bricker.)

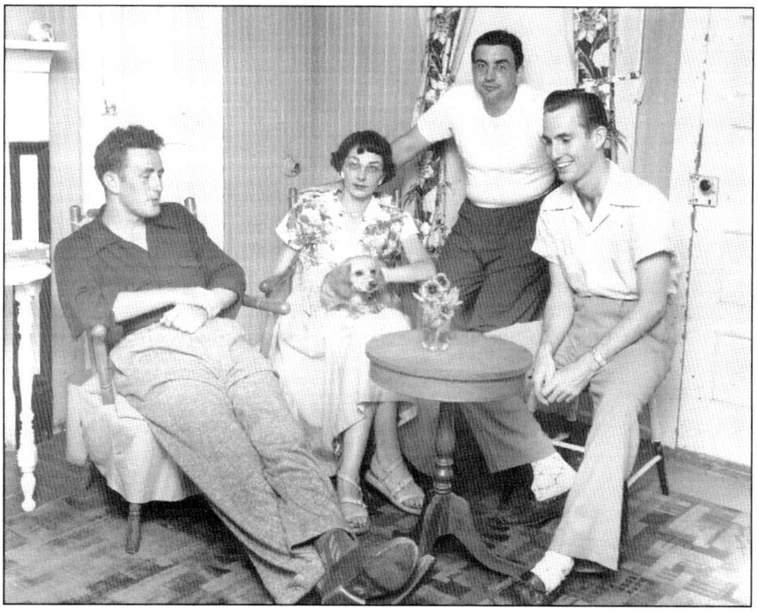

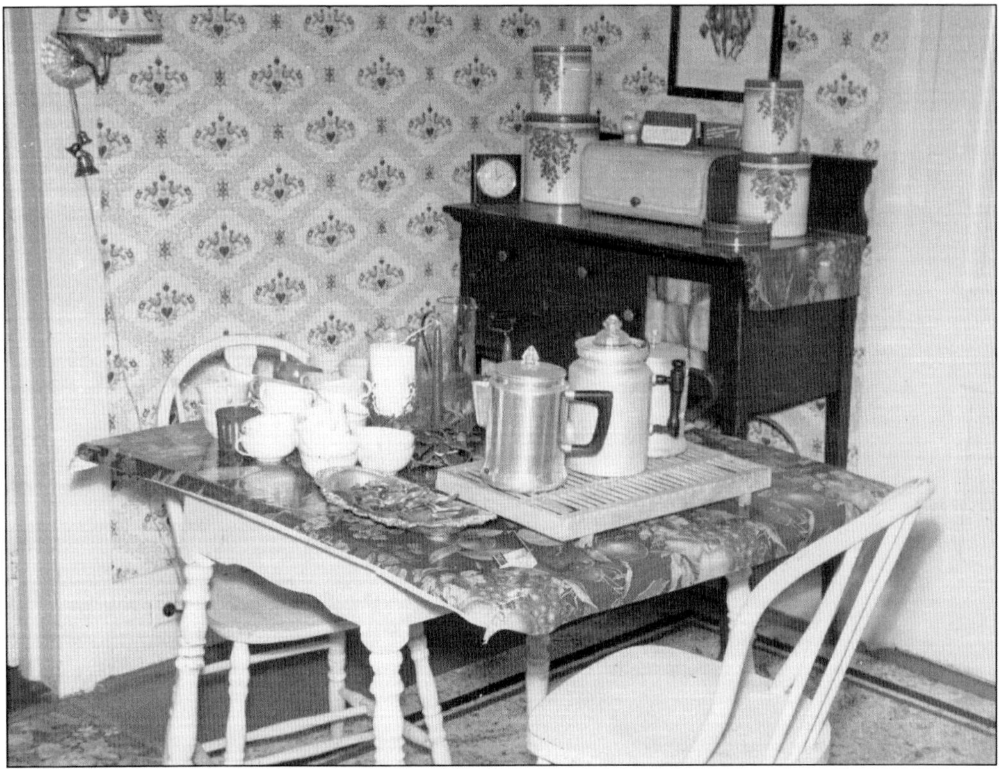

Two important rooms of mid-20th century Forsyth County home places are shown here. Note the minimal furniture in the dining room, above. Below, the kitchen has everything needed to feed a household at a time when one would run to the corner store to purchase daily groceries without any thought of tomorrow. (Courtesy M. Bricker.)

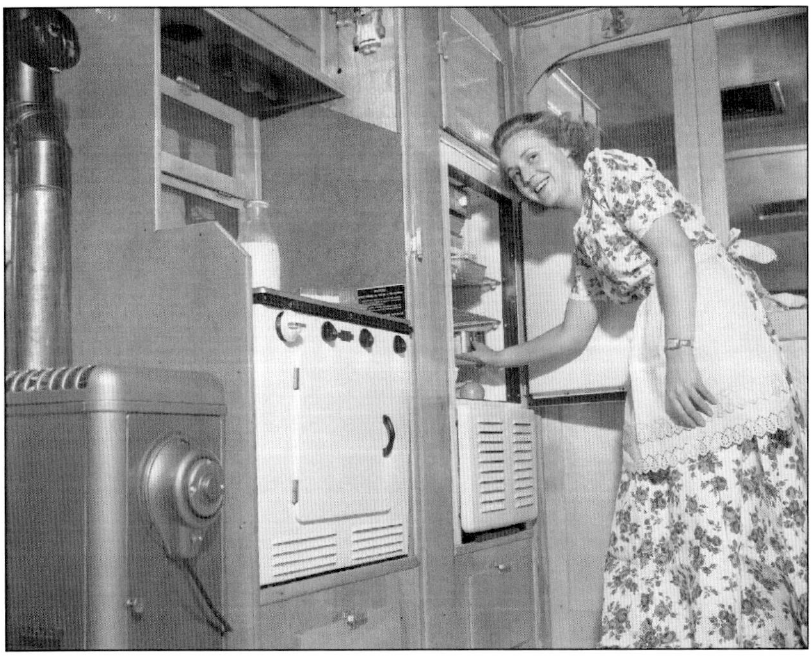

With the advent of the automobile in the early 20th century, travel became the norm throughout Forsyth County. One way to travel was with the camper trailer, and many Forsyth residents would hitch up their trailer and head off on an adventure on the weekends. (Courtesy M. Bricker.)

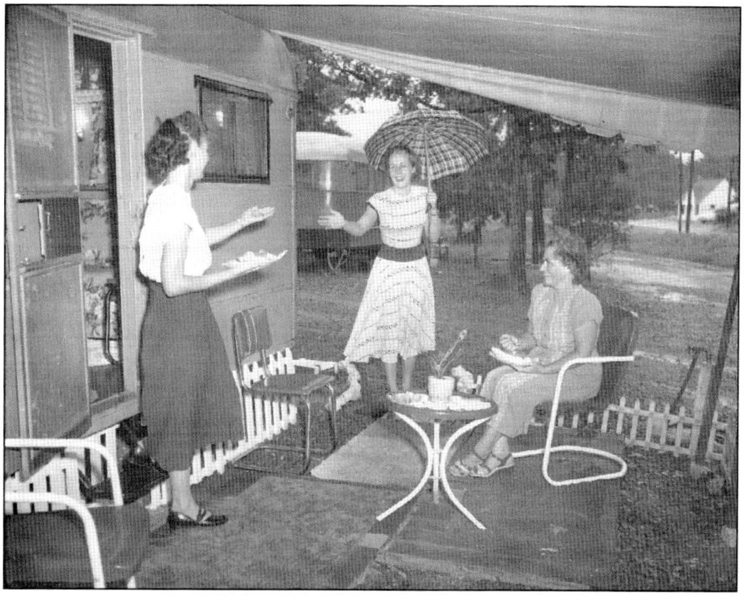

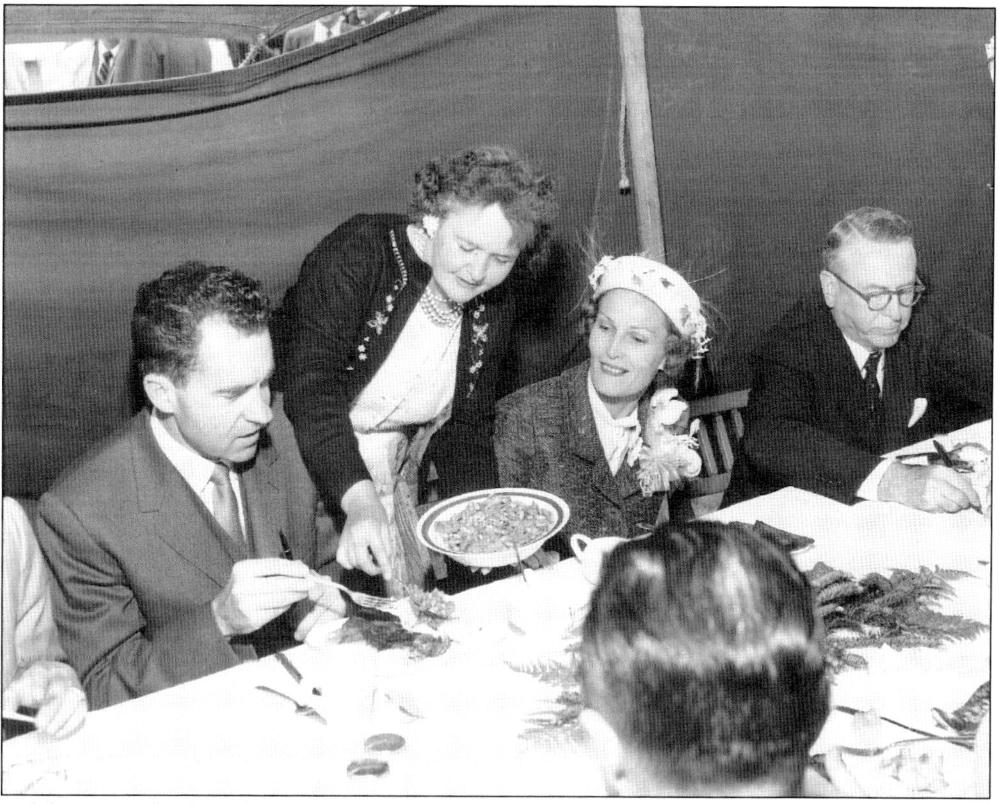

Celebrities and political leaders have often found Forsyth County an important stopping point, whether pitching a movie or themselves. This 1950s photograph shows Pres. Richard Nixon and his wife, Patricia, at a fundraiser for his reelection campaign. Many dignitaries, beginning with George Washington (who visited Salem in the 18th century), have visited Forsyth County. Recently, Pres. Barack Obama visited Forsyth Technical College. (Courtesy FJ/WSHA.)

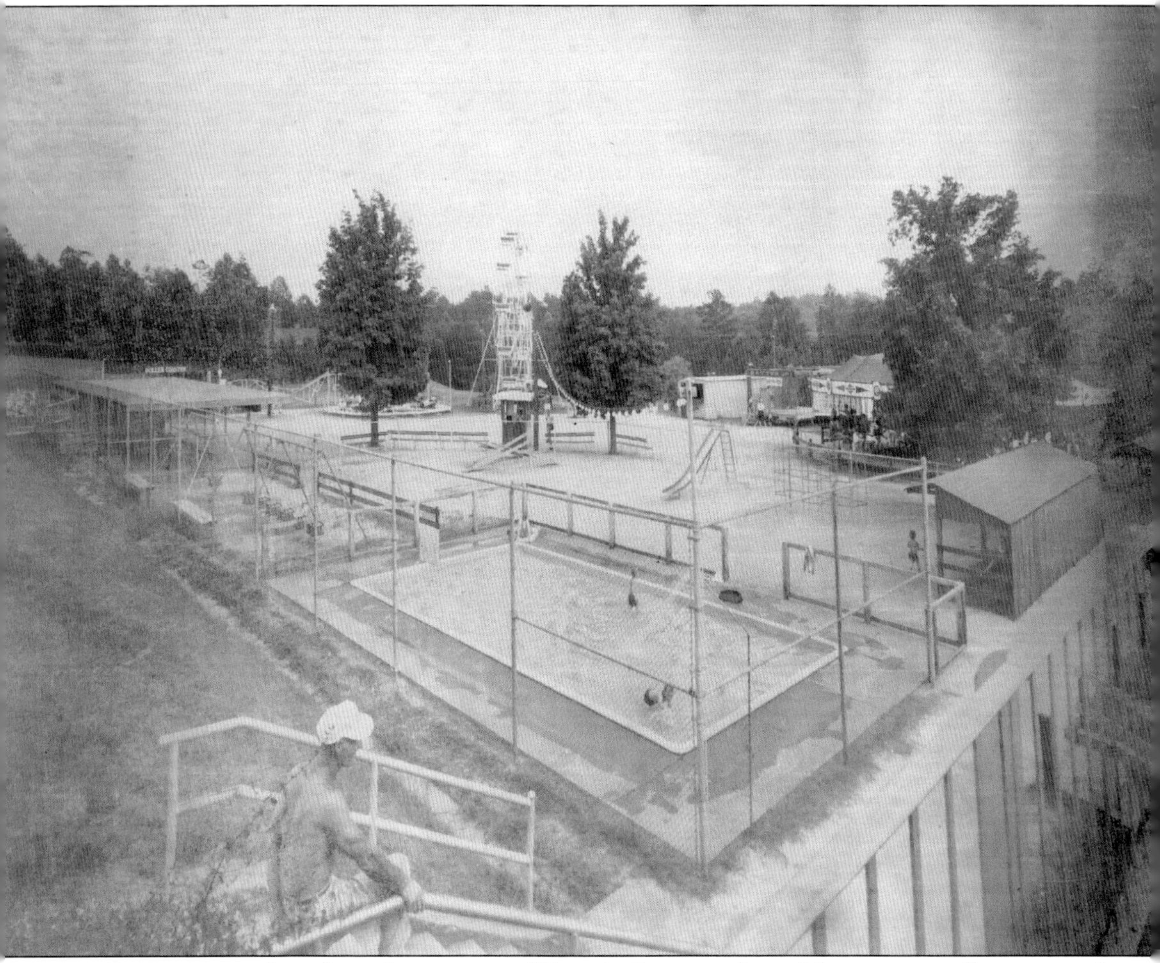

Entertainment has always been a part of Forsyth County culture. Here is an excellent piece of 20th-century Americana. Reynolds Park, shown here in the 1950s, was a playground for the young and young at heart. To the right (outside of the photograph) was an Olympic-size swimming pool. Also surrounding the carnival scene was an 18-hole golf course. A few of the features were a small Ferris wheel, a miniature roller coaster, a playground with swings, a small miniature golf course, a merry-go-round, shooting gallery, and, of course, a miniature train, which would transverse the area through tunnels and over hill and dale. This was a wonderful gift to the city and county by the Reynolds family. (Courtesy of WSHA.)

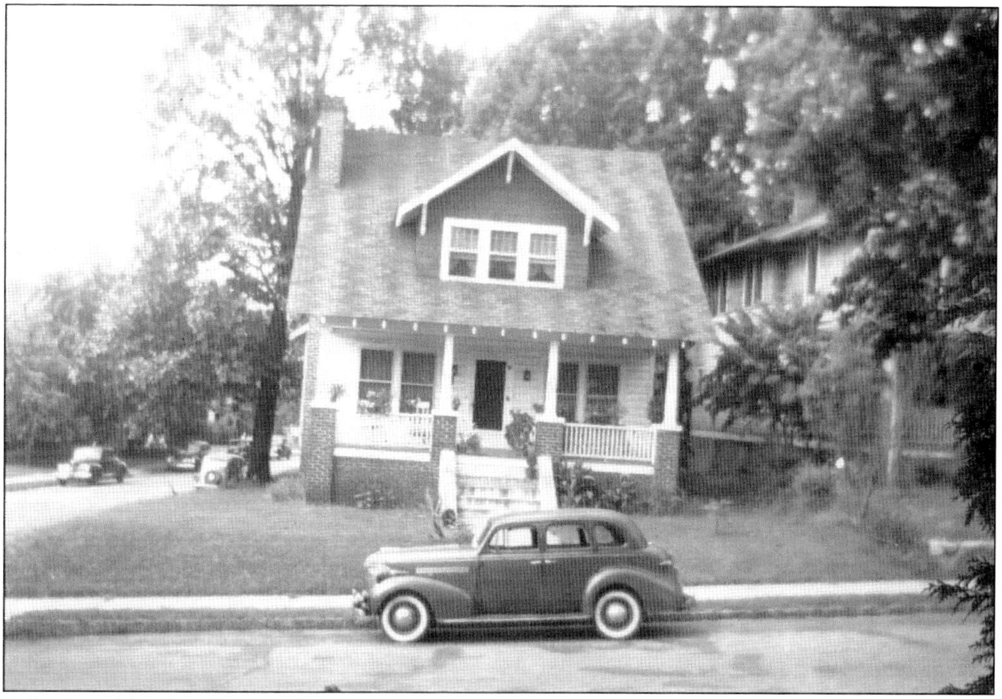

A lost neighborhood is found at Park Circle near the dividing line between Winston and Salem. The neighborhood originated around 1917 with the growth in the area's factories and mills. Pictured is the Grady Chatman home in the 1920s. Many residents populated the older neighborhoods, which began as county neighborhoods. Winston and Salem grew to include two-thirds of Dobbs Parish, later Forsyth County. (Courtesy WSHA.)

As an older resident during the later years of the Park Circle neighborhood, Mary Young Bricker of 132 Park Circle enjoys a quiet time at Easter with her favorite flowers, Easter lilies, which were encircled by the cedars of the homestead. Both this and the Chatman home above fell to the wrecking ball for the BB&T baseball field. (Courtesy M. Bricker.)

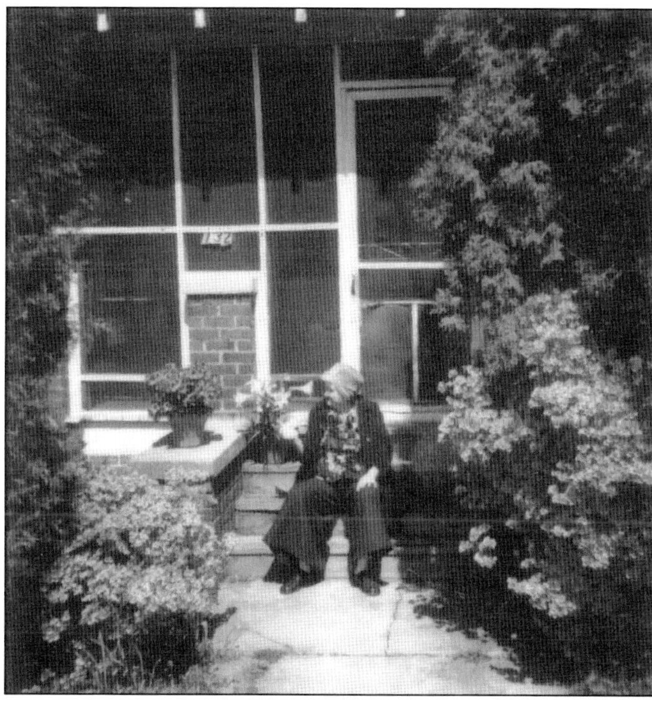

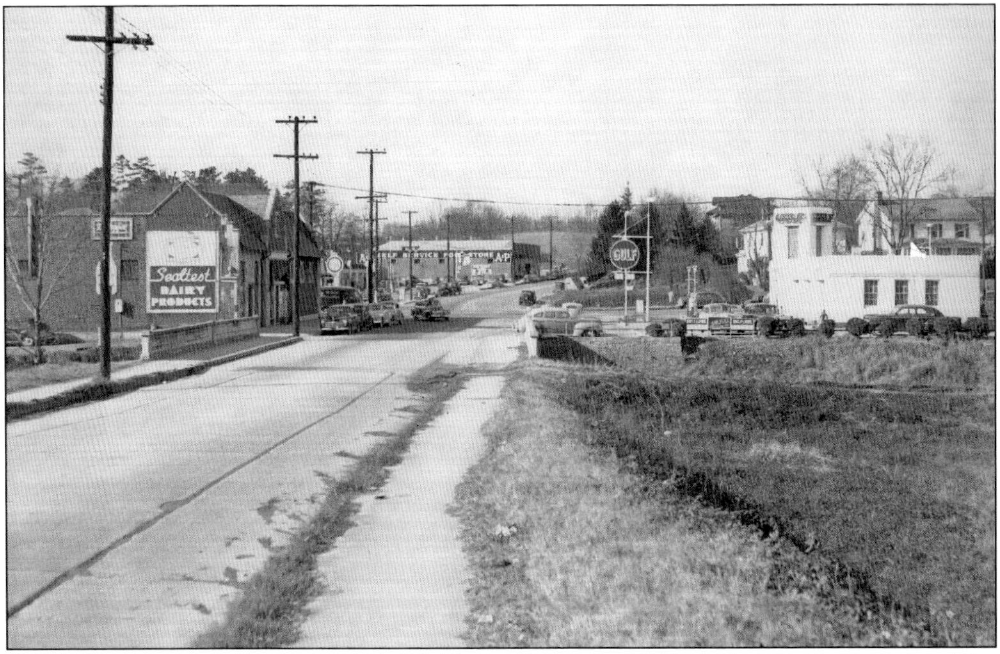

The Old Shallowford Road extended from the Yadkin River and brought travelers to Salem. The photograph above shows First Street, formerly Old Shallowford Road. Small shops and businesses line the street to the left. On the right is a 1930s service station, and beyond is the new A&P grocery store. A&P was one of the first commercial grocery stores to arrive in Forsyth County in the 1910s. The photograph below shows First Street looking east toward US 158, the way old travelers did down Old Shallowford Road headed to Salem. This road divided the West End neighborhood to the left and West Salem to the right. The intersection today is West First Street at Hawthorne Road. (Courtesy M. Bricker.)

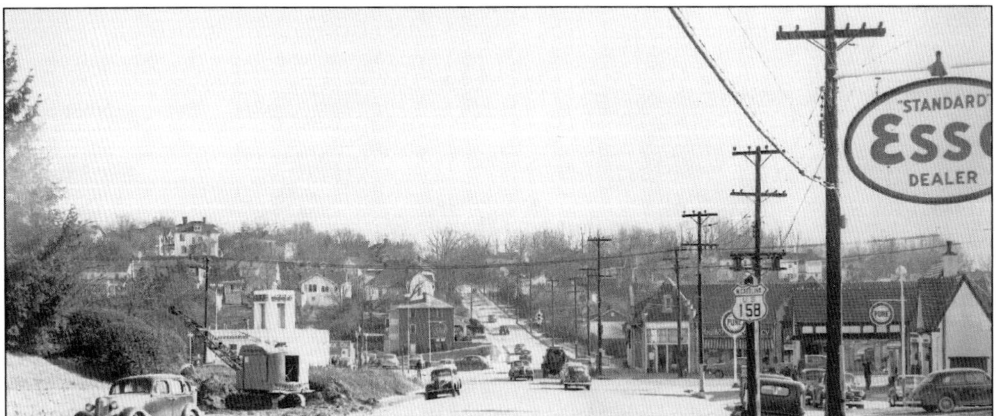

The original West End neighborhood of Winston became a showplace for the early tobacconists and successful businessmen of the late 19th century. This photograph from the 1960s shows Effird's family homestead. The 1880s brownstone showcased the family's success in tobacco, retail stores, and grocery stores. Mary Young Bricker and her son Donald Bricker pose in front of Mary's homestead at 228 North Green Street. (Courtesy M. Bricker.)

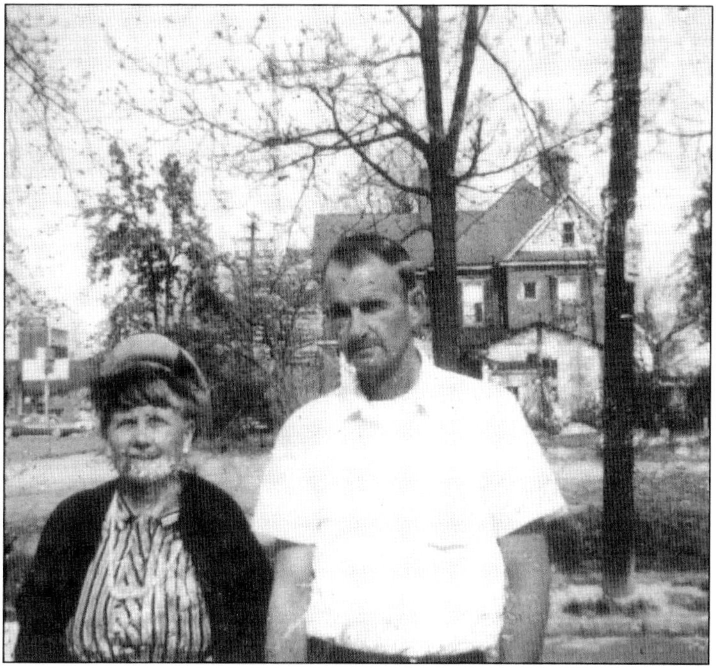

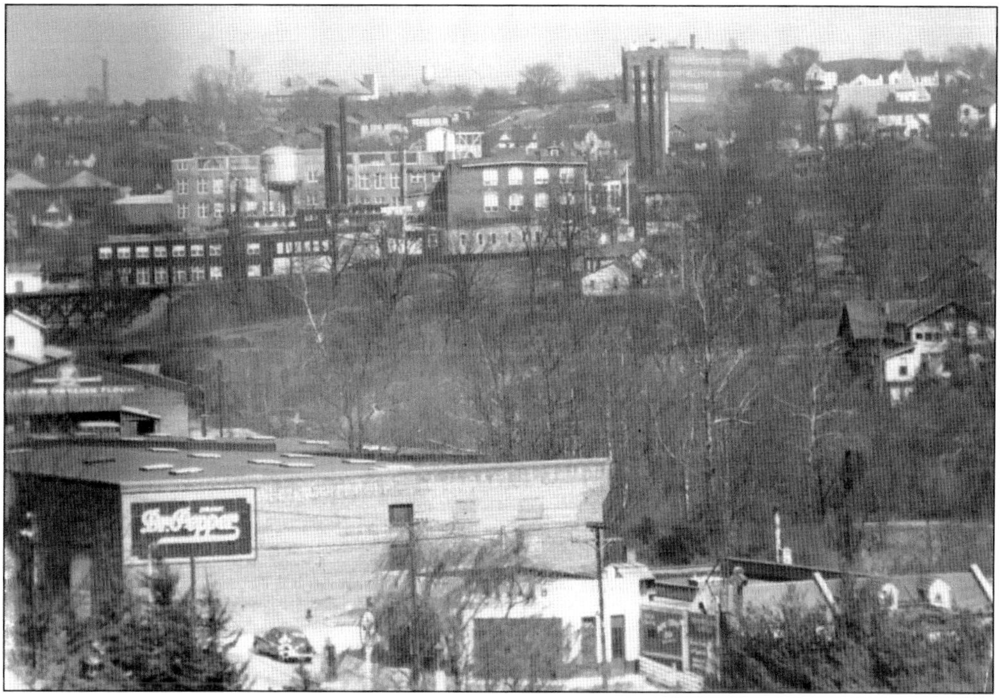

The lost neighborhood surrounding the Chatman Manufacturing Company, which once housed the Western Electric Complex and parts of the West End neighborhood, is shown in this c. 1950 photograph. The bottom part of the photograph shows the businesses and industry along Reynolda Road at Hanes Park. During the 19th century, this area was once part of the brush arbor of the Old Mulberry Church located along Reynolda Road and later, the Children's Home. (Courtesy FJ/WSHA.)

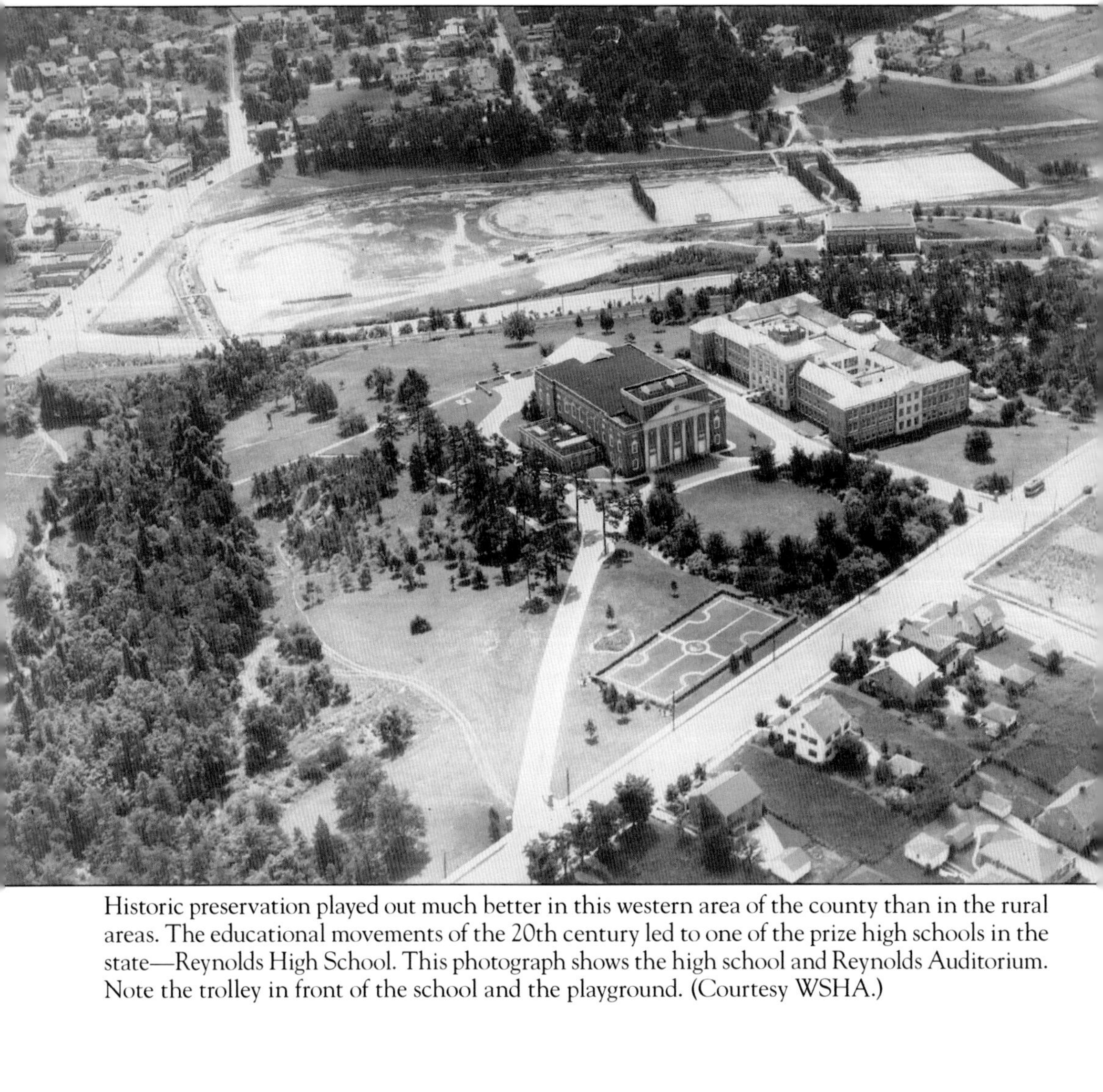

Historic preservation played out much better in this western area of the county than in the rural areas. The educational movements of the 20th century led to one of the prize high schools in the state—Reynolds High School. This photograph shows the high school and Reynolds Auditorium. Note the trolley in front of the school and the playground. (Courtesy WSHA.)

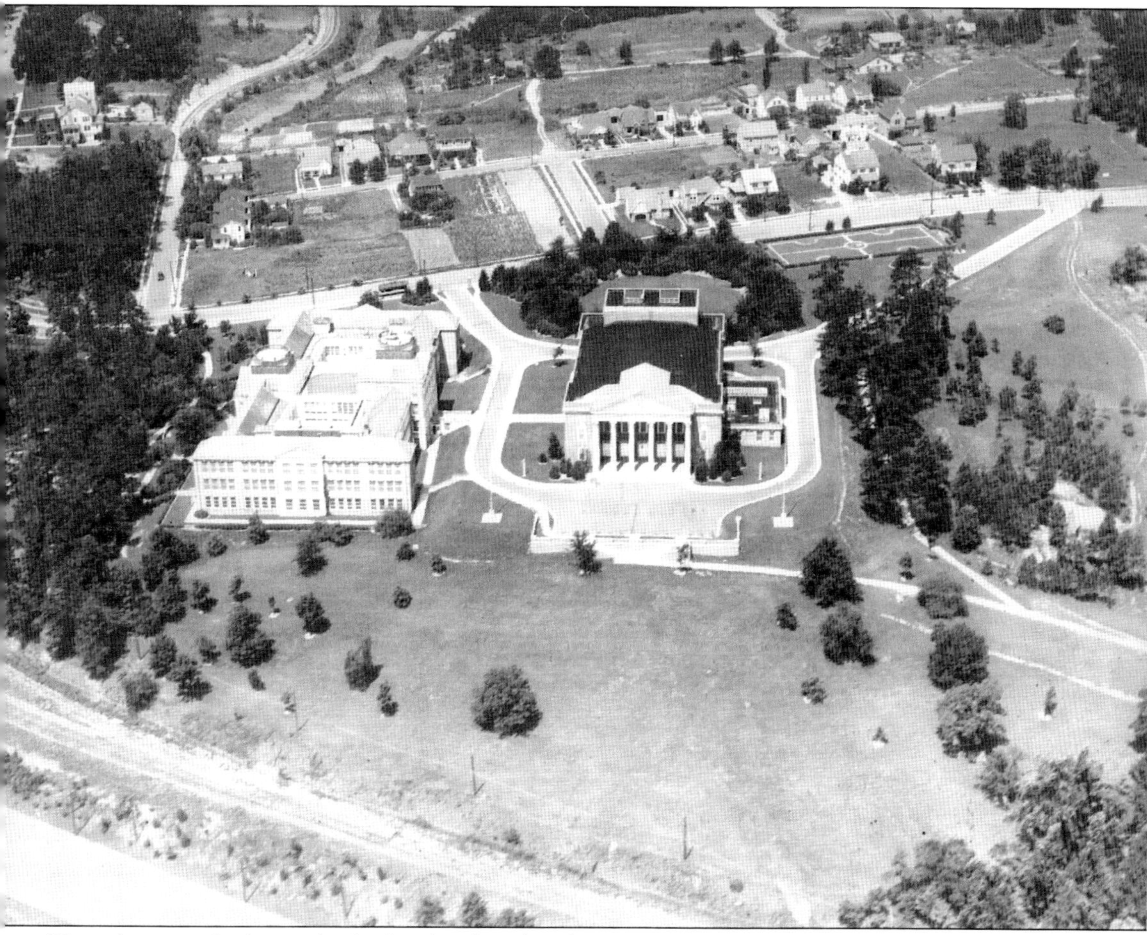

This photograph shows the high school and auditorium from the east along with the early development around the school. An older neighborhood existed here as part of a large farm in the 19th century. This farm had slaves who lived in this area as well. The top part of the photograph shows an African American neighborhood and cemetery. Legend has it that a shaman was said to reside here who provided support and protection for his people. (Courtesy WSHA.)

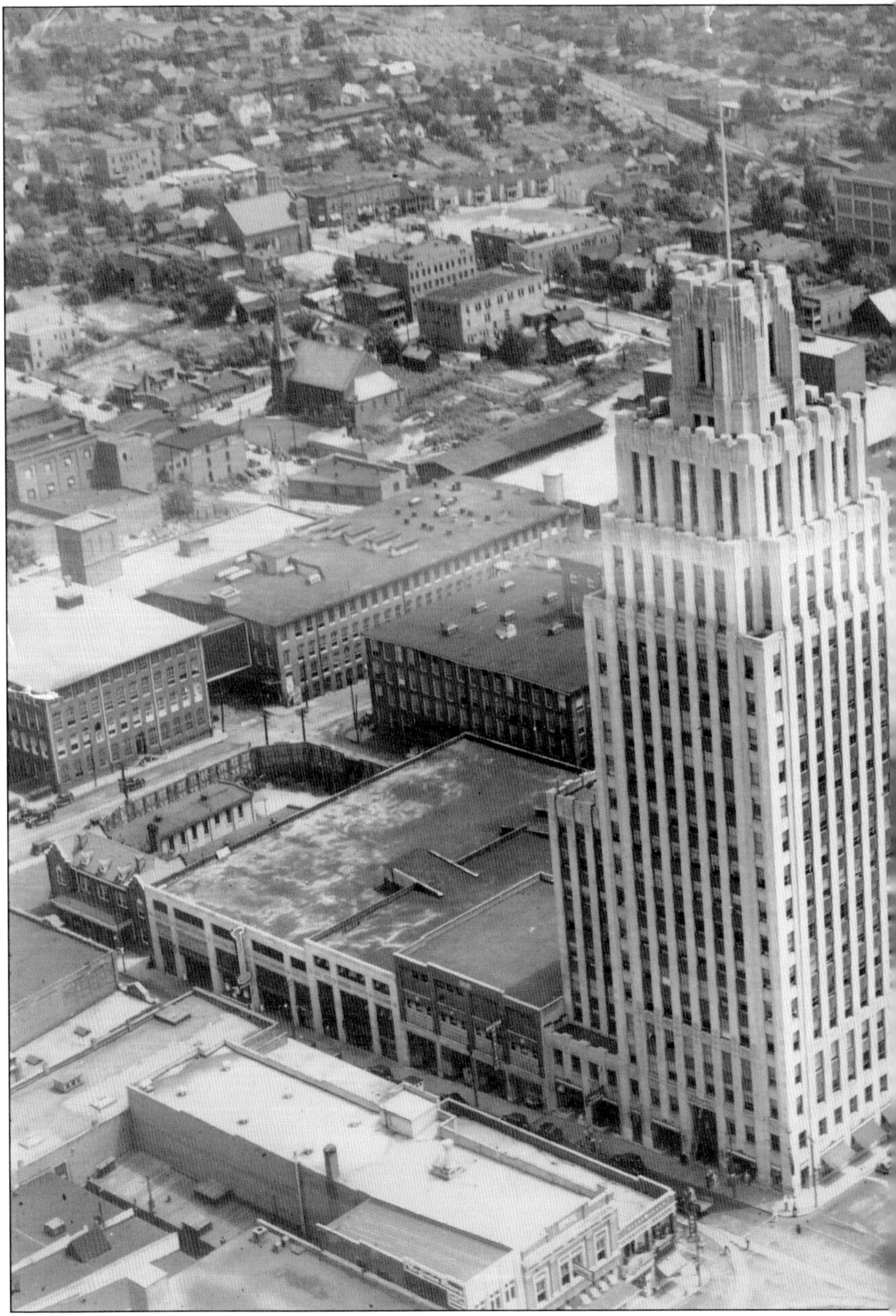

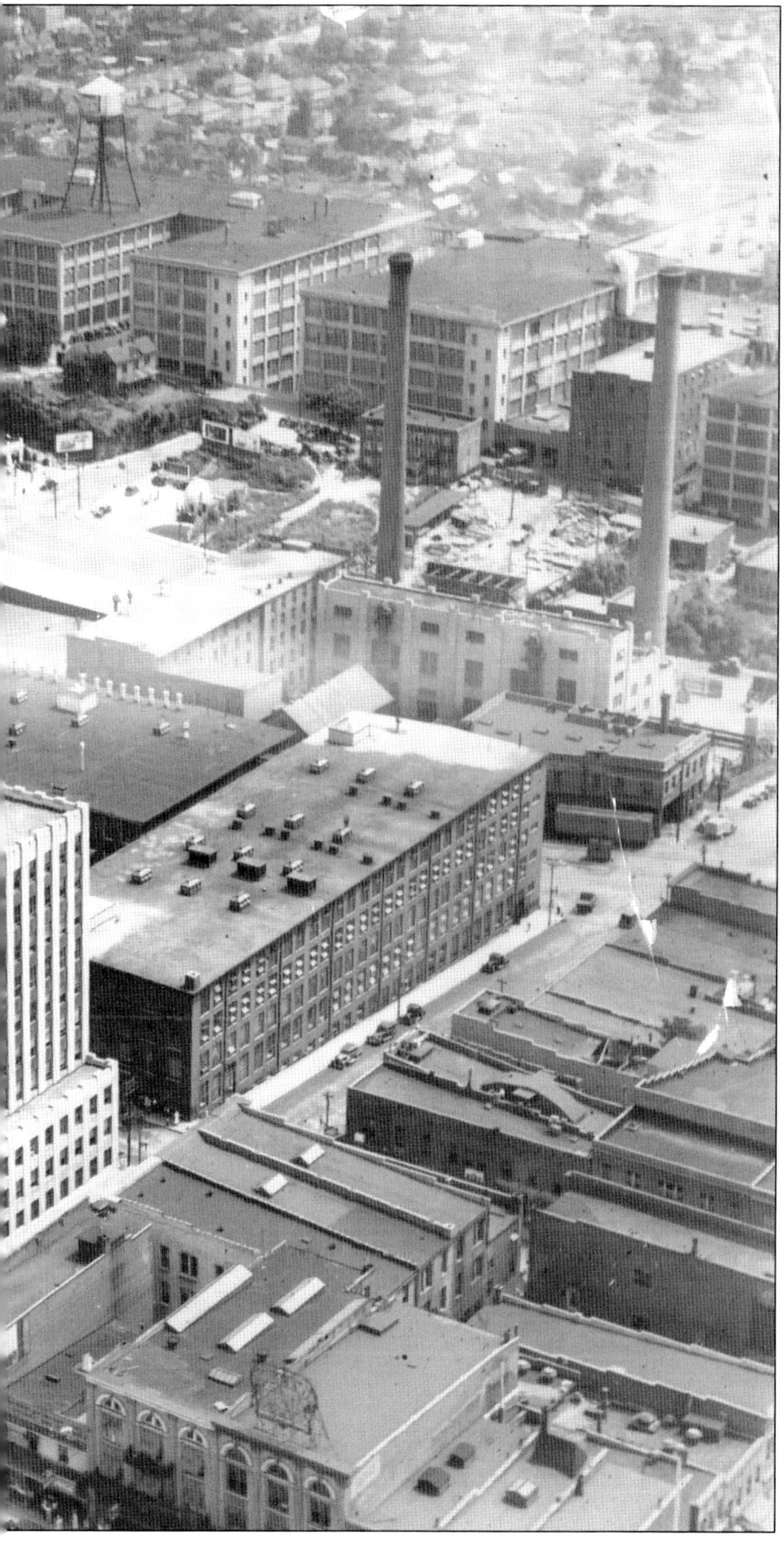

The central town of Forsyth County is shown with its centerpiece, the prototype of the Empire State Building in New York City, the Reynolds Building. The factories of Reynolds Tobacco Company surround the central building. The lost c. 1930 neighborhood of East Winston is in the upper left corner. The streets include Depot (Patterson Avenue), East Fifth, East Sixth, East Seventh, East Eighth, and Linden. East Fourth at Main is in the foreground. These structures were the dividing line of the African American businesses. Along East Fourth Street are the Lincoln, Lafayette, and Rex Theaters. To the west of the African American businesses were the white establishments along Main Street, including Piedmont Federal Savings and Loan, the Schuler Dry Goods Store, and the Forsyth County Jail. (Courtesy M. Bricker.)

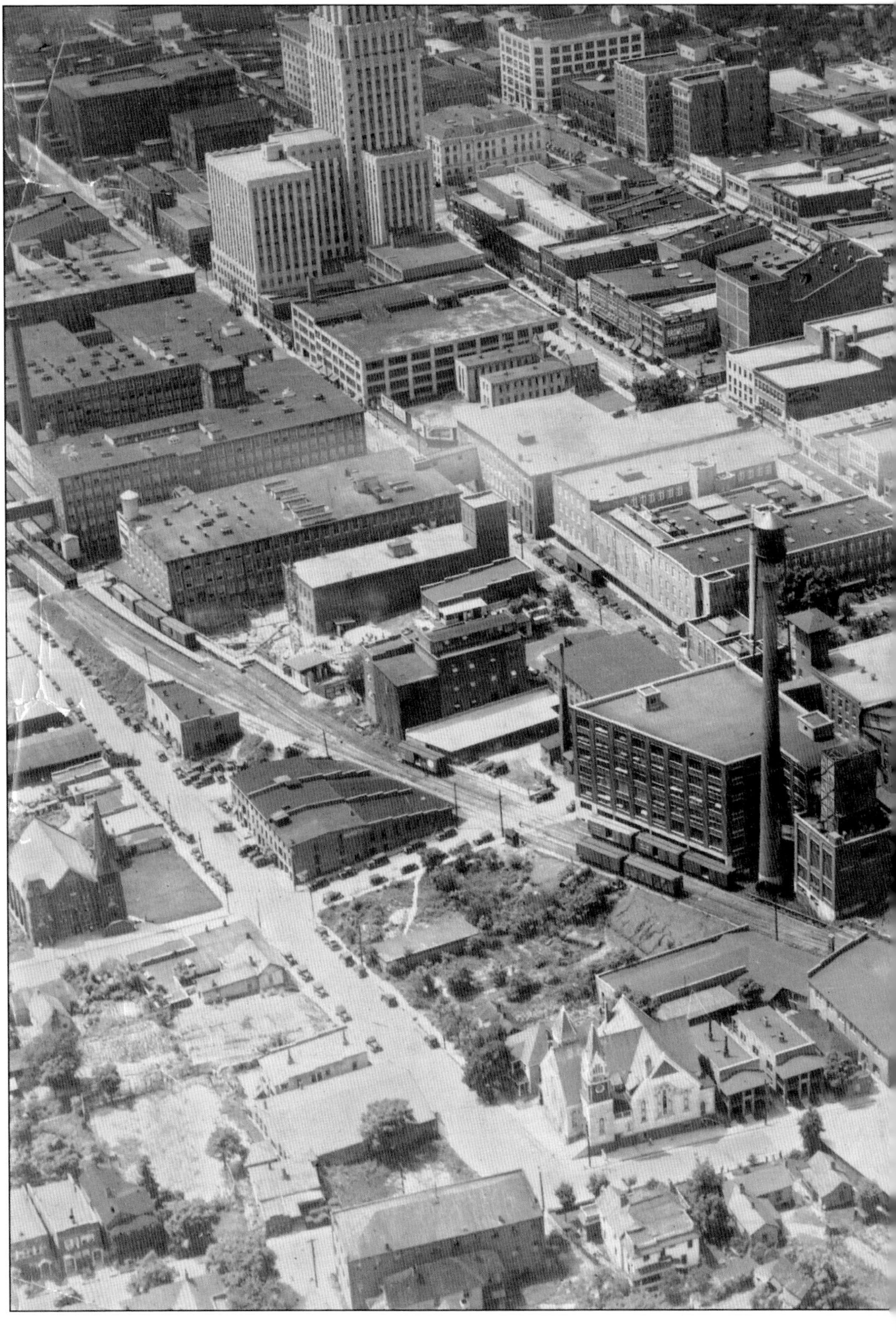

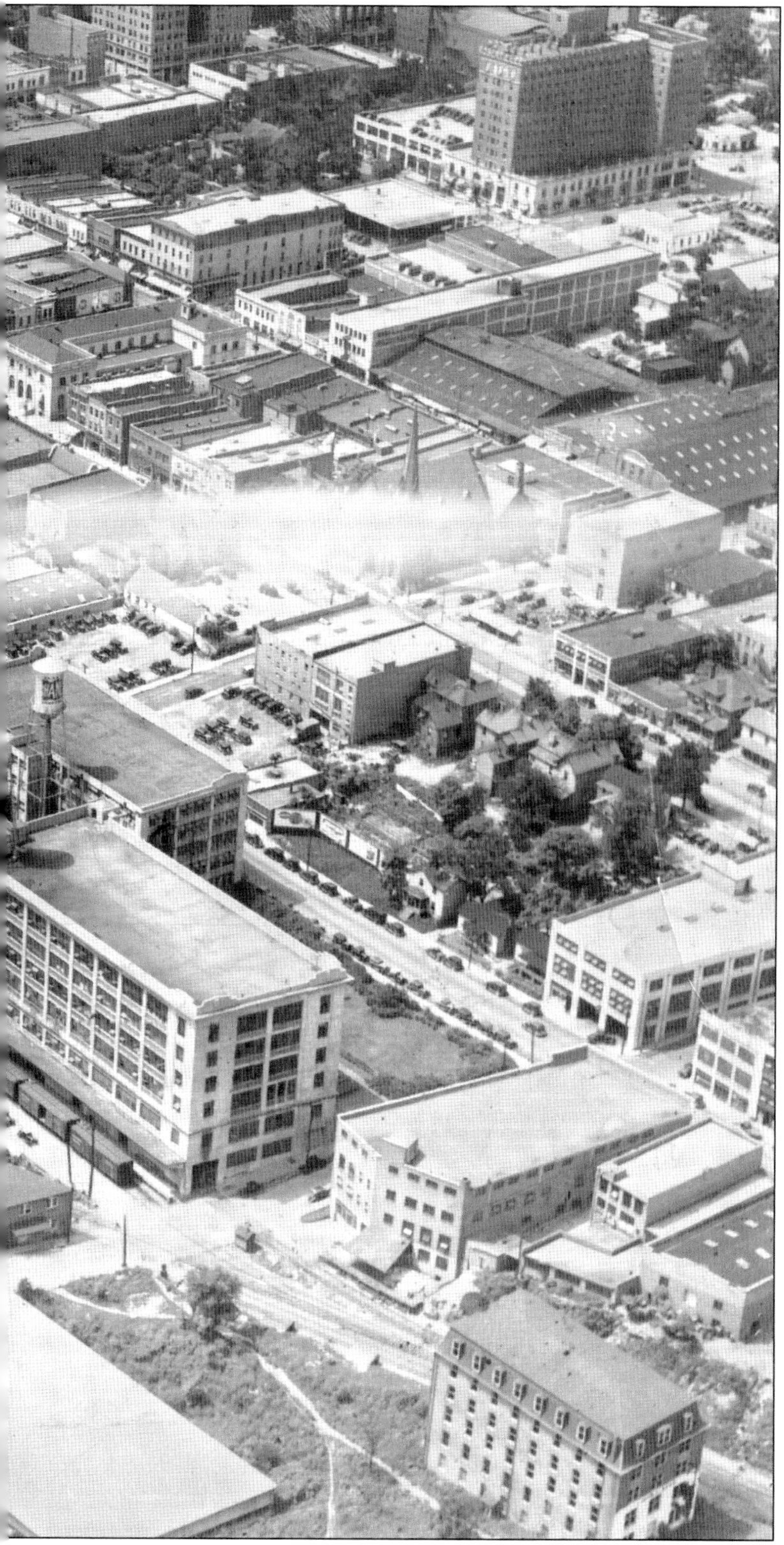

The west downtown area is shown in this c. 1930 photograph. Factories and businesses, including the State Theater, the Crest Building, and the Forsyth County Jail, were centered in the area of Fourth, Fifth, Trade, Liberty, and Church Streets, which are shown here. Churches and homes were also found here. The Robert E. Lee Hotel, built about 1923, was the dominant hotel for business and entertainment. The Nissen Building, built about 1926, is also shown. The boundaries of the new section of town were Fourth, Cherry, Marshall, and Fifth Streets. The central part of the photograph shows trees and homes amongst the buildings. Several of these homes were part of the early settlement before Winston expanded and included this county town into its fold. (Courtesy M. Bricker.)

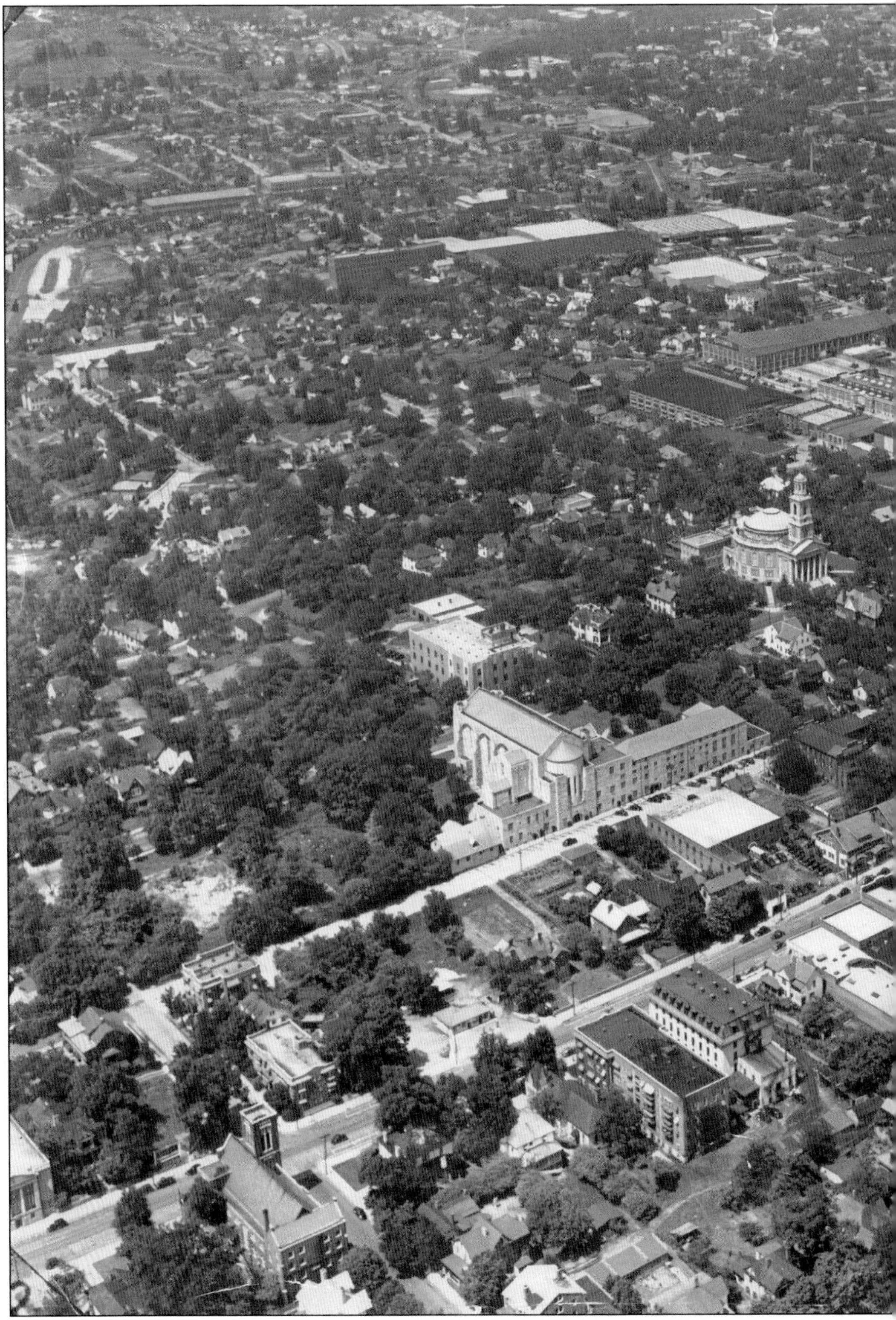

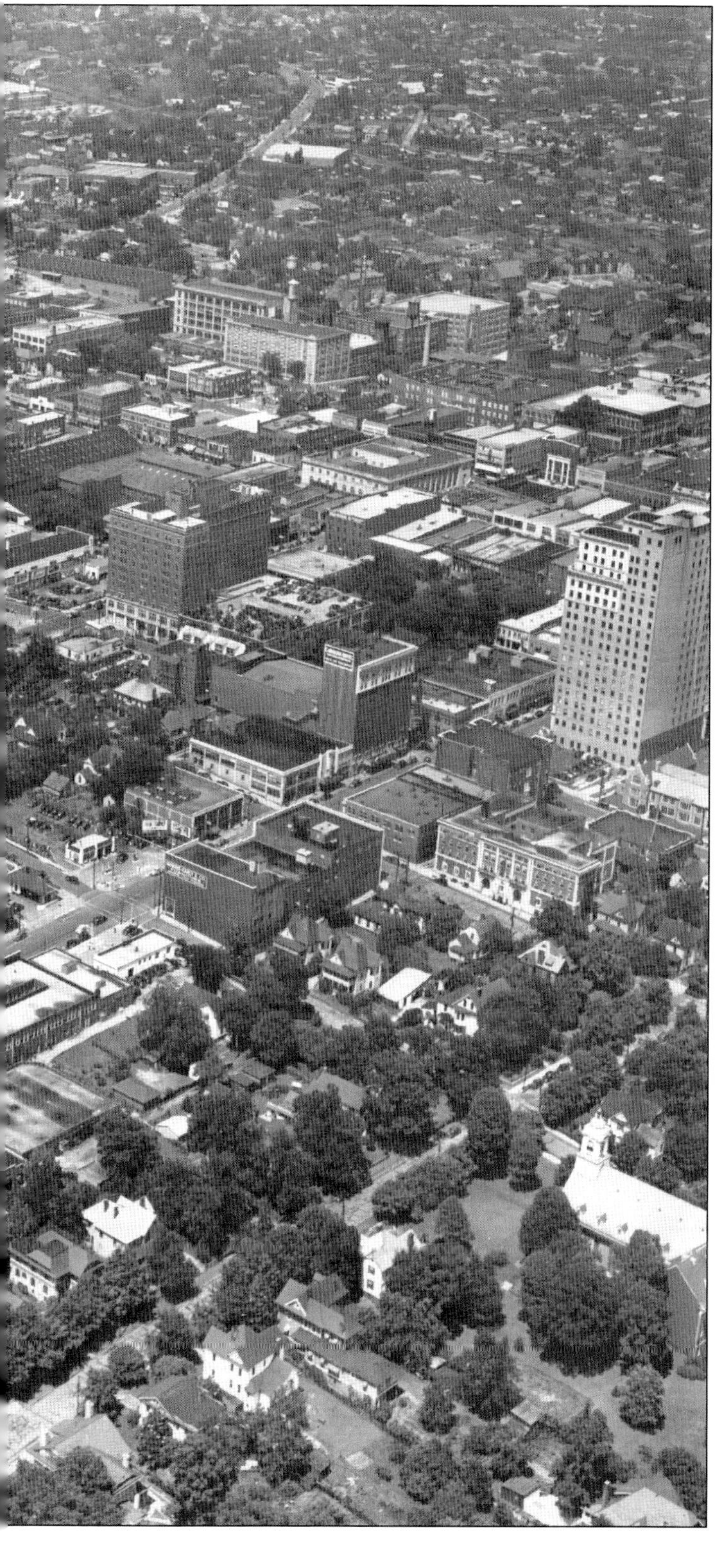

The homes located here were part of the North Cherry Street community. It included warehouses, churches, and individual businesses such as grocery stores and feed stores. Most of this area was razed due to the expansion of the highway system of the Cherry-Marshall Street corridor in the 1960s. From the west, the area beyond the buildings was part of eastern Winston-Salem. The largest building, the Nissen Building, shown to the right, was built by the Nissen family after they sold Nissen Wagon Works and began investing in real estate. The Holly Avenue neighborhood, shown in the foreground, originated with the Calvary Moravian Church, built in the 1870s. This was a pocket neighborhood. (Courtesy WSHA.)

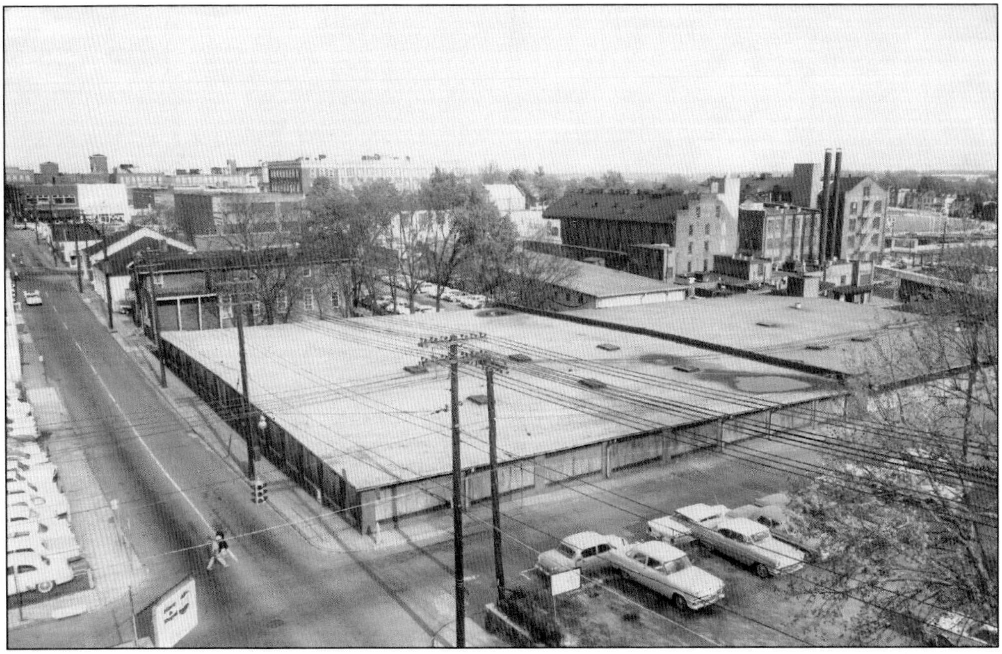

The Brown and Williamson Tobacco factory is shown at right in this 1890s image. In the 1840s, the first schoolhouse in Winston and the first house built by Thomas Wilson were located on this block. The lines of autos to the left were part of the Blue Bird Cab Company, one of the oldest taxi services in town. This was also the original location of the first suburb of Winston in the 1870s. (Courtesy FJ/WSHA)

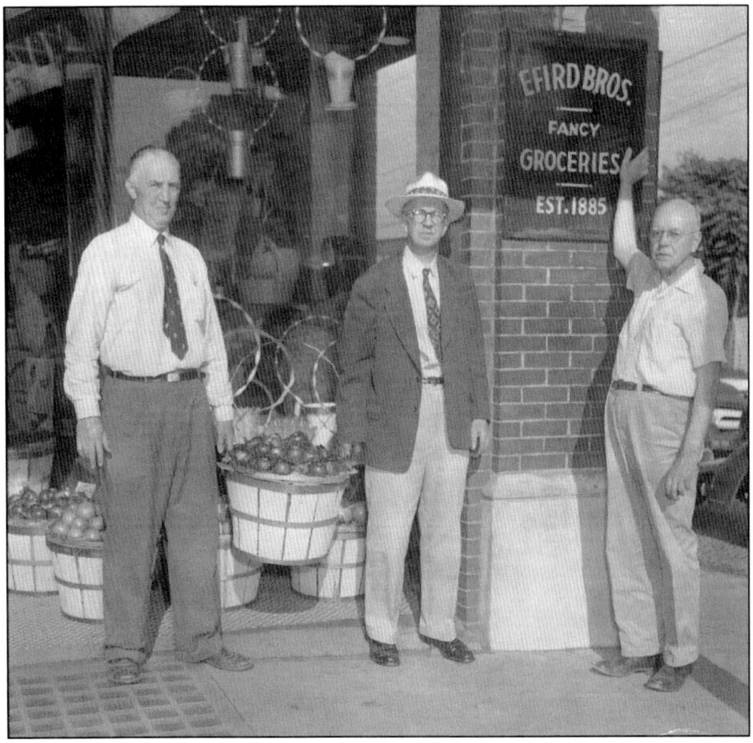

The location of lost neighborhoods and lost cities should be a factor in deciding what is to be restored and preserved and what is not. The Efird Grocery Store is an example of the many grocery stores that exisited in the central town of Forsyth. The city was known for having a grocery store on every corner. (Courtesy WSHA.)

These ladies were decorating their upper apartment in the old Trade Street business district of the central city of Forsyth County. Throughout the 19th and early 20th century, tobacco farmers throughout Forsyth County brought their wares to this stretch of roadway to sell. Additional stories were added to the buildings along Trade Street, which became living quarters above the businesses. (Courtesy FJ/WSHA.)

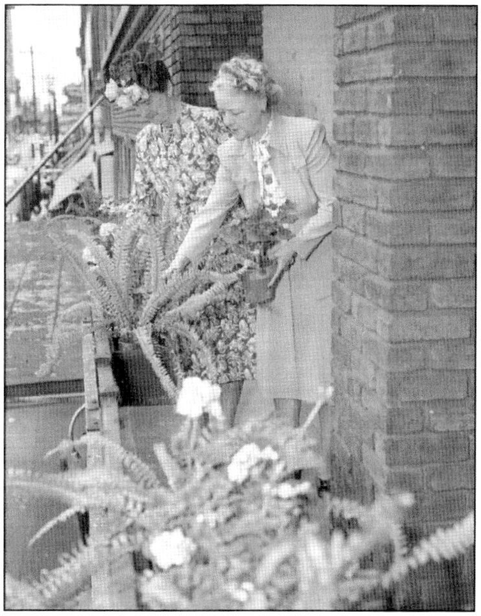

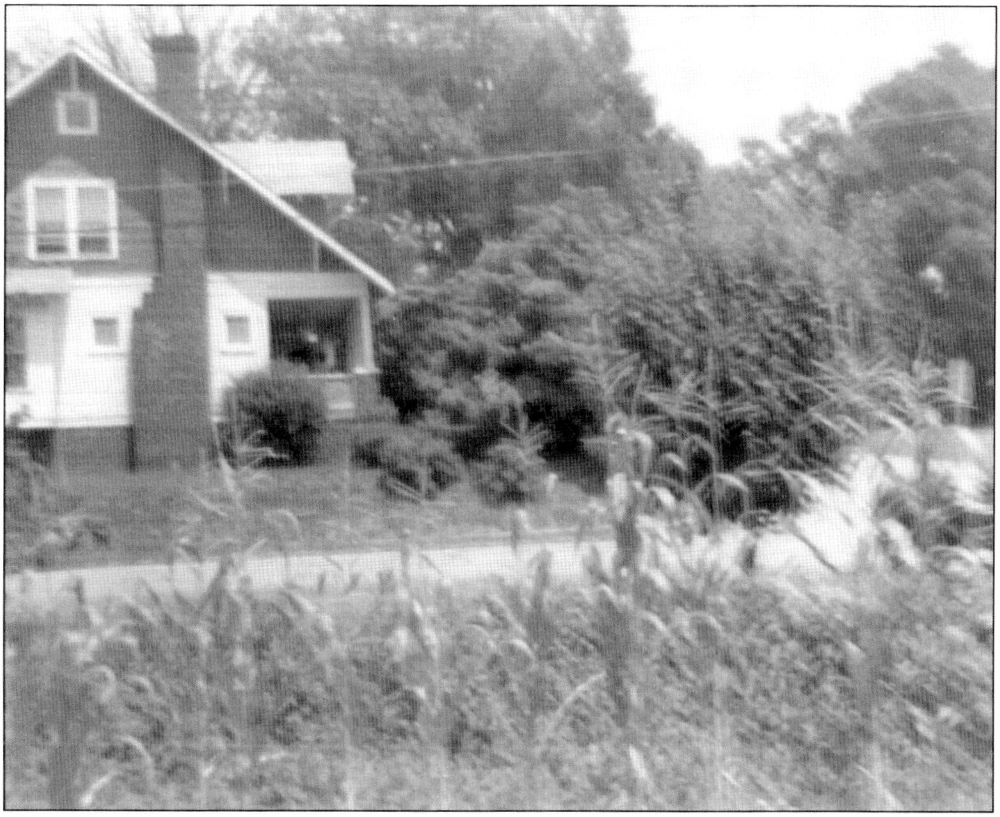

The lost neighborhood of Park Circle and Watkins Street is shown in the early 1970s. This garden was dedicated by the Holcomb family to memorialize the Victory Gardens that were prevalent throughout Forsyth County towns and neighborhoods during World War II and the Great Depression. (Courtesy M. Bricker.)

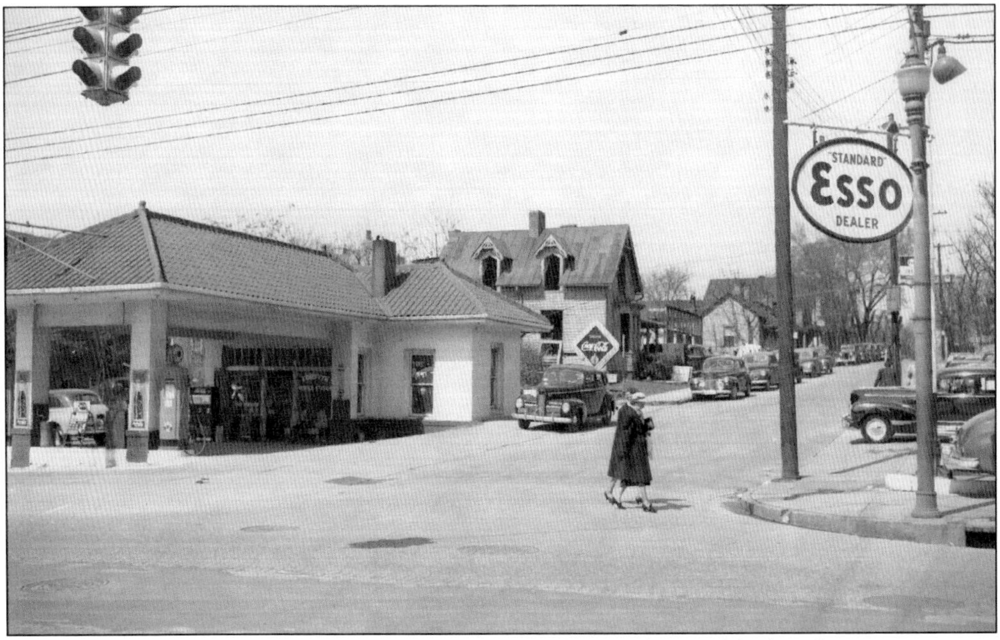

The lost neighborhood of West Fourth Street is pictured here. This neighborhood was an extension of older ones found throughout Forsyth County. Often, the neighborhoods in downtown business areas were comprised of merely one or two city streets. Residents often built a line of homes in proximity to the early business districts. (Courtesy M. Bricker.)

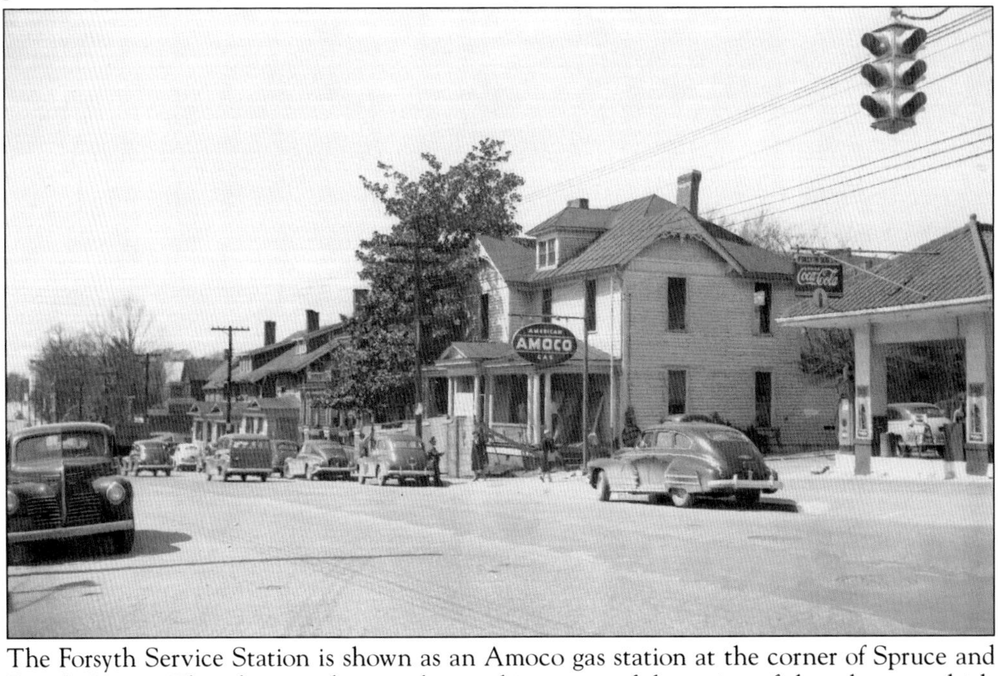

The Forsyth Service Station is shown as an Amoco gas station at the corner of Spruce and Fourth Streets. This photograph was taken within a year of the razing of these homes, which were located in one of the earliest neighborhoods in downtown Winston. Like many towns across Forsyth County at this time, many of the earlier neighborhoods and businesses were replaced in the 1950s. (Courtesy M. Bricker.)

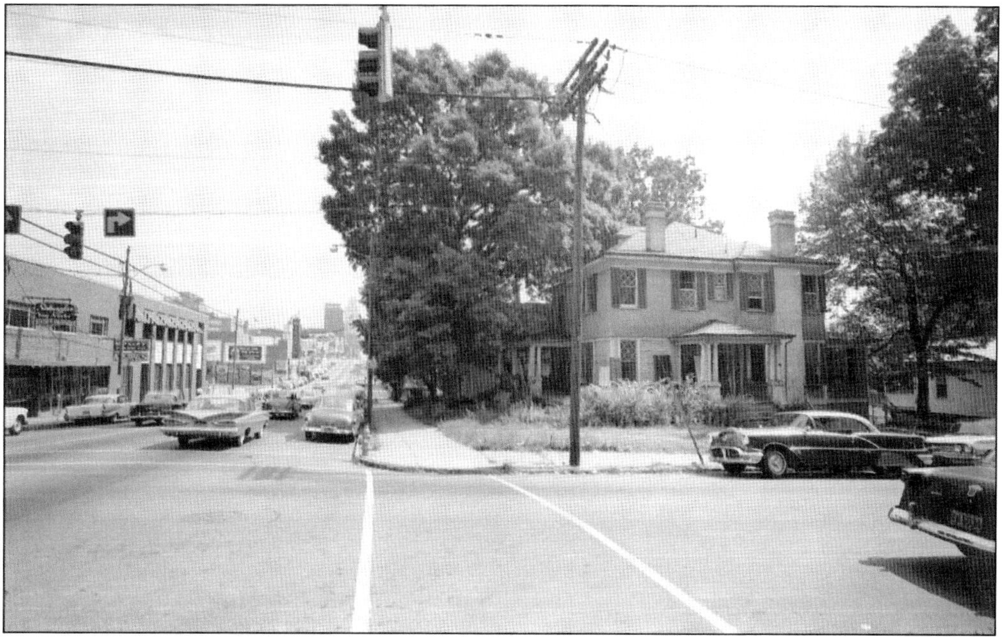

This large mansion at the corner of Spring and Fourth Streets was the last remnant of this early downtown neighborhood. The streetscape to the left of the home was the location of the older neighborhood in the previous photograph, which was razed. Unfortunately, progress without historical preservation has eliminated many rich architectural wonders that once existed throughout Forsyth County. (Courtesy M. Bricker.)

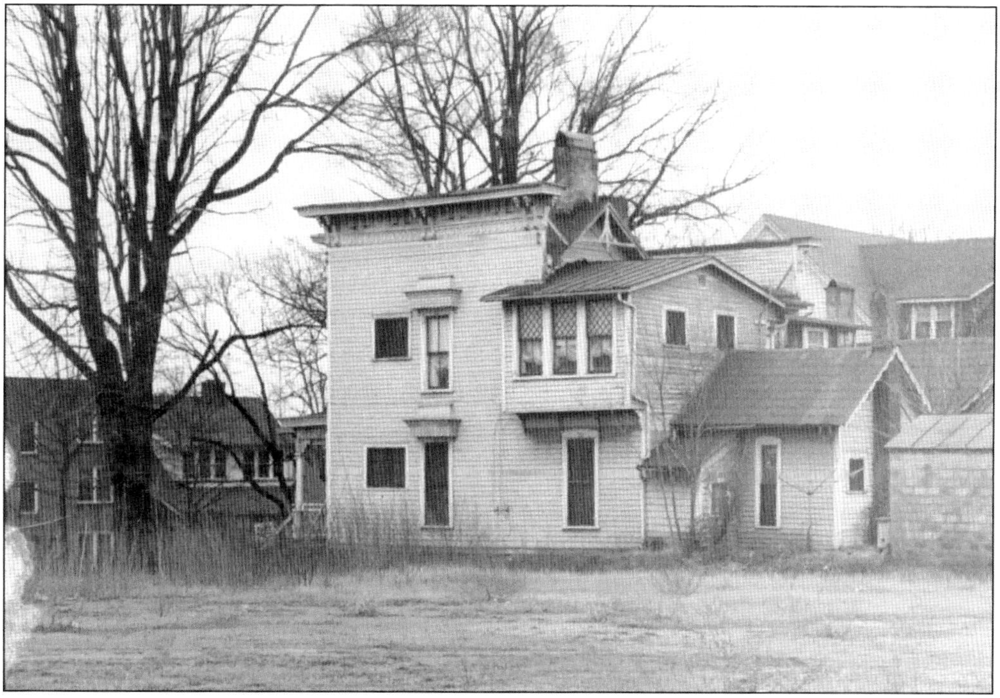

Many homes that were built in the 19th century evolved as the years passed. This older home place on Fourth Street shows numerous additions. (Courtesy WSHA.)

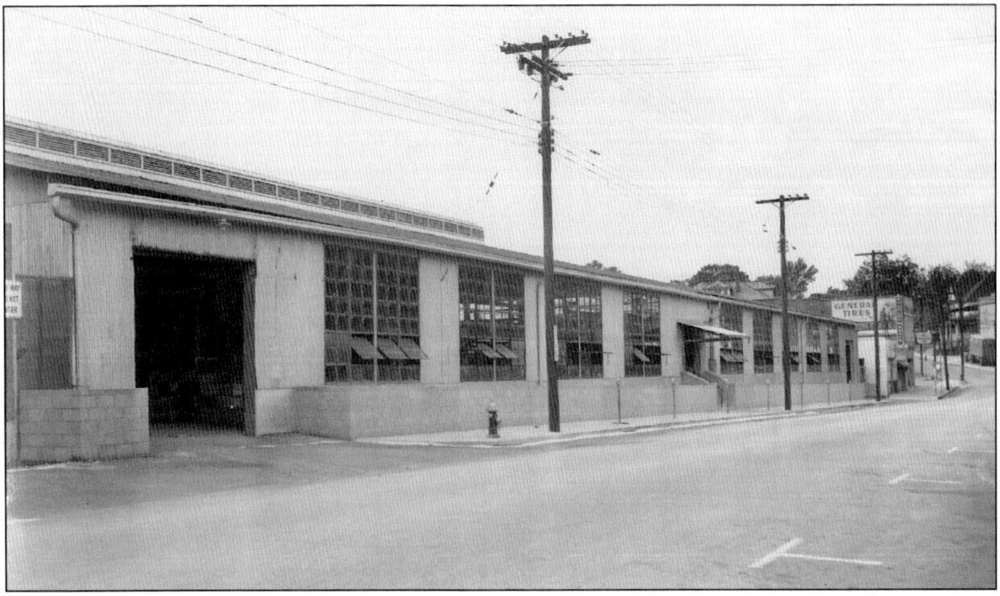

This is an example of a tobacco warehouse. Planters Warehouse, located in the central business area along Trade and Cherry Streets, burned in the 1960s. It was replaced by the W.G. White Grocery Store. White was a long-time businessman in the downtown area. (Courtesy FJ/WSHA.)

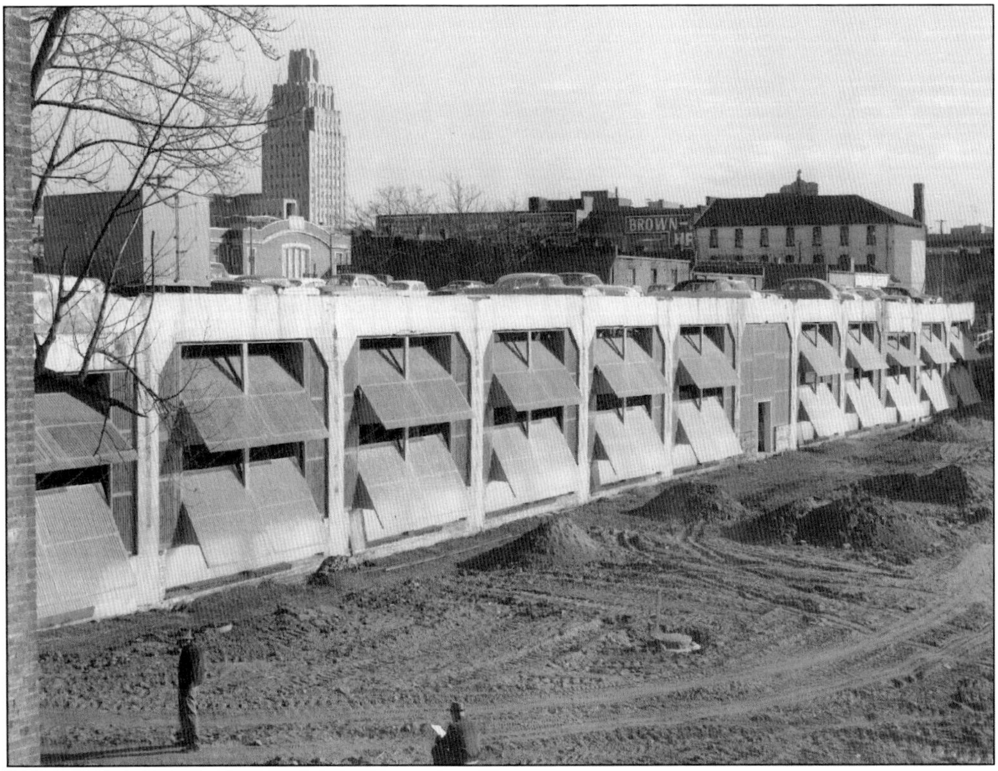

The advent of automobiles generated a parking problem through the 1950s. This photograph shows one of the earliest multilevel parking garages located in the tobacco farmers' premiere spot, Trade Street. In the distance looms the Reynolds Building. (Courtesy FJ/WSHA.)

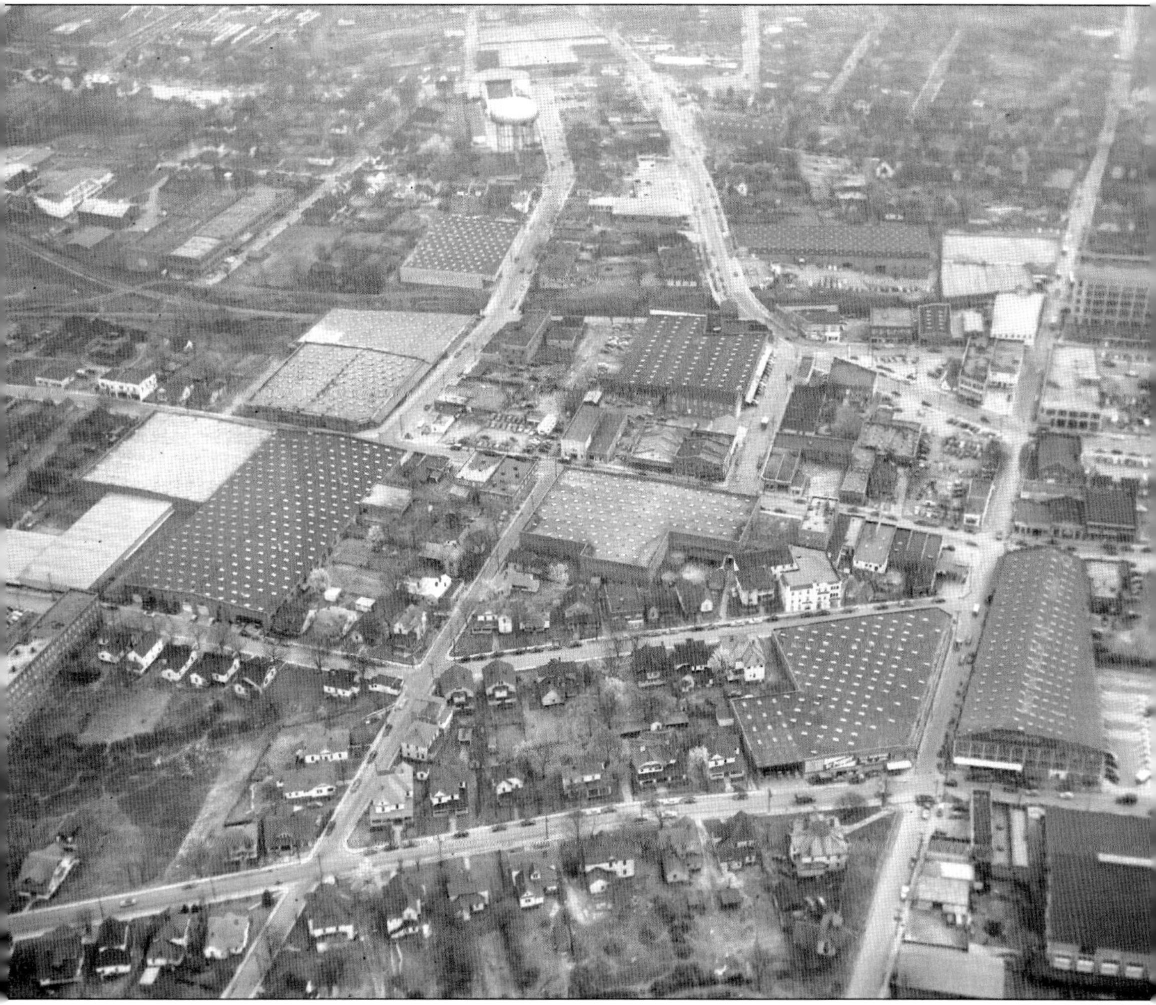

As the business area of Forsyth County's largest town expanded, another neighborhood was very close to being lost. The Cherry-Marshall neighborhood grew up around the hubbub of the tobacco warehouses and the tobacco sells that had permeated the town for more then 100 years. The upper part of this c. 1950 photograph shows Old Liberty Street as it winds out of the town, passing remnants of the old town of Liberty (incorporated about 1800) before changing to Old Walkertown Road. (Courtesy WSHA.)

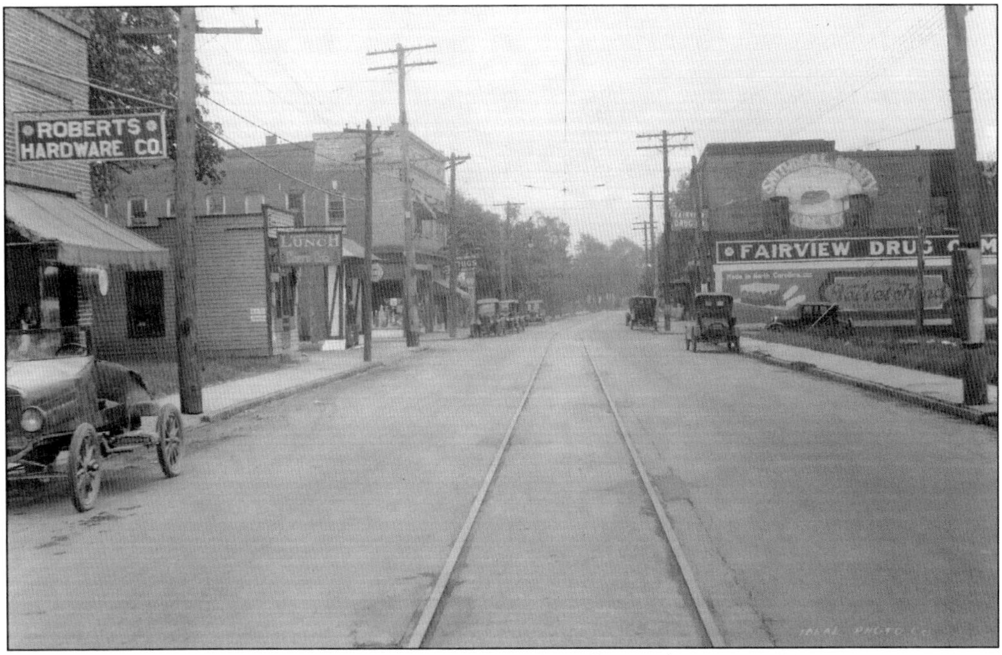

This c. 1915 photograph shows a small, older hamlet of Forsyth County. Fairview was a town within itself. It was once part of the Old Liberty Street corridor, which included the town of Liberty. The streetcar line ran from Winston and ended in the Fairview neighborhood. The larger two buildings, Fairview Drug Company and the two-story building across from it, still exist as potential landmarks along this area of North Winston. (Courtesy M. Bricker.)

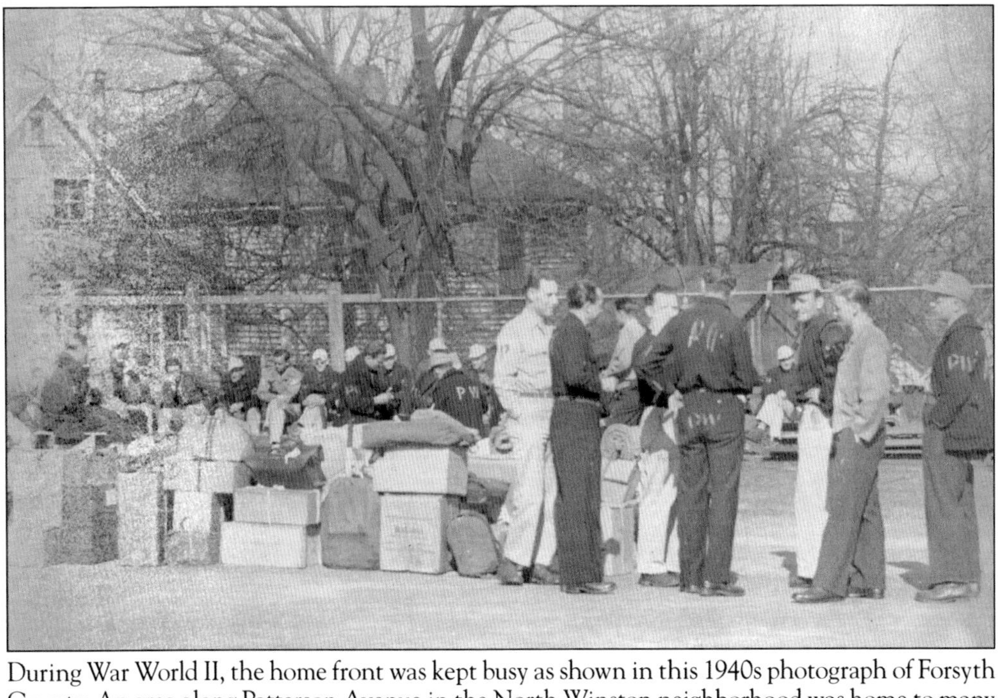

During War World II, the home front was kept busy as shown in this 1940s photograph of Forsyth County. An area along Patterson Avenue in the North Winston neighborhood was home to many captured German soldiers. (Courtesy WSHA.)

Four

LOCAL LANDMARKS

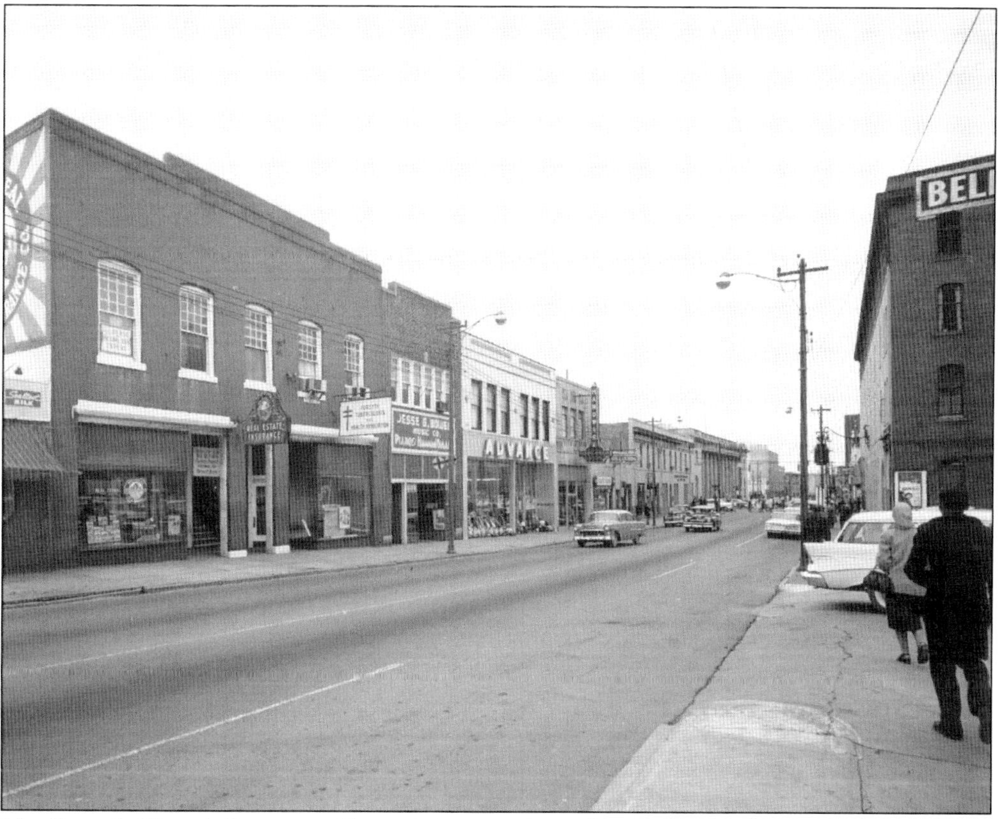

The Forsyth Historic Resources Commission was formed to oversee and maintain historic sites and landmarks. The central town of Forsyth, Winston-Salem, lies in the middle of the county, and the commission is located here, under the jurisdiction of the Winston-Salem Planning Board. A local landmark, the US post office, built about 1914, is shown along Fifth Street. (Courtesy FJ/WSHA.)

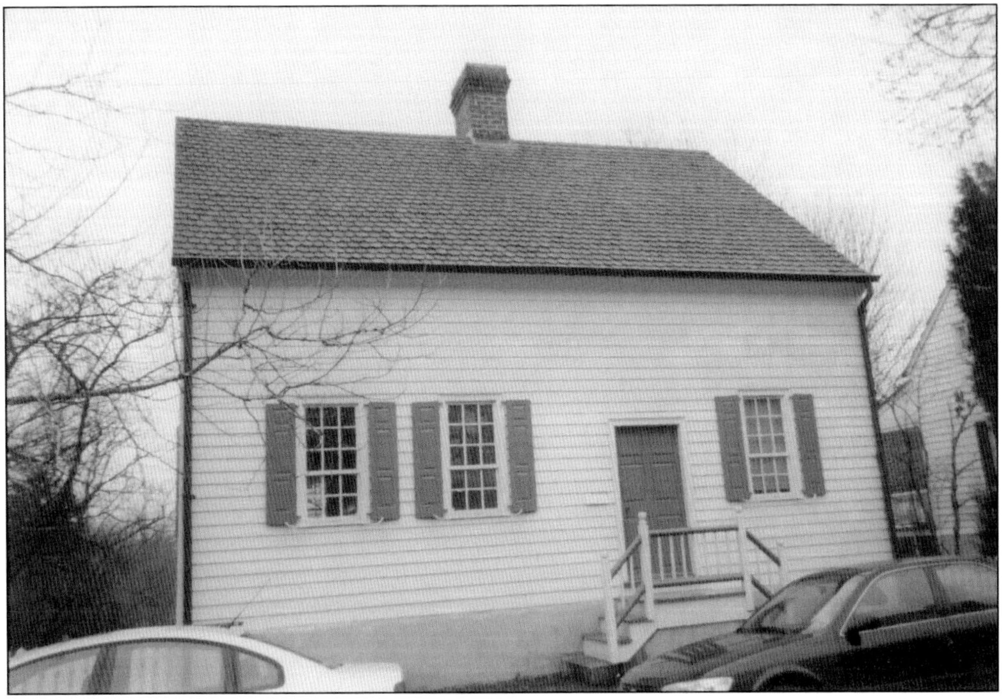

The largest concentration of local landmarks appearing on the Forsyth County Resource Commission's list is located in the Old Salem Historic District in East Salem. However, the West Salem Historic District, which with East Salem comprises the Salem town lot, has no designated landmarks. Shown here is the Levering Home, a landmark in the Old Salem Historic District in East Salem. (Courtesy M. Bricker.)

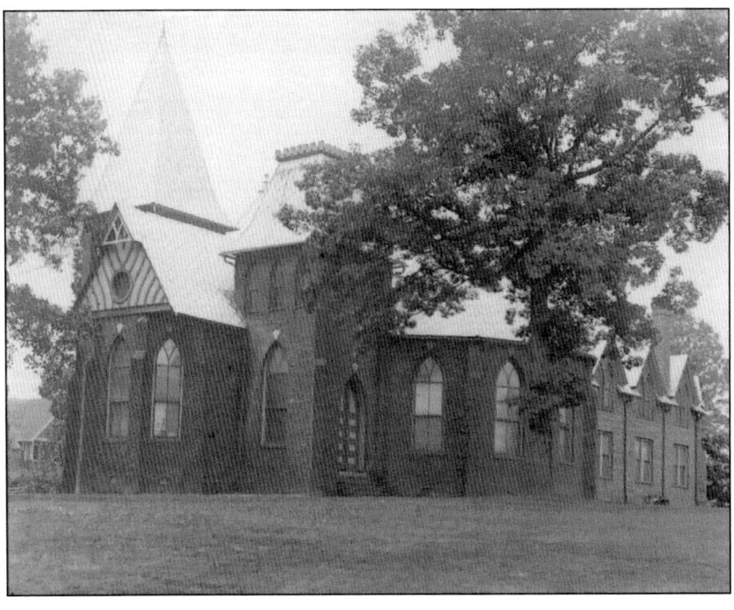

Although not designated an official local landmark, the Christ Moravian Church on Academy Street dates to around 1920. The church represents one of 100 19th-century structures located in the West Salem Historic District. The asymmetrical facade and arched windows are key features of this structure. (Courtesy M. Bricker.)

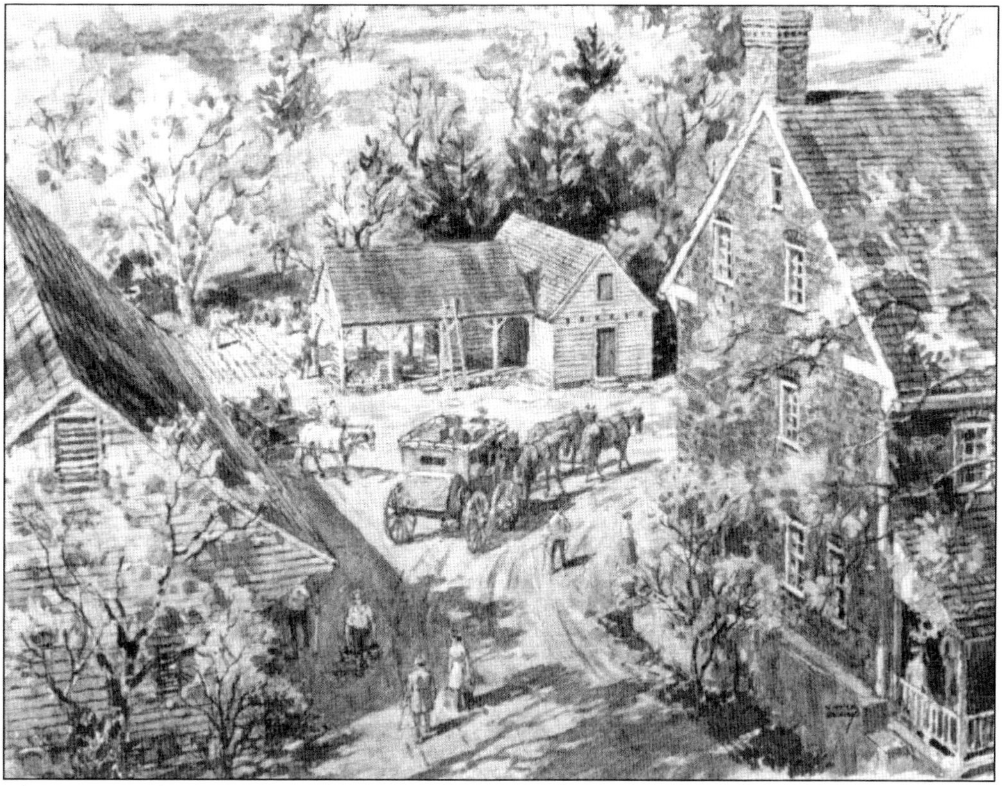

This painting depicts a piece of Forsyth History and was used during the reconstruction of Old Salem beginning in 1950. The Salem Tavern, built about 1784 and a local landmark, is visited by the Hattie Butner stage line from Clemmonsville. The outbuilding and barn to the left were built in the 1740s. The barn was part of the E. Beverly Jones farm, started about 1847, and is located north of Bethania on Tobaccoville Road. (Courtesy Moravian Archives/WSHA.)

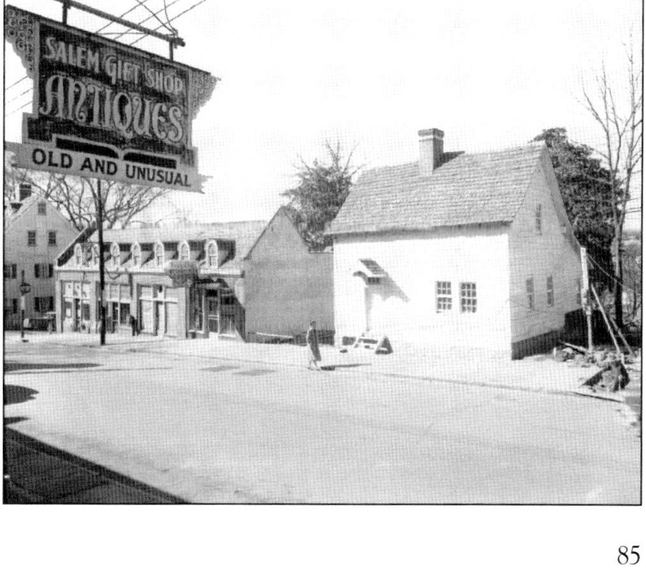

This small white building was home to the Miksch Tobacco Shop, which opened about 1771 on Main Street in Salem. Note the contrast with the later building on the left, the c. 1930s Krispy Kreme, which was razed at the cost of preserving one historical building over another. Forsyth County residents in other hamlets voiced indignation over the preservation of certain buildings at the expense of others. (Courtesy FJ/WSHA.)

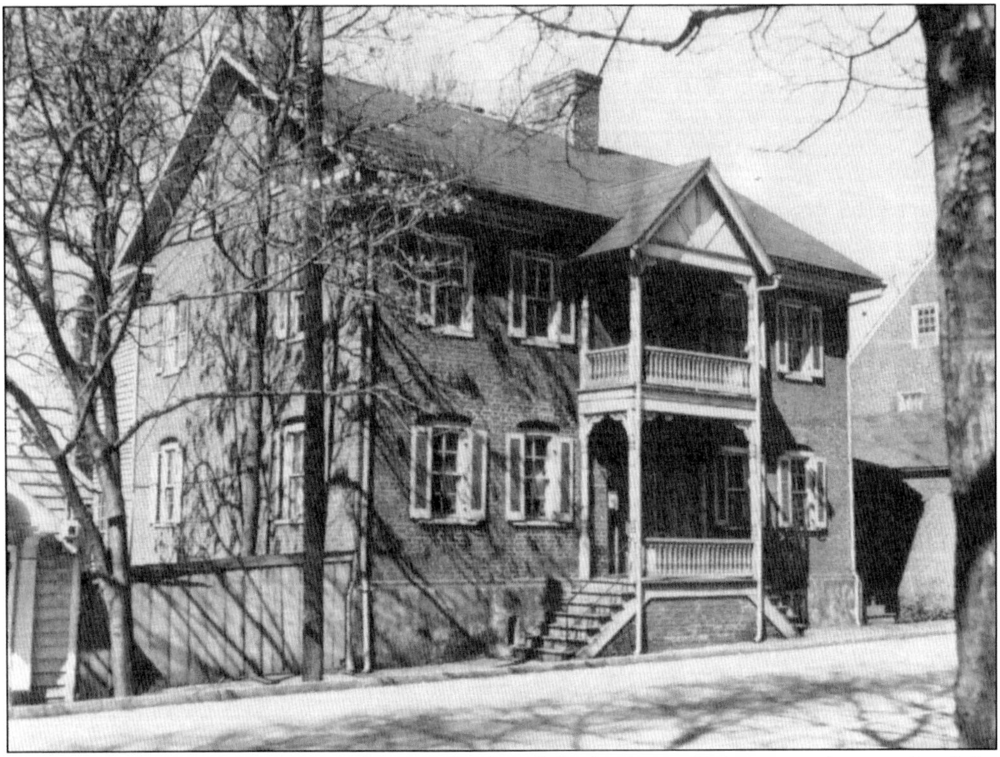

The Christopher Vogler House, a historic landmark built about 1797, is a good example of the change experienced by those who lived in Salem between the 1870s and the 1960s. Francis Miller purchased the Vogler House and added a second story and a Victorian stoop. Christopher Vogler was a gunsmith, and was followed by a long line of craftsmen in Salem. (Courtesy Moravian Archives/WSHA.)

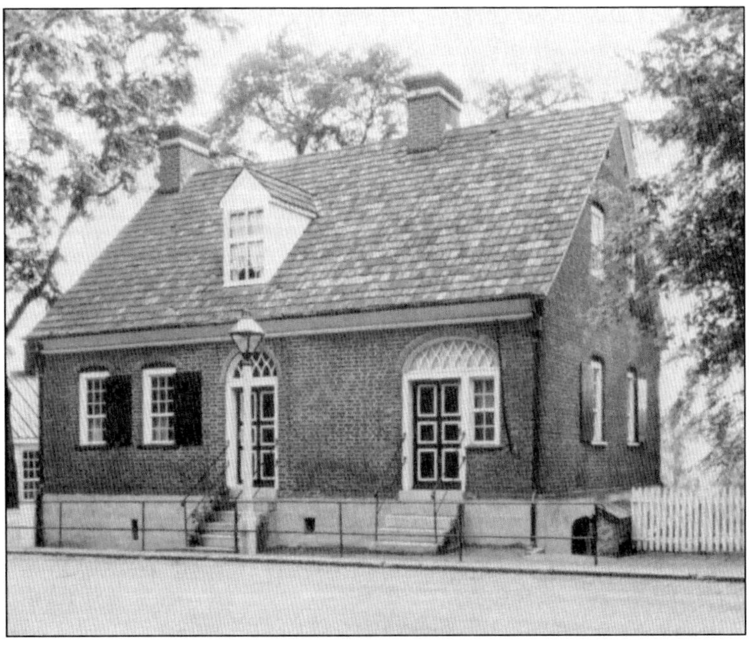

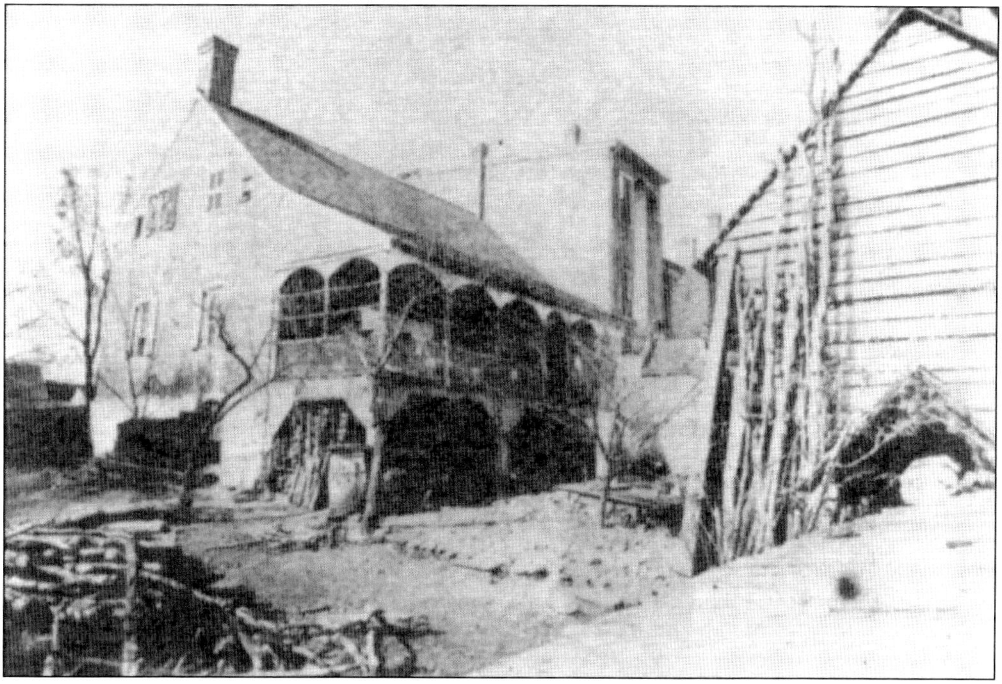

Another major change affecting many local landmarks was the addition of shops to residents' homes. The Targott Leinbach House, built about 1824 by silversmith and pioneer Dauerrean, had separate entrances to his shop and living quarters. In the 1850s, he built a long, three-story addition, pictured above. In 1912, the home and addition were razed. The southern part of Main Street moved toward modernization much like Winston-Salem, beginning in the 20th century. Today, the reconstructed original building has returned, pictured below. (Courtesy Moravian Archives/WSHA.)

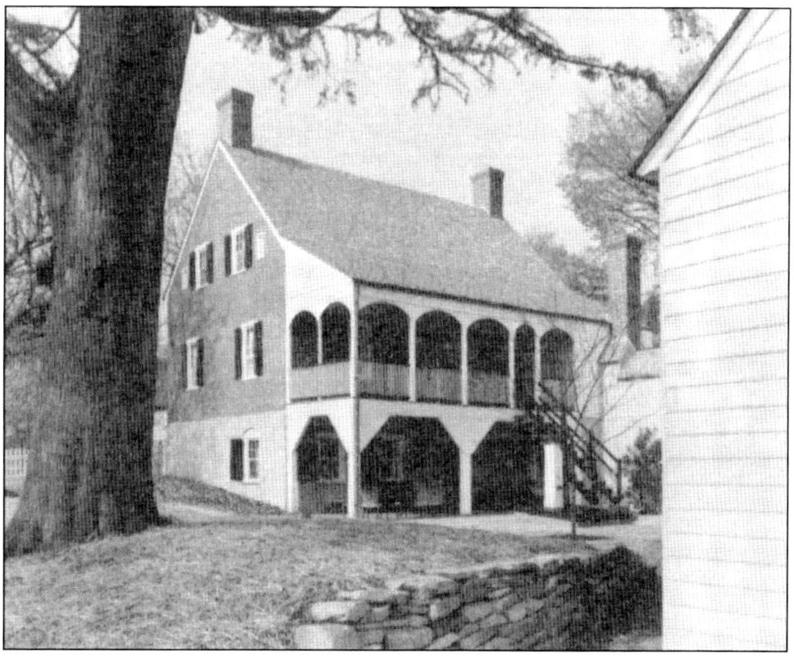

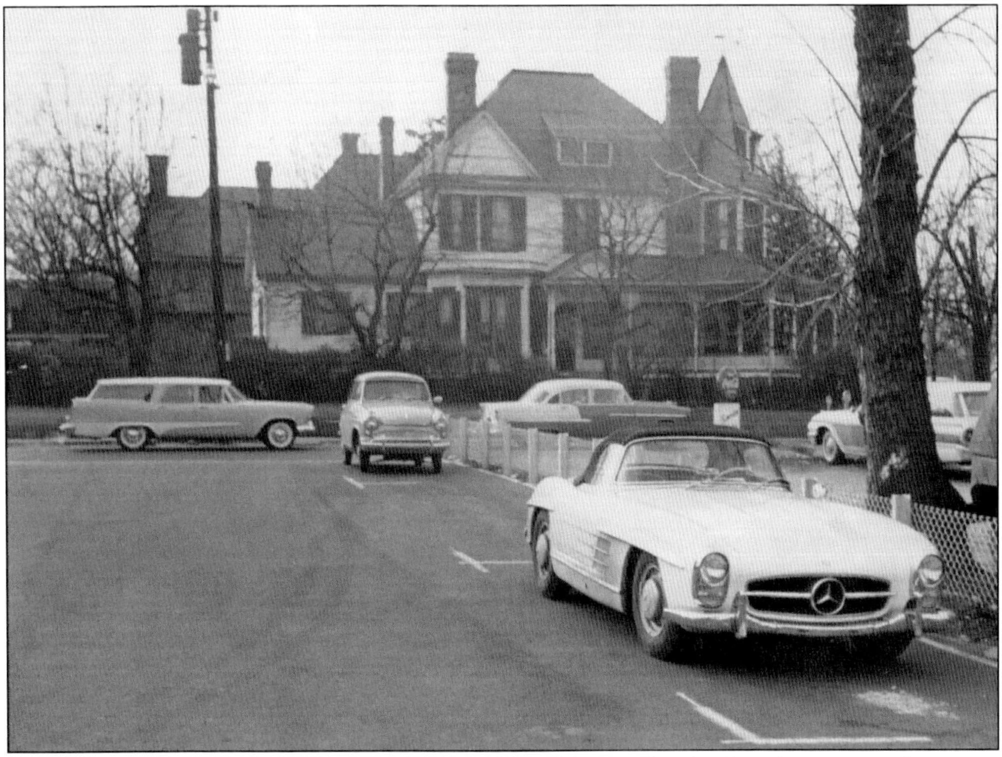

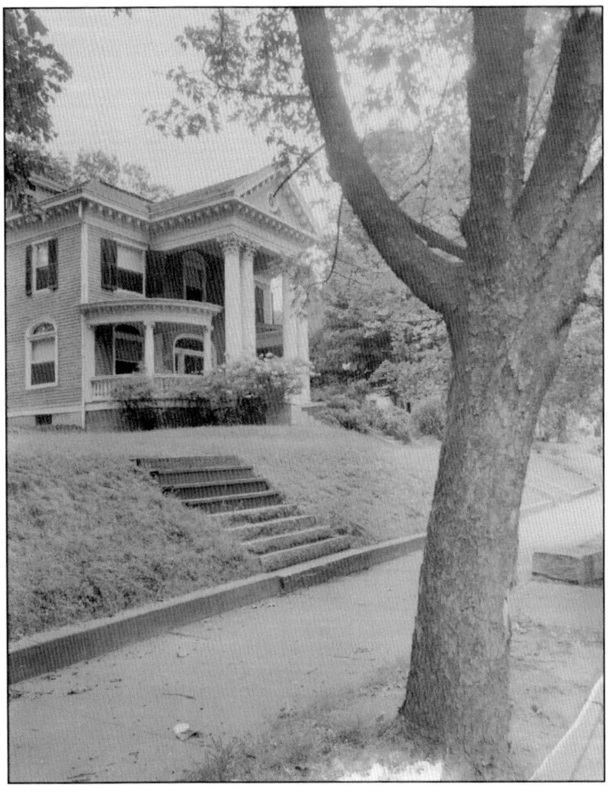

One landmark mansion that speaks of the wealth and prosperity of the Victorian era in Forsyth County is the H.D. Poindexter House, built about 1892 and pictured above about 1960. Poindexter was a successful hardware merchant. The building that housed his business, one of the oldest in Winston, survives at the corner of Trade Street near Fourth Street. A Queen Anne house at the corner of Fifth and Spruce Streets in Winston, the Poindexter was moved in the 1970s to the West End Historic District. At left is the Rosenbacher House, built about 1909 and pictured in the 1950s. Alladin Rosenbacher, a clothing merchant, built his retail store at the corner of Liberty and Fourth Streets. His store advertised: "Boys and Children's Clothing in varied styles—we carry the largest stock in North Carolina." (Courtesy FJ/WSHA.)

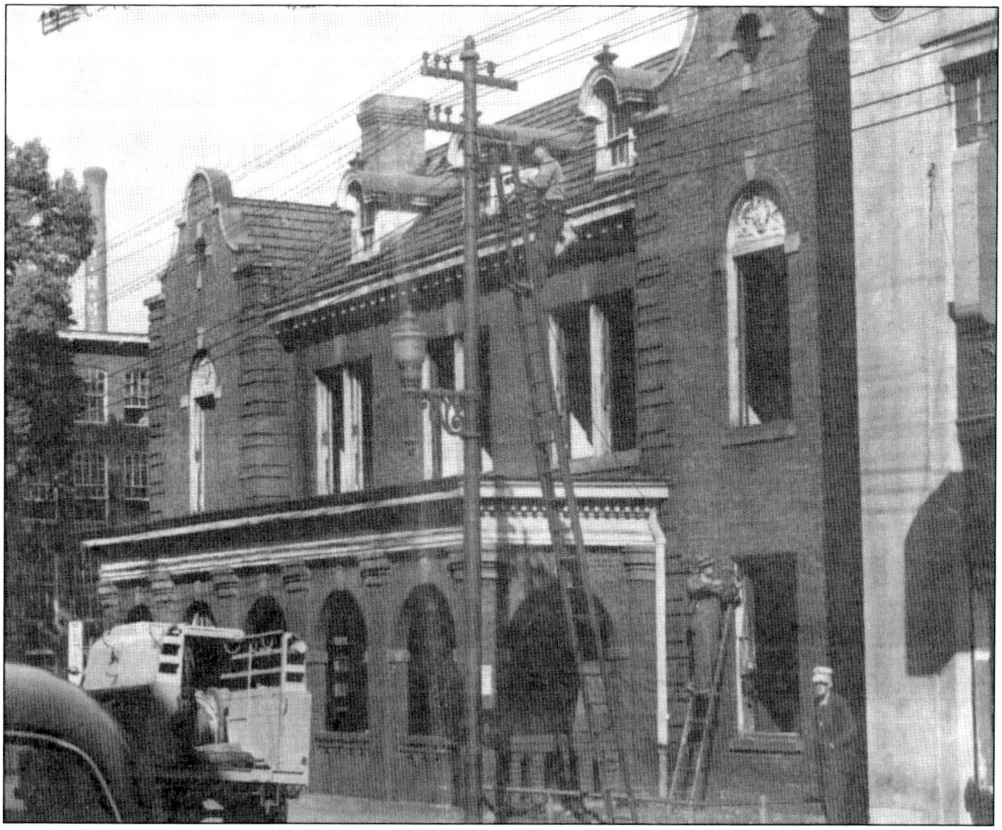

Another landmark, if only in archival photographs, is the Old Forsyth County Jail, which was located in the county seat of Winston. Pictured in the 1950s, the jail served the county from the reconstruction period after the Civil War (1870s) to the 1950s. In his 1925 book *Winston, Fifty Years Ago,* Henry Foltz gives his account: "The Jail was 2 stories high, constructed of brick, and boasting a large basement, Joe Master, the jailer, and his family lived on the first floor while the prisoners were kept in the basement."

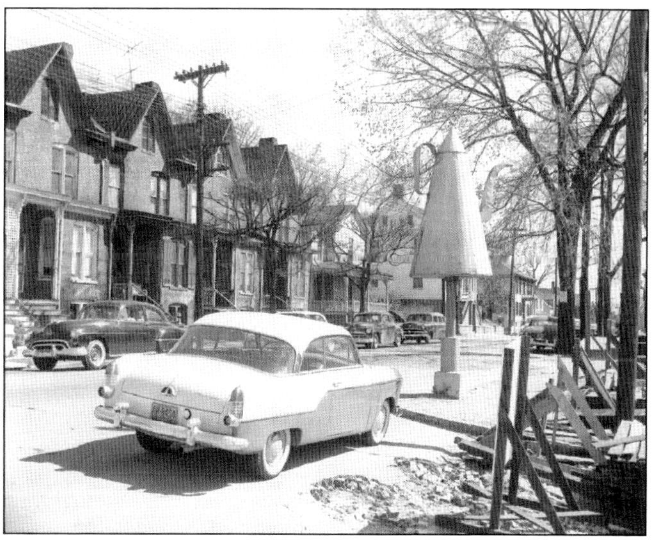

The creation of Old Salem Inc. around 1950 began the first concentrated movement for historic preservation in Forsyth County. Central Main Street's nickname, "Highway 52," was falling into disuse, but not without a price. A few weeks after the c. 1956 photograph at right was taken, all the structures in this block except for the Salem Teapot would be gone. (Courtesy FJ/WSHA.)

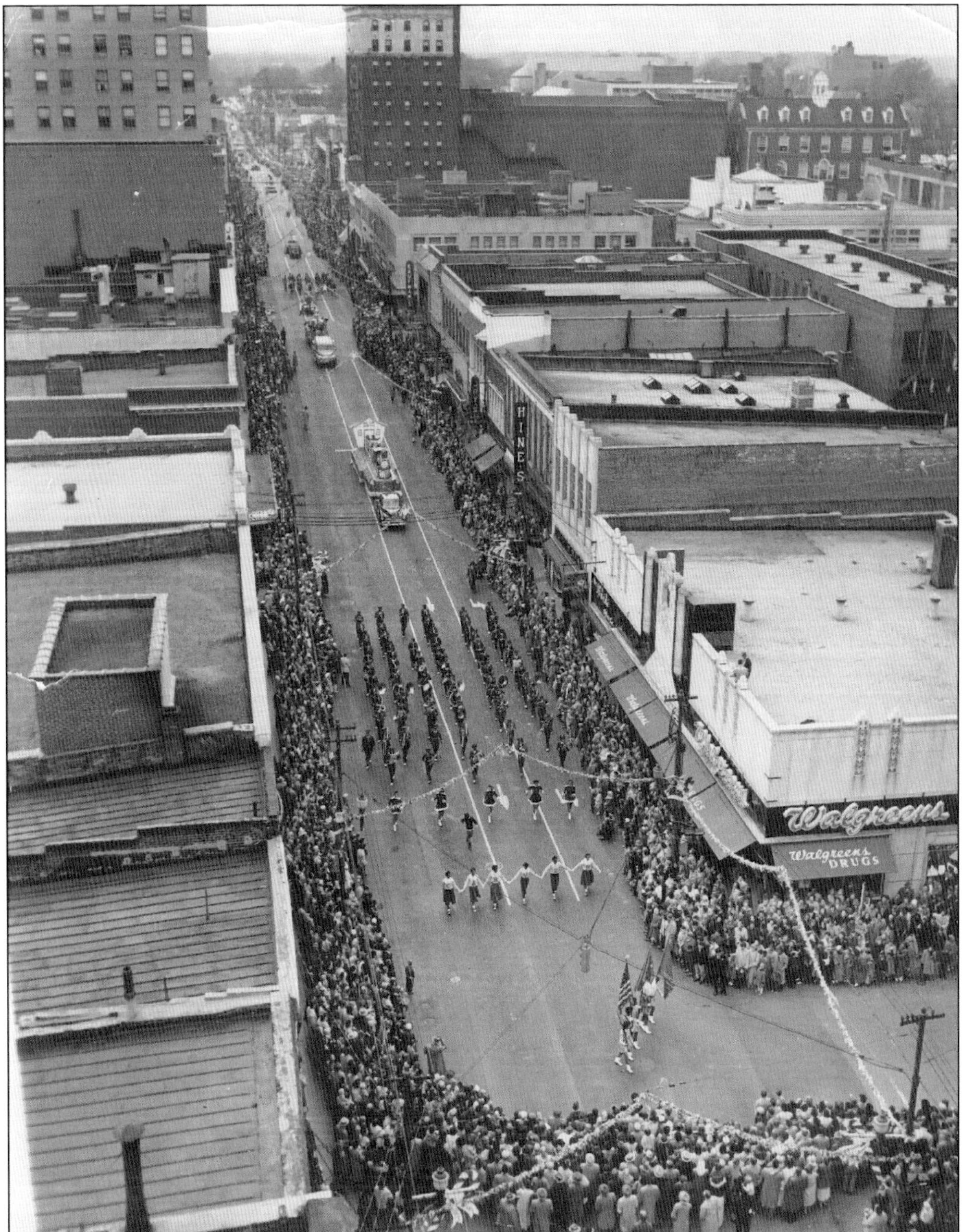

Pictured here is a celebration dating to the 19th century—The Merchants Christmas Parade. High school marching bands and decorated floats from schools and hamlets across the county participated. (Courtesy M. Bricker.)

The parade continues in this 1960s photograph of the merchants' parade. The miniature locomotive and train from Reynolds Park is an iconic landmark. Beginning in the 1940s, Reynolds Park followed in the footsteps of the 19th-century Nissen Park in Waughtown. One may call these "Memory Landmarks." (Courtesy FJ/WSHA.)

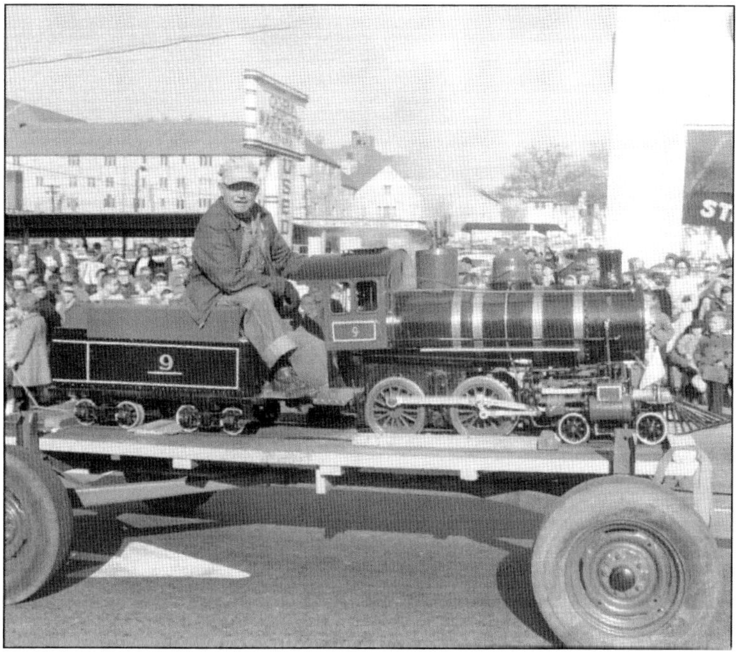

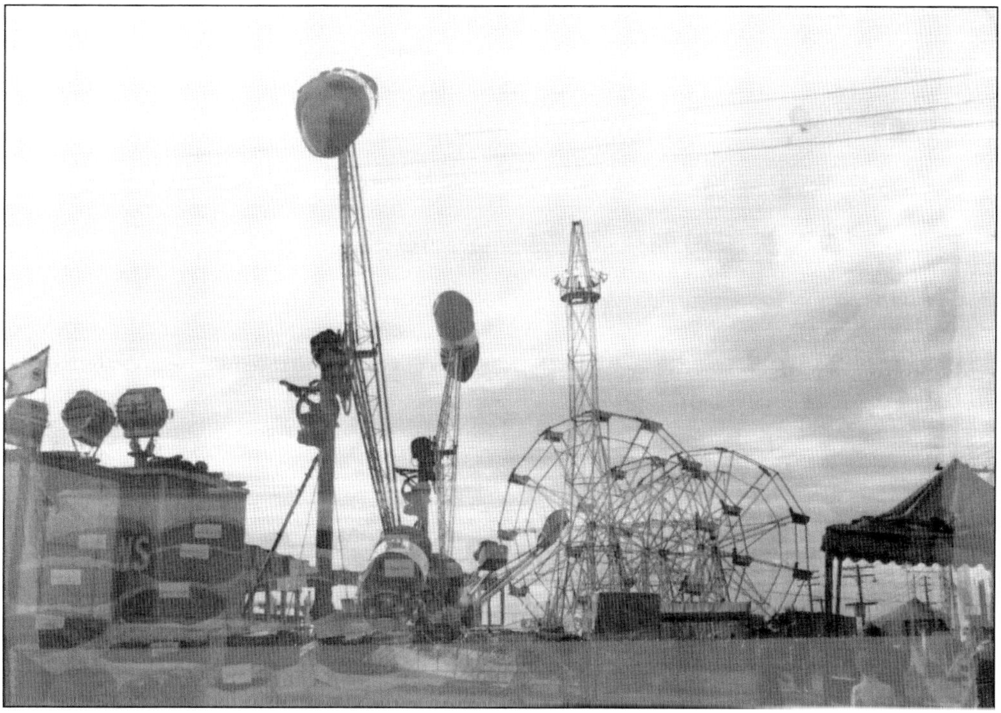

Piedmont Park in northern Winston on North Liberty Street (or as old-timers like to call it, "The road to Walkertown") was home to another landmark of entertainment—the Forsyth County Fair. "The World of Mirth" arrived to the fairgrounds with every fair ride imaginable, as this 1940s photograph shows. The Forsyth County Fair saw its earliest years in Browns Warehouse on North Main Street. The warehouse was a backdrop to the tobacco market in Old Winston in the 1880s. (Courtesy WSHA.)

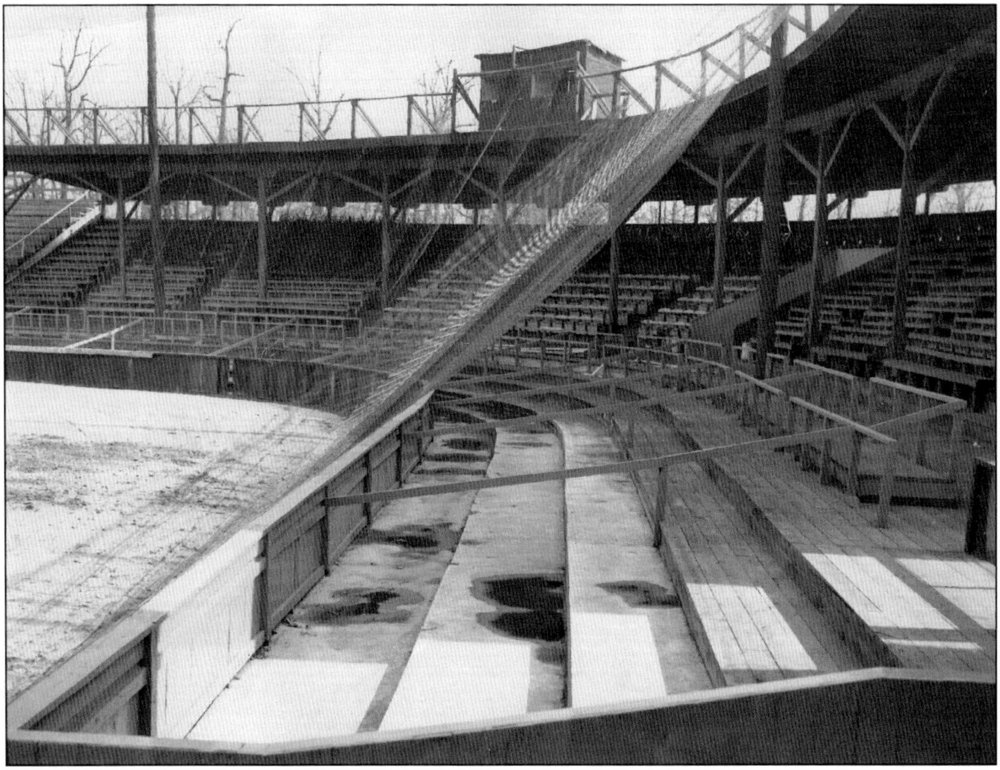

Forsyth summers were not complete without a trip to the ball field. Southside Ball Park, built in the 1920s, was the premier baseball park. Located near Gray High School in south Salem, local celebrities and athletes graced the park. The first professional boxing match and heavyweight championship in the Twin City and Forsyth County was fought here between Jack Gross and Billy Dugans. (Courtesy FJ/WSHA.)

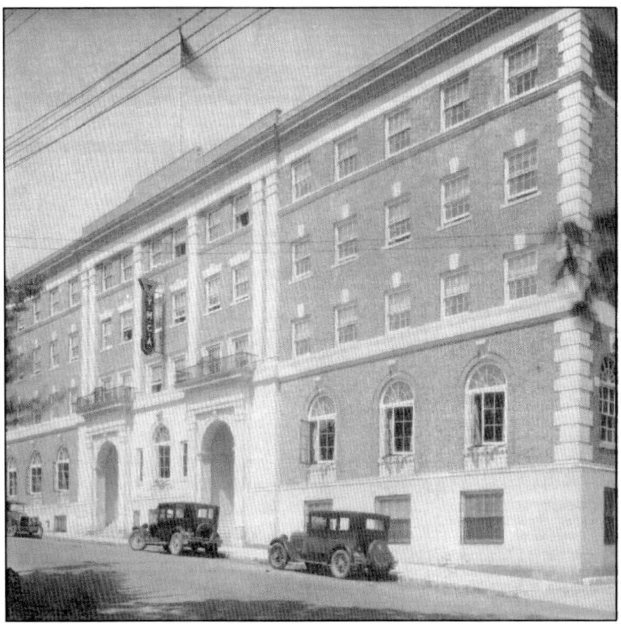

The YMCA and YWCA arrived in Forsyth County in the late 19th century and the early 20th century, respectively. Beginning on Fourth Street in Winston, the YMCA grew in importance and is pictured here about 1930. There was one entrance for boys and one for men, and small apartment rooms available for young men coming to the city seeking their fortunes. The YWCA built a spacious building about 1920 on Church Street to entertain many of the young ladies coming from surrounding Forsyth County farms to work in factories on the "Baby Line" of the R.J. Reynolds Tobacco Company.

The yearly Forsyth County Parade in downtown Winston-Salem showcased the variety of tastes and sights of the county's residents during the Christmas season. This scene along Fourth Street shows the popular shopping district.

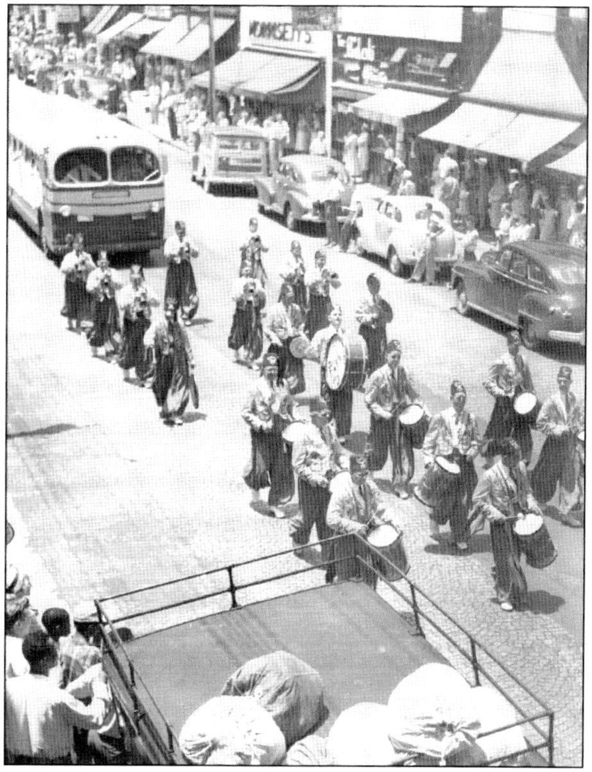

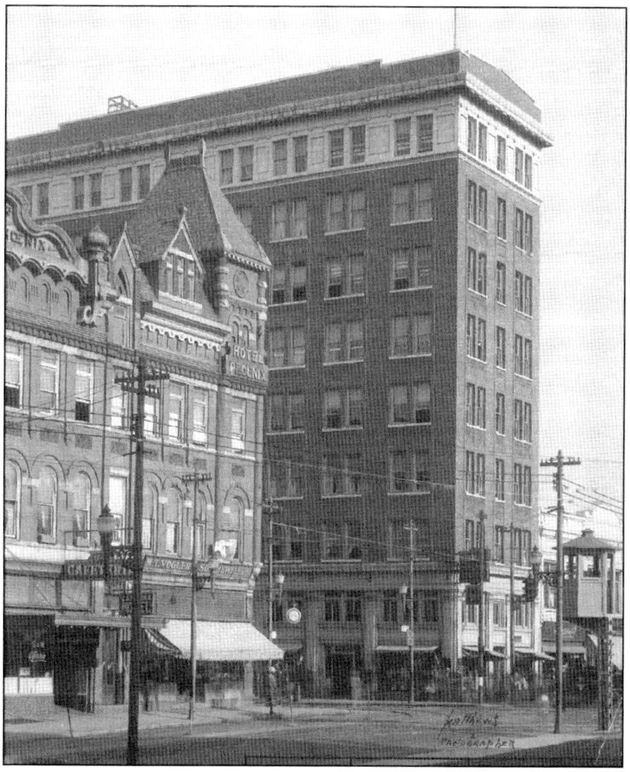

This photograph shows the OHanlon Building, a local landmark, and the Phoenix Hotel, a lost landmark, in the 1920s. (Courtesy M. Bricker.)

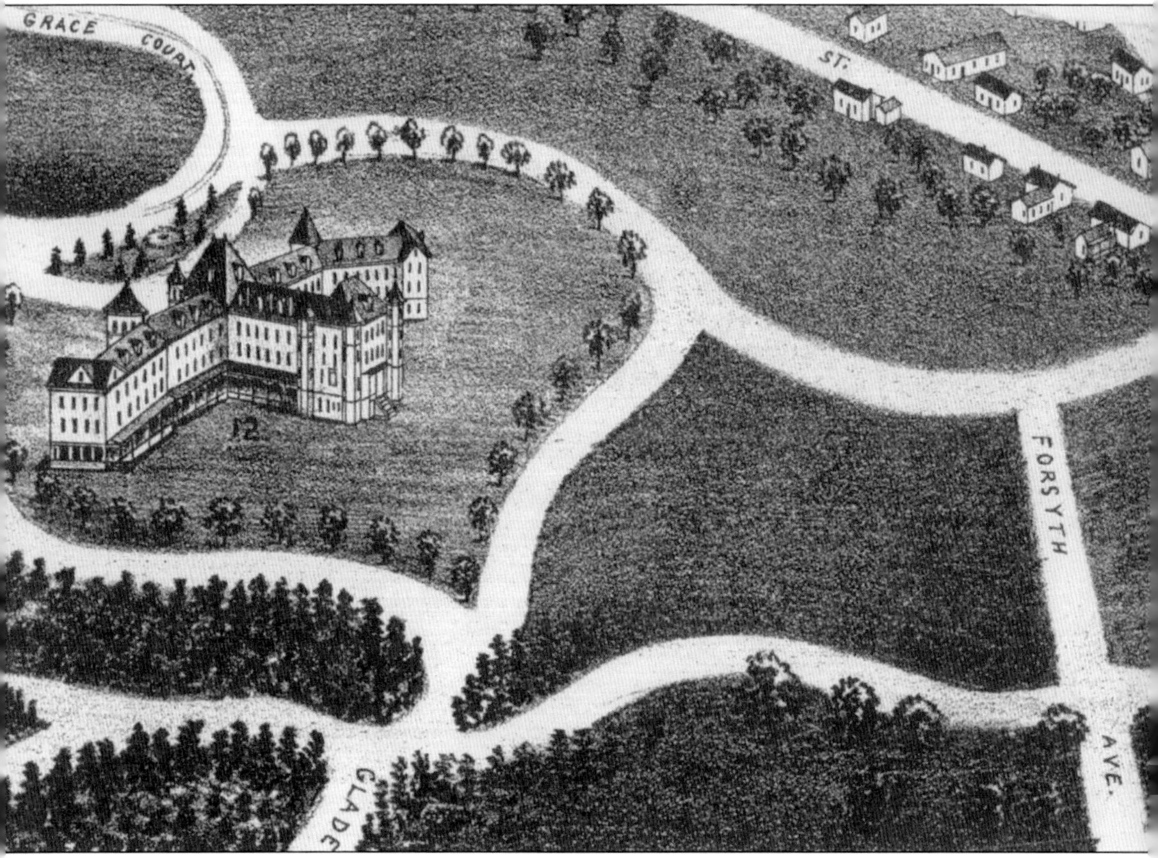

After the Grand Zinzendorf Resort hotel (shown here on an 1891 map) burned in 1892, a new Zinzendorf Hotel was born. The structure was not a resort hotel, but a grand Victorian with a veranda supporting a multitude of rocking chairs. The new Zinzendorf contained a large ballroom and the most elaborate salon in town. (Courtesy Bird's Eye Map/WSHA.)

Five

CITY AND STATE VISITED

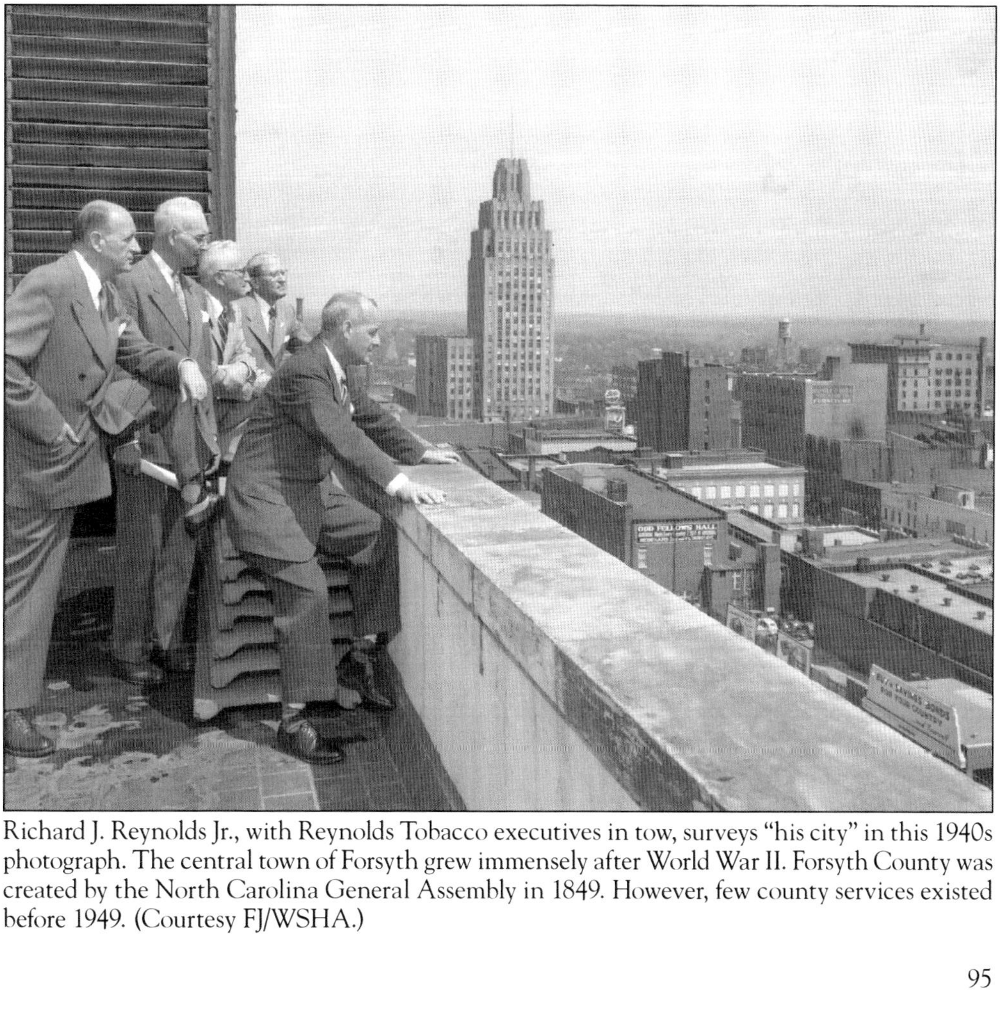

Richard J. Reynolds Jr., with Reynolds Tobacco executives in tow, surveys "his city" in this 1940s photograph. The central town of Forsyth grew immensely after World War II. Forsyth County was created by the North Carolina General Assembly in 1849. However, few county services existed before 1949. (Courtesy FJ/WSHA.)

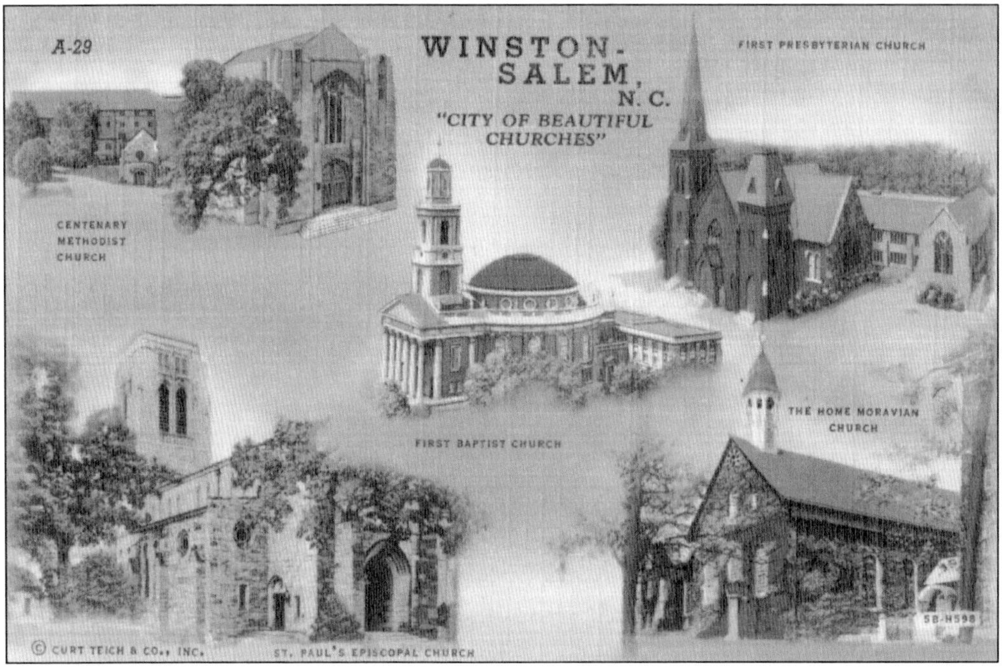

Throughout the 20th century, Reynolds Jr. and "his city" competed with what some called a "higher force"—the church. Winston was called the City of Churches and purportedly had a church on every corner. Some of the largest and most beautiful are pictured in this 1950s postcard. (Courtesy First Baptist Church Archives.)

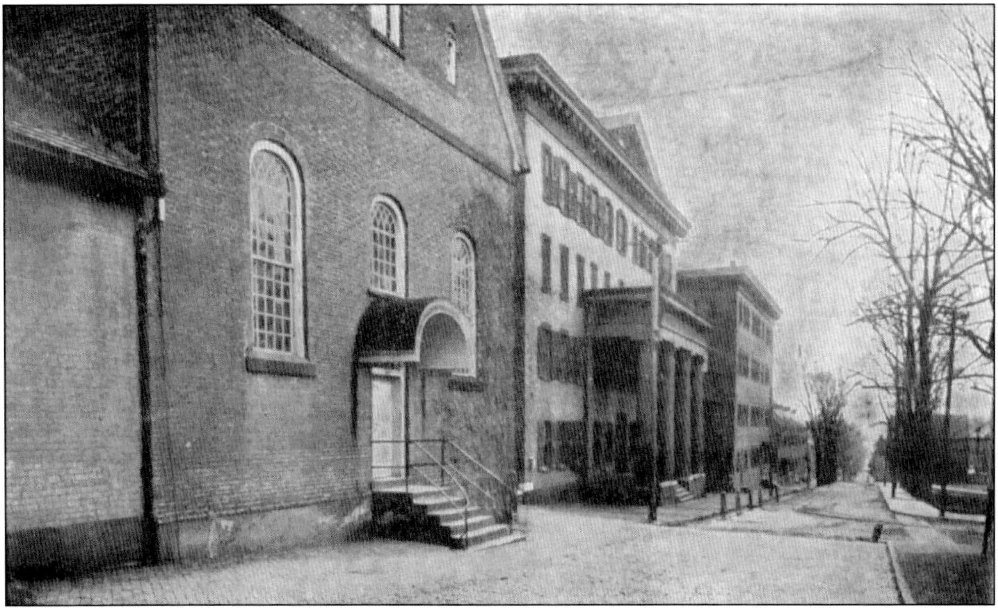

Pictured about 1910, the Gracious Home Moravian Church, built about 1800, and one of its Moravian offspring, Salem Academy and College, oversaw the central town of the Moravians. Until 1850, Home Moravian Church, the central church of all Moravian congregational towns surrounding Forsyth County, endorsed "The Lease." The Lease, meaning the laws of Dobbs Parish, was handled by the Gracious Home Moravian Church. (Courtesy M. Bricker/WSHA.)

The Lease, which Salem and Bethania shared early on, led to two competing towns. They seesawed back and forth for the honor of most-populated. The two towns were different in one very important way. Bethania allowed "outsiders," non-Moravians, to live in the central town. Salem prohibited them in the congregational town. Edward Rondthaler (pictured around 1920) oversaw Salem for 50 years between 1877 and 1927. (Courtesy WSHA.)

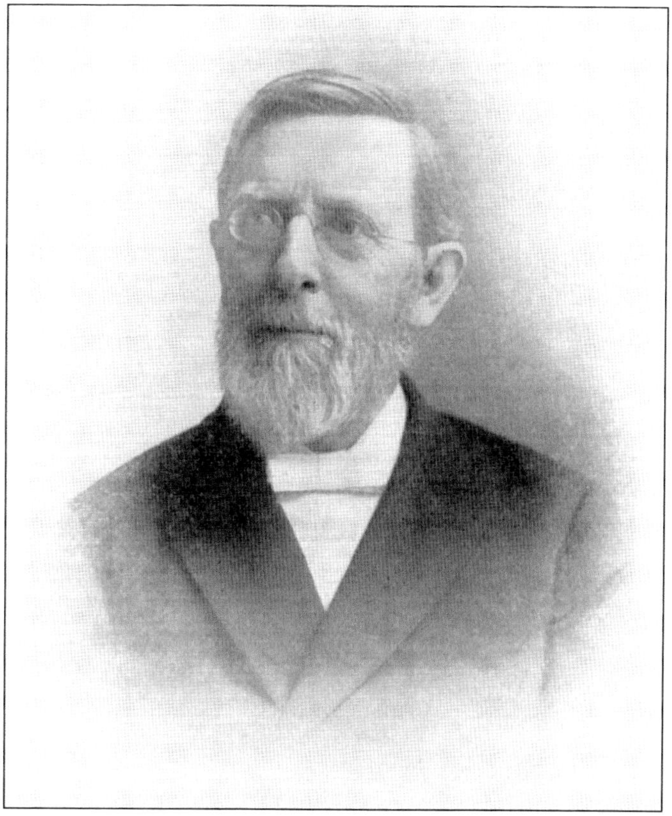

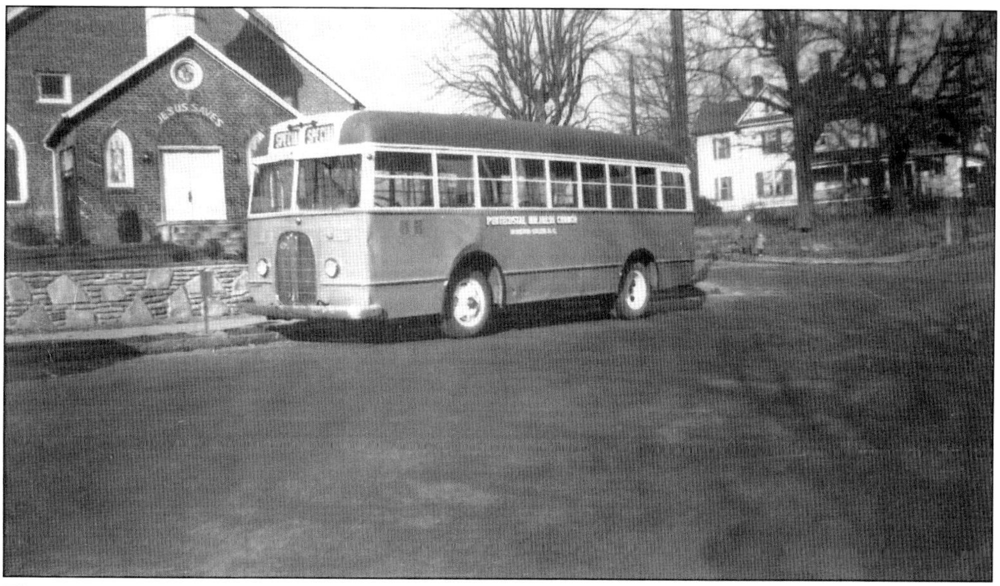

The Moravian, Baptist, Methodist, and German Lutheran were the dominant churches in Forsyth. One new, lesser-known group was the Pentecostal Holiness, appearing in the central town of Forsyth in 1908. The church was a fixture in East Winston for nearly 30 years before arriving here in 1936 on the corner of Broad Street and Brookstown Avenue. The Walkertown Pentecostal Holiness Church began in 1956. (Courtesy First Pentecostal Holiness Church Archives/M. Bricker.)

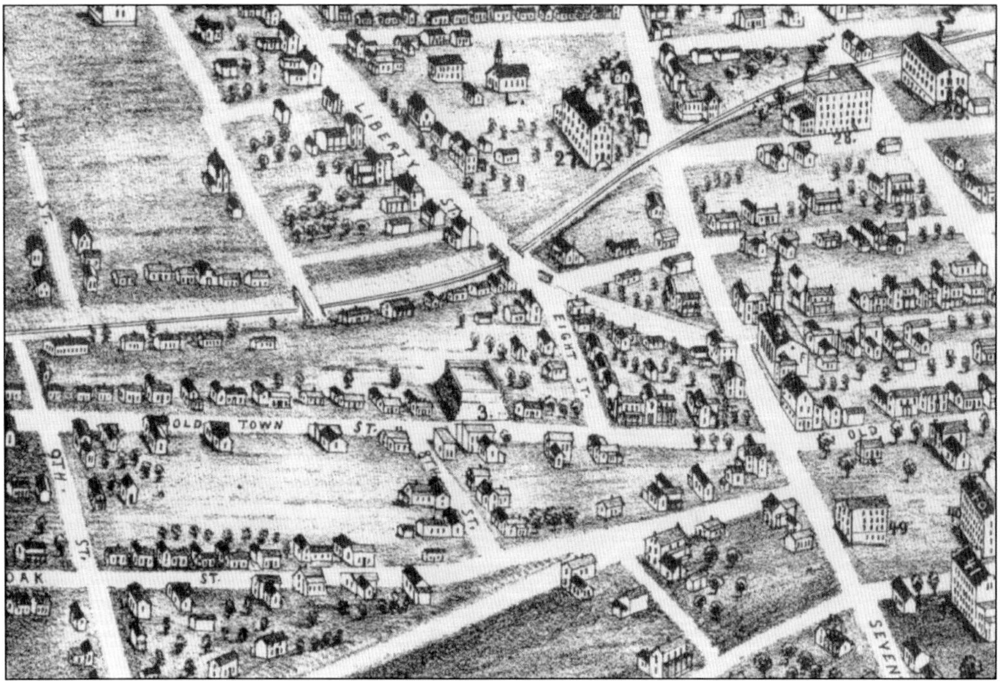

This Bird's Eye Map shows the Methodist church as the premier church at Eighth and Liberty Streets. The Methodist churches were among the earliest denominations in Dobbs Parish. The Methodists outnumbered other churches for much of the 19th century. The oldest Methodist church, Concord, began in the Lewisville Community around 1881. The Knight's Meeting House of Worship in Clemmonsville and Love's Church in Walkertown were both early 18th century county churches. (Courtesy Bird's Eye Map, M. Bricker.)

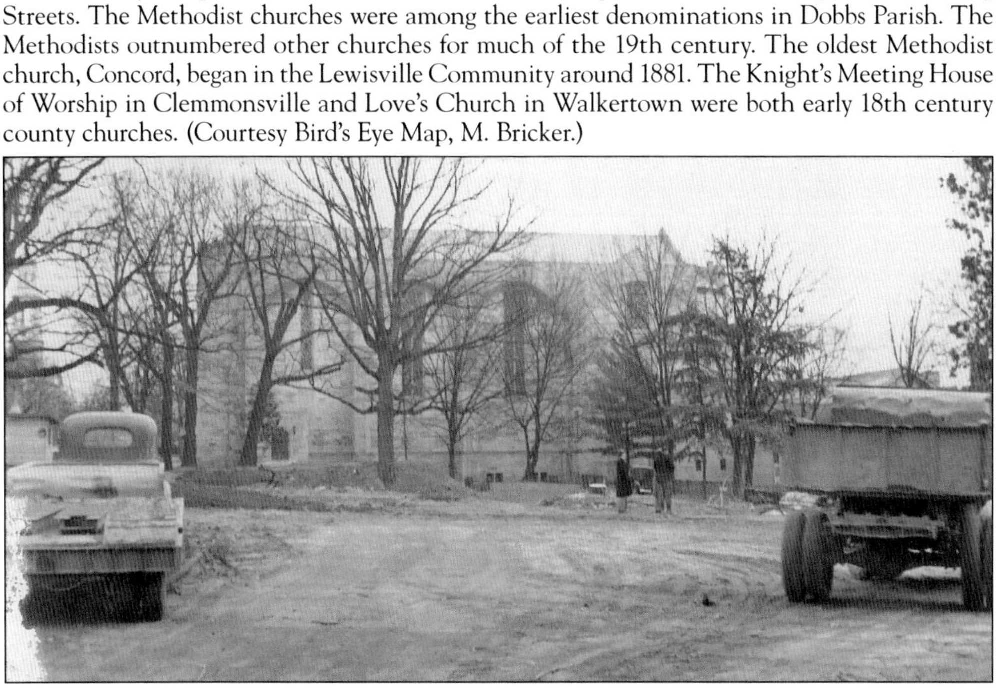

By the time of Prohibition, Winston was known as the Town of Churches. The majestic old Centenary church, built about 1884, was located north of Winston on Liberty Street. As populations moved westward in Winston, so did the largest Methodist home, Centenary, built about 1931. This c. 1950s photograph of Centenary Methodist Church shows preparation for its new neighbor, the Forsyth County Library on Fifth Street. (Courtesy FJ/WSHA.)

Baptists arrived in the 18th century, but their stay was short-lived at first. Before 1774 the Baptists and Moravians were allies. Both preached and ministered in each other's community. But the Baptists were asked to leave by the Moravians and would not return to Dobbs Parish for 100 years. In 1874, Alfred Holland and congregation built the First Baptist Church, pictured here, at Second Street in Winston. (Courtesy First Baptist Church Archives.)

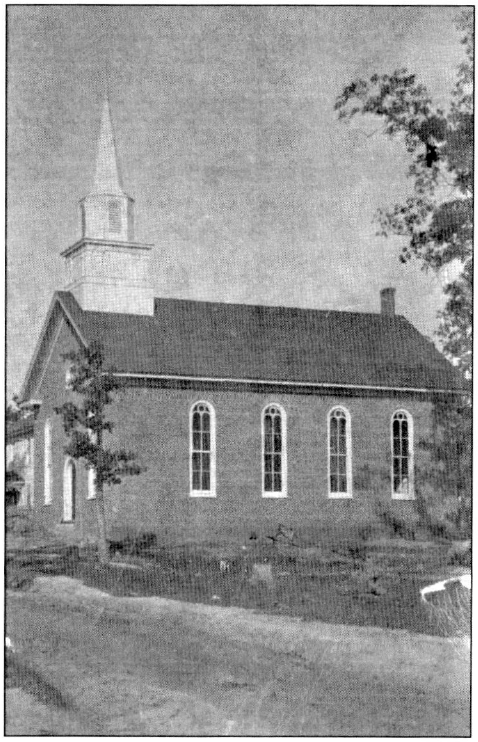

The first African American Baptist church and its white counterpart began in a similar fashion to the black and white Methodist churches. Before the Civil War, prayer meetings in homes and brush arbors were numerous. In the early 1800s, The Old Jerusalem Church was organized in a brush arbor on the grounds of the Children's Home on Reynolda Road. The First Baptist Church, pictured here on Second Street, was extended in the 1800s. (Courtesy First Baptist Church Archives.)

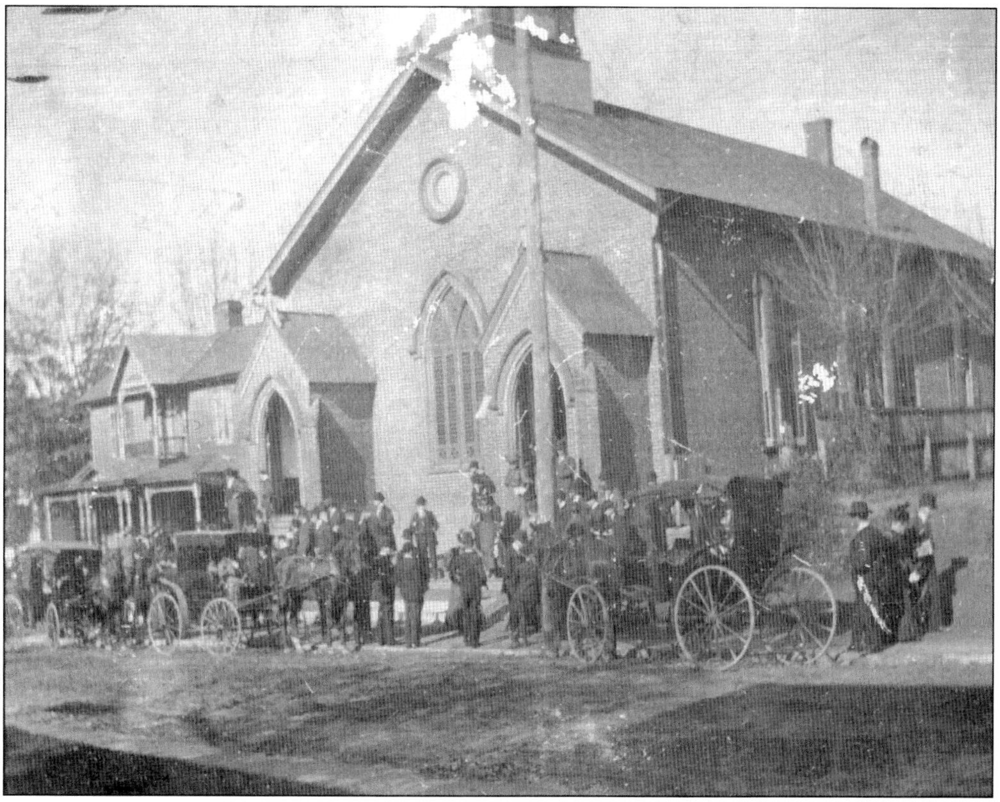

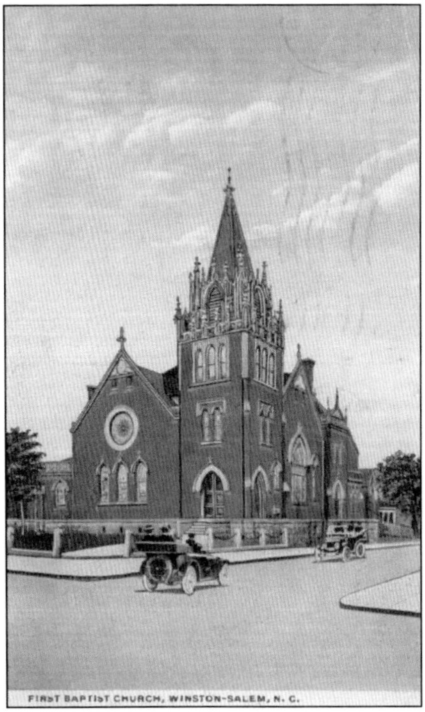

Welsh preacher James Younger was an early Baptist leader. He moved to the Abbott's Creek Settlement in southeast Forsyth County about 1753. Abbott's Creek became the home of the first Baptist church in Forsyth County. In the late 18th century, German Baptist dunkards (baptisms) began taking place in Muddy Creek (southwest Forsyth County) and in Clemmons township (at Old Fraternity Church of Brethren). The First Baptist Church at Second and Chestnut Streets is pictured on this c. 1916 postcard. (Courtesy First Baptist Church Archives.)

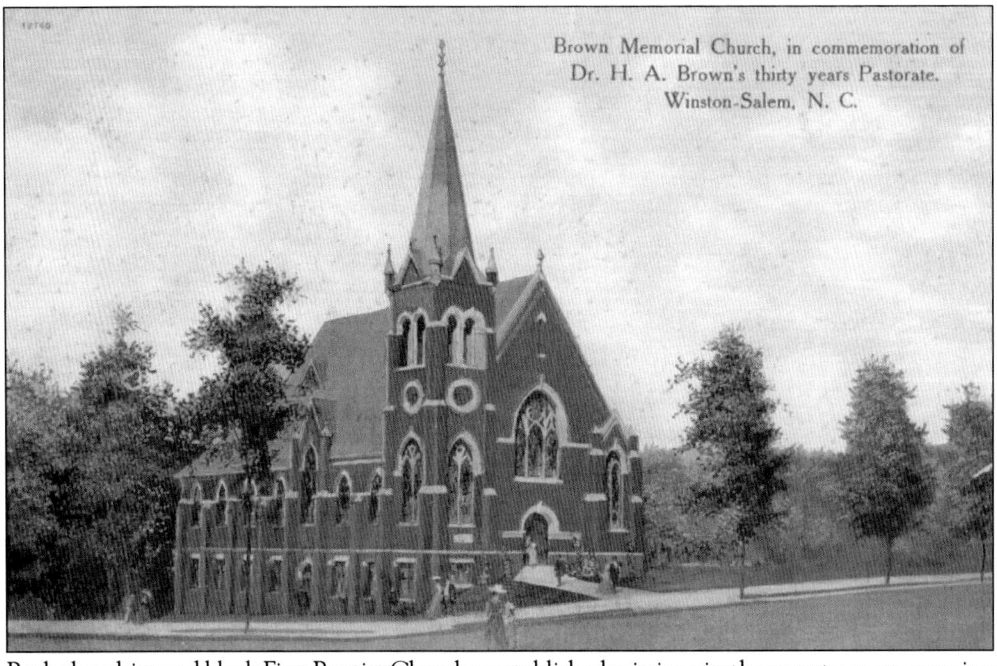

Both the white and black First Baptist Churches established missions in the county, many growing into independent churches. Congregations of Salem, West Salem, Southside, Waughtown, and North Winston originated from the white First Baptist Church. The black First Baptist Church helped create First Institutional, West End, Mount Zion, and New Bethel. The Brown Memorial Church at Fourth and Spring Streets, pictured in this c. 1911 postcard, was named for Baptist mission pioneer H.A. Brown. (Courtesy First Baptist Church Archives.)

The greatest positive social change in "church and state" after the Civil War was the growth of churches and their missions throughout Forsyth County. Dr. Henry A. Brown of First Baptist Church and fellow minister Dr. Jesse B. Weatherspoon are shown in the c. 1920 photograph at right. Doctor Brown helped to organize social missions across denominational lines, working with Methodists, Episcopalians, Lutherans, and Moravians. The Roaring Twenties helped to erase much of the church's social movement. The cities' churches were spurred on with the New Freedom programs of Pres. Woodrow Wilson. Social reform programs were created by churches to help the increasing industrial workforce arriving in Winston-Salem. The companies in Winston-Salem employed a large part of Forsyth County's residents. Below, the congregation at First Baptist Church is pictured around 1930. (Courtesy First Baptist Church Archives.)

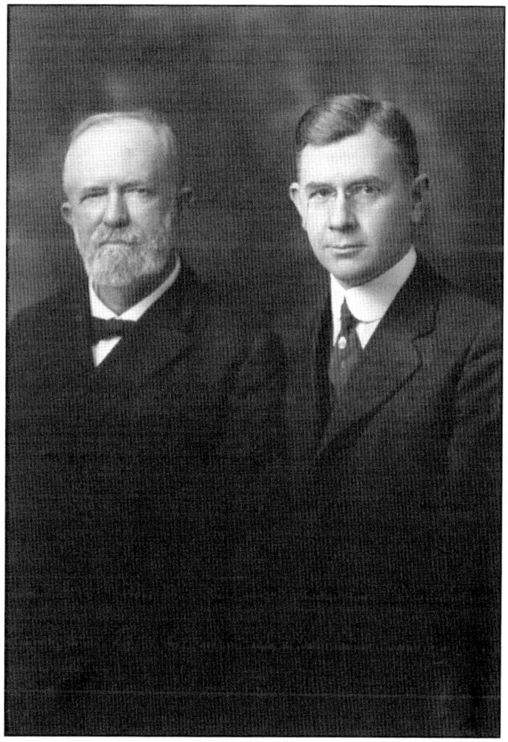

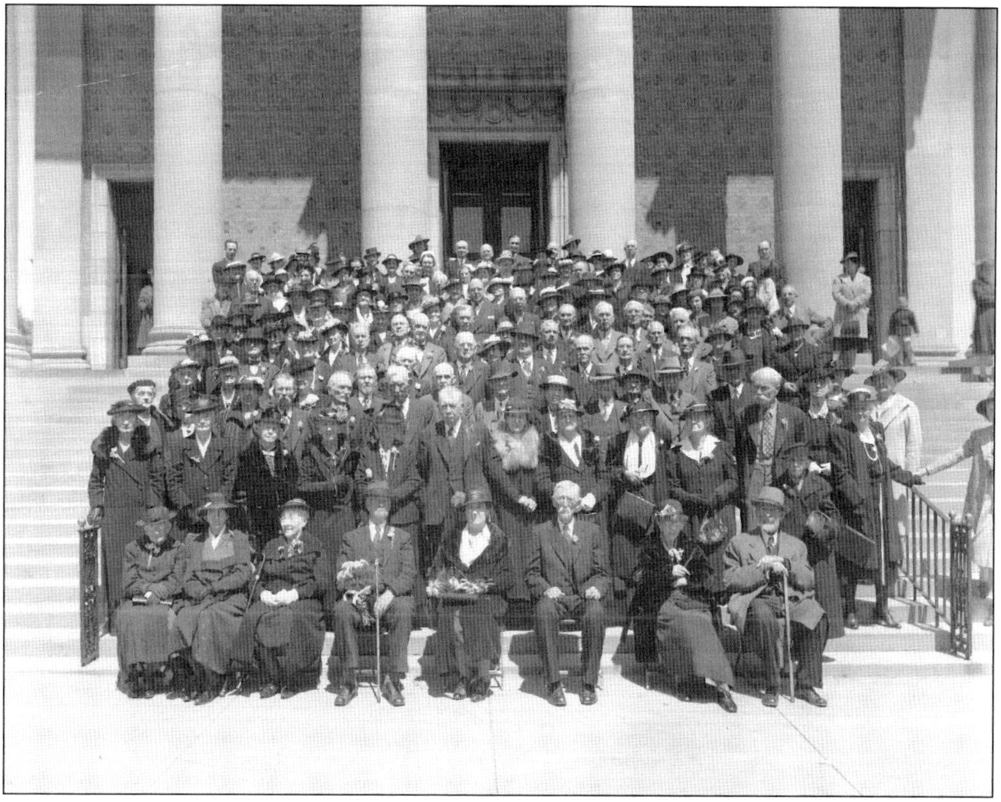

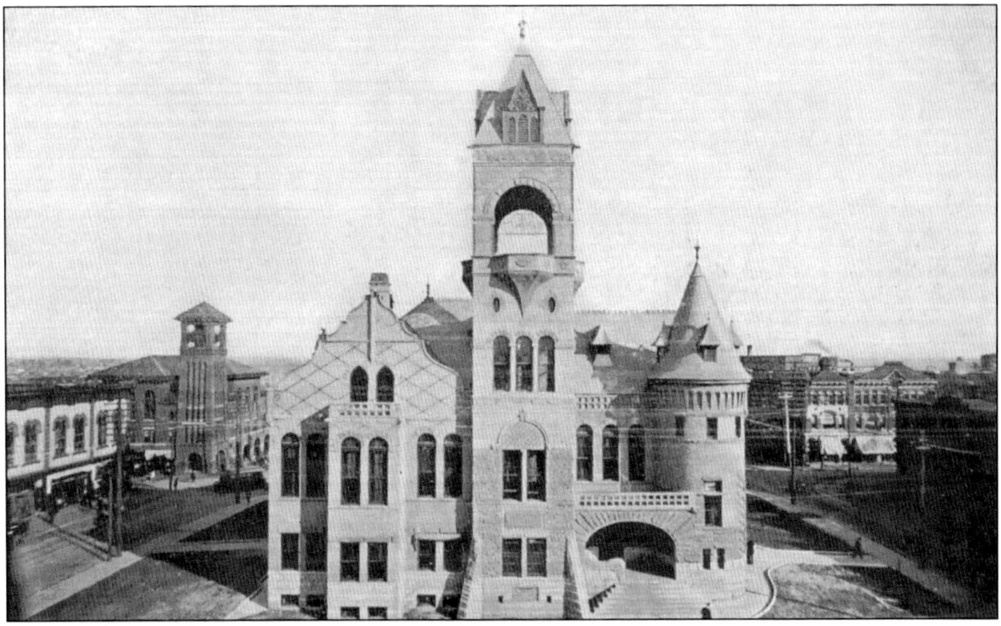

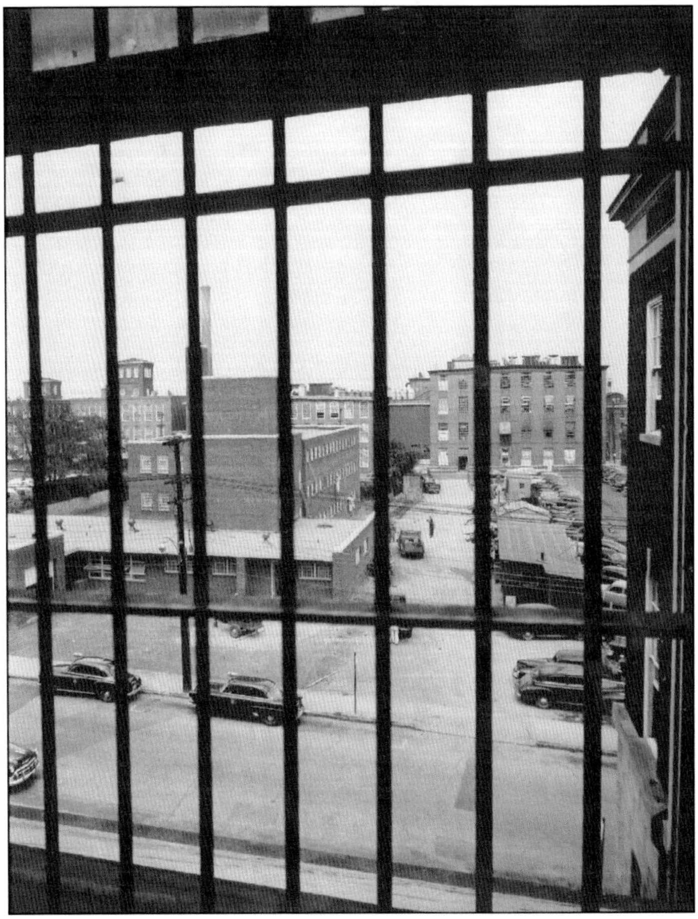

County government was founded during the Colonial period in Dobbs Parish. The parish helped the Moravians and surrounding hamlets of Scots-Irish and English residents to form a type of independence from other locales in North Carolina. Between 1754 and 1849, the parish practiced its own form of government. By 1896, the first Forsyth County Courthouse had been replaced by this Romanesque structure, pictured around 1900. (Courtesy M. Bricker/ WSHA.)

This c. 1950 photograph, taken from city hall in Winston, shows the new Forsyth County Jail. (Courtesy FJ/WSHA.)

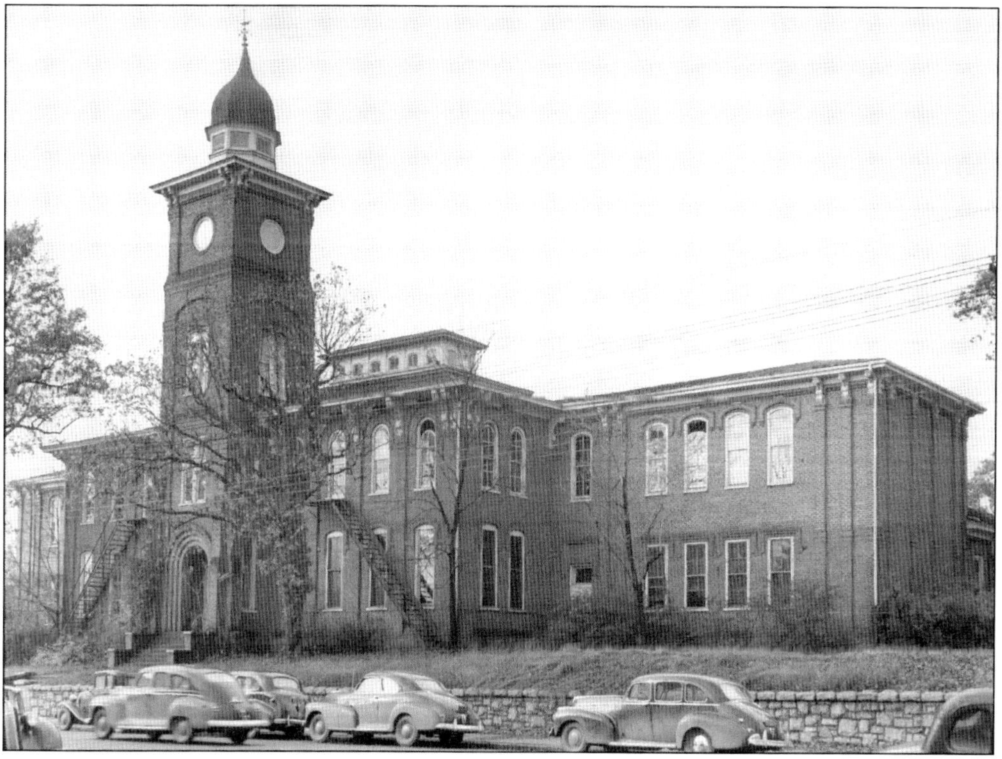

Government schools were established between 1830 and 1850. Free School Houses served Forsyth residents who worked as laborers in mills and factories. Dr. Calvin Wiley, minister and educator, helped create the Free School House Movement for the federal government. If not for the movement, only the wealthy would have been educated beyond the Sunday schools of the early churches. The Civil War saw the movement end, and education did not return for the masses in Forsyth County until 1874. The first modern schoolhouse helped unify the Church and State Program. The Winston Graded School was built in 1882 and was later renamed West End School. The school is pictured above in the 1940s before demolition and below in the mid-1940s. The Winston Graded School was razed about 1948 to make way for the new Sears and Roebuck building. (Courtesy FJ/WSHA.)

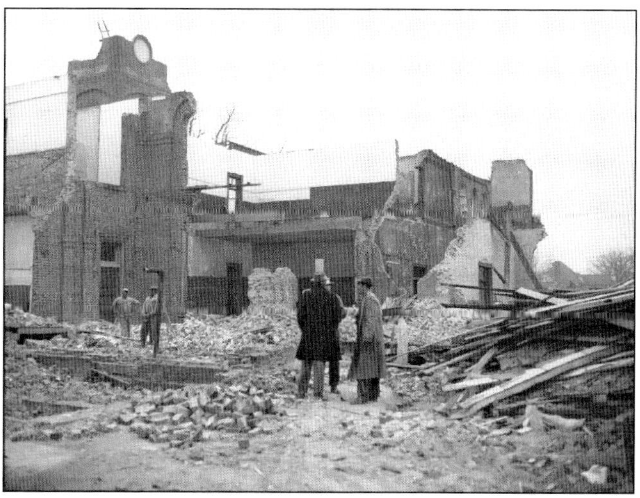

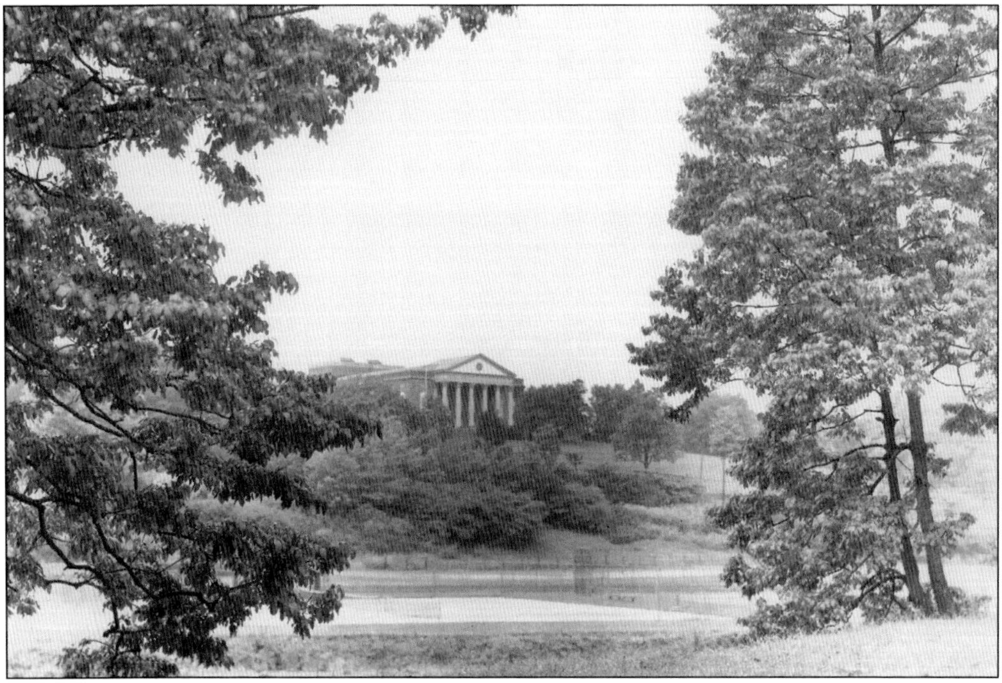

Many churches, schools, and government buildings were built in the 1920s. Reynolds High School, overlooking Hanes Park, is noted for its architecture. Mrs. R.J. Reynolds built the elaborate structure, pictured above in the 1960s, in honor of her husband. The 1960s photograph below shows the bridge over Peters Creek Parkway that connected Ardmore and Latham. (Courtesy FJ/WSHA.)

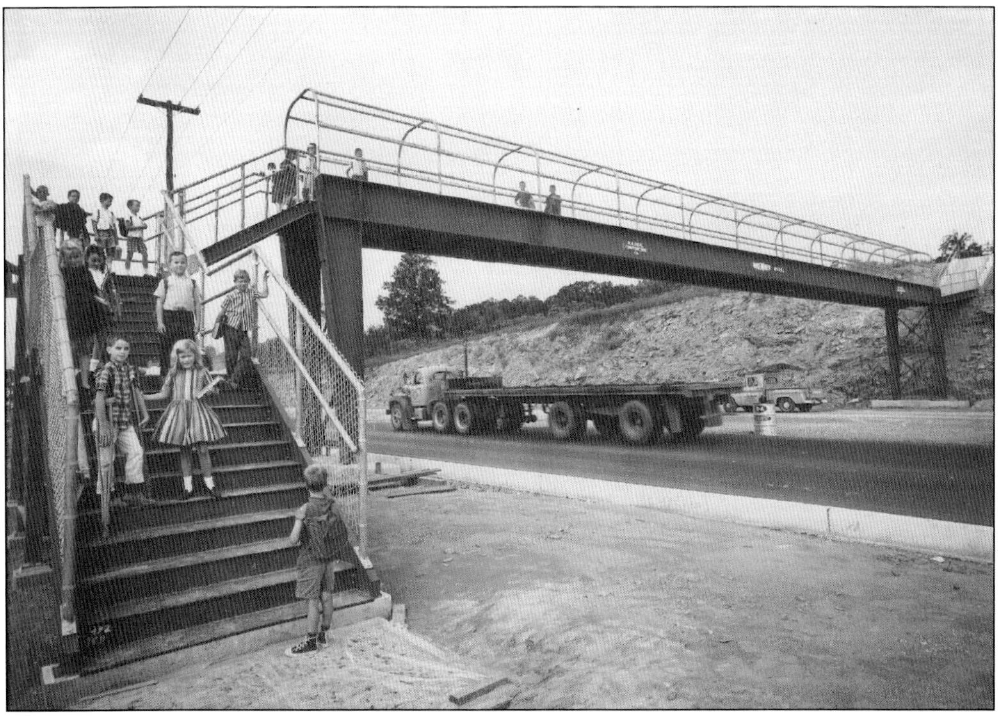

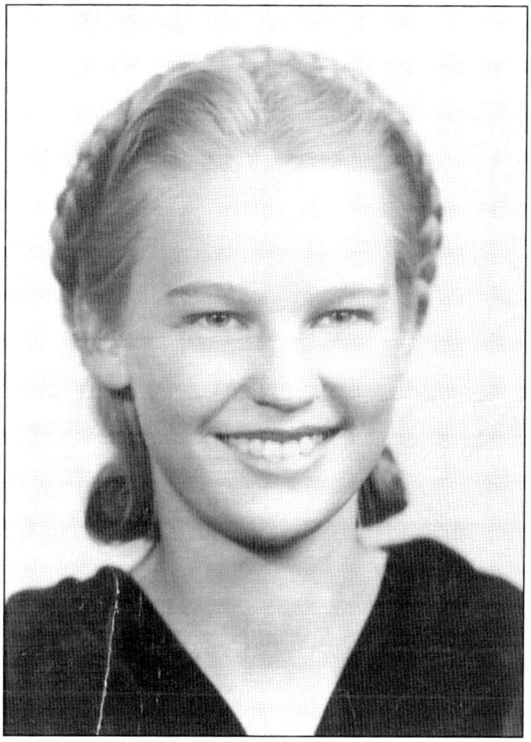

Forsyth County saw lean times during World War II. Rationing of food and gasoline, along with practiced electrical blackouts, were regular occurrences during wartime. Lucy Johnson Branscome, pictured at right in the 1930s, experienced rationing. Her husband, Ernest, ran the Konnoak Hills Food Market at South Main Street and Wall Town–Clemmonsville Road. Pictured below is a c. 1940 war ration booklet from the US Office of Price Administration. (Courtesy Branscomb collection.)

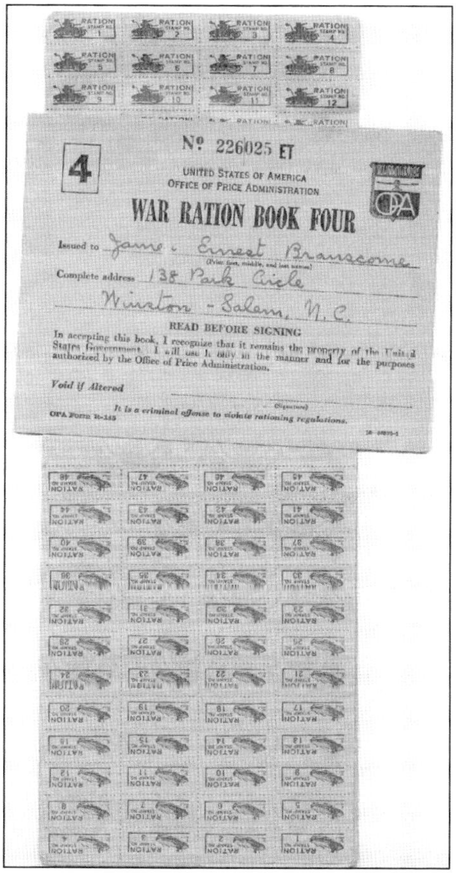

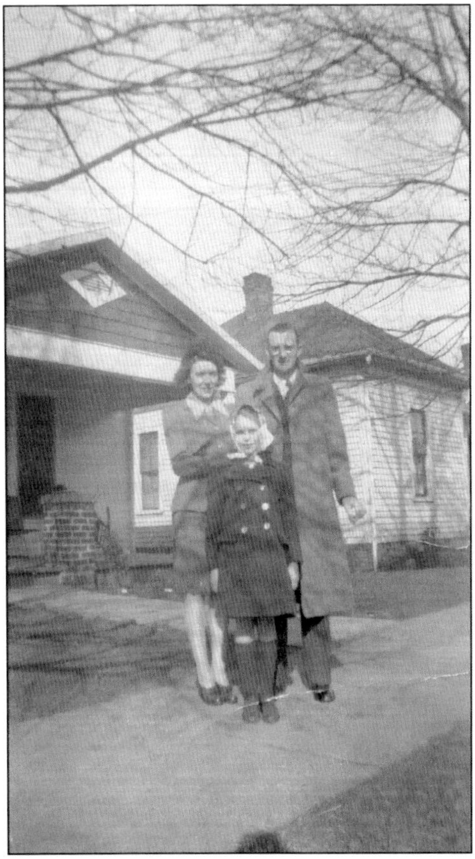

LaNelle Hunter Church (center) is pictured in the 1930s with her aunt Drew and uncle Jim. After War World II, Forsyth County, like most counties in North Carolina, returned to normal, but there was much to be done. In general, a revolution had begun between the central city of Winston-Salem and the county. The merger of the city-county health department, the founding of the city-county planning board, and the establishment of a city manager, which continues in today's Forsyth County, occurred at that time. Pictured below is Church's alma mater, Gray High School, which became the North Carolina School of the Arts. (Courtesy LaNelle collection.)

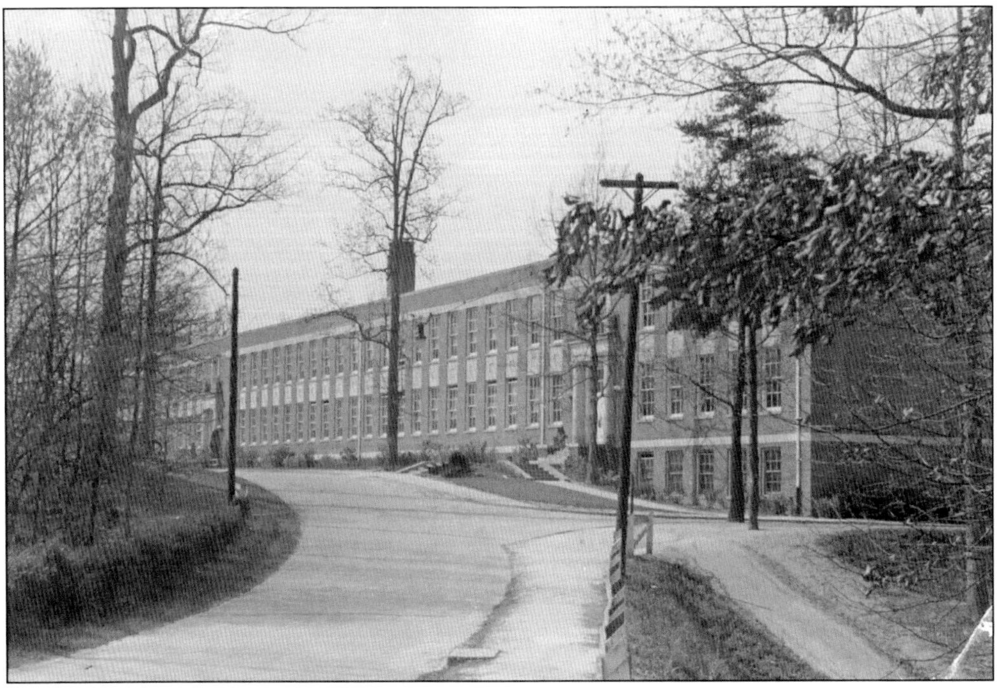

Six

Business, Science, and Industry

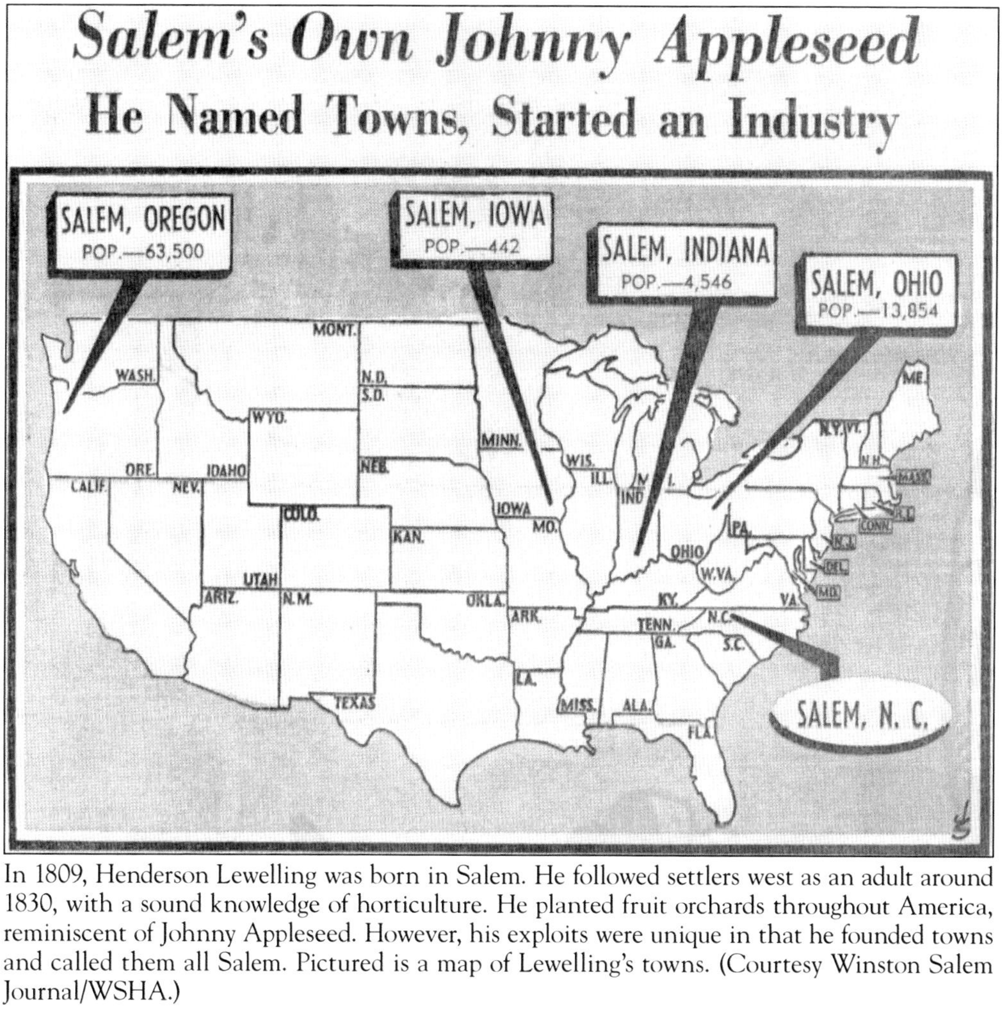

In 1809, Henderson Lewelling was born in Salem. He followed settlers west as an adult around 1830, with a sound knowledge of horticulture. He planted fruit orchards throughout America, reminiscent of Johnny Appleseed. However, his exploits were unique in that he founded towns and called them all Salem. Pictured is a map of Lewelling's towns. (Courtesy Winston Salem Journal/WSHA.)

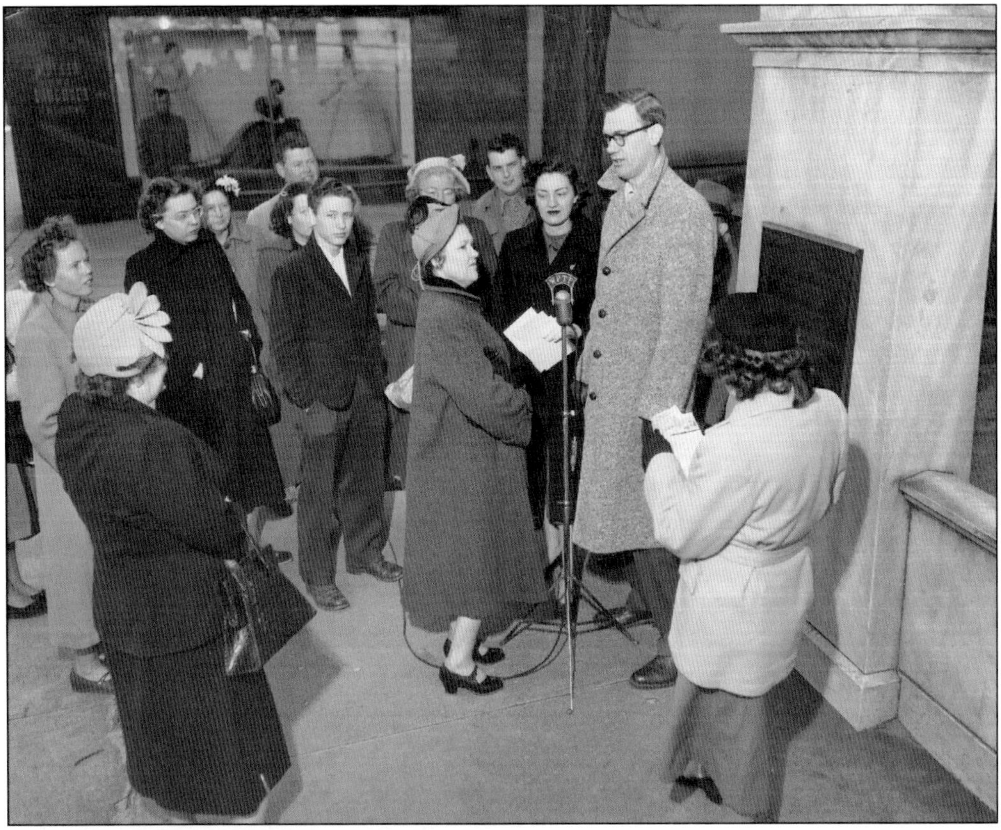

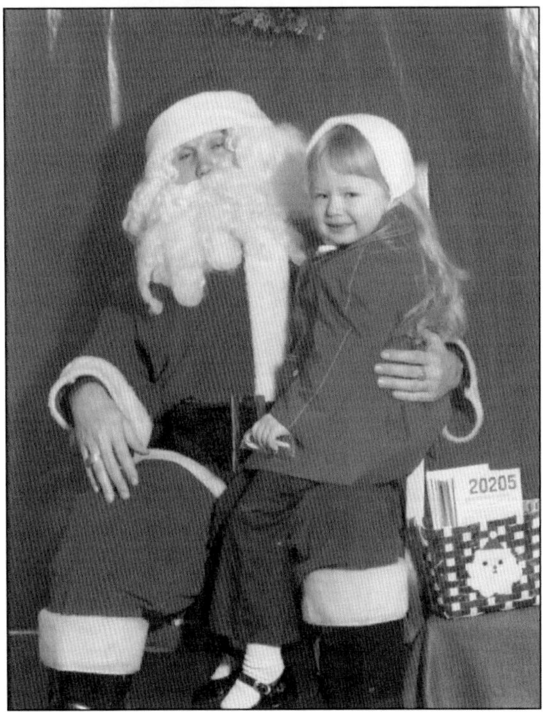

The c. 1950s photograph above shows the Anchor Company on Fourth Street. In the photograph at left, Tommie Howell enjoys the company of Santa Claus in a downtown store around 1970. (Courtesy FJ/Branscomb collection.)

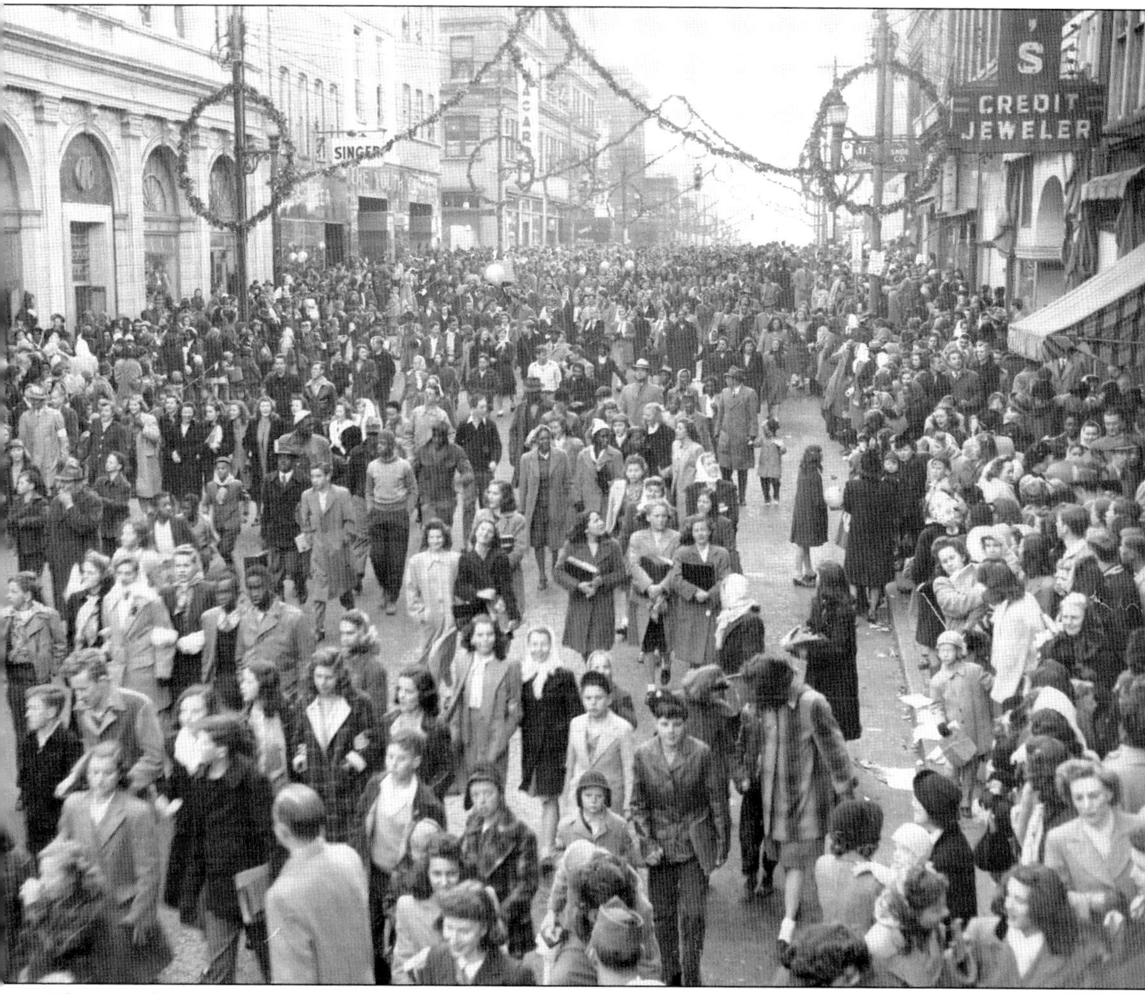

The parade was over, and downtown shopping was about to begin in this c. 1948 photograph. Christmastime saw more Forsyth County residents in one place than any other time of the year. (Courtesy M. Bricker.)

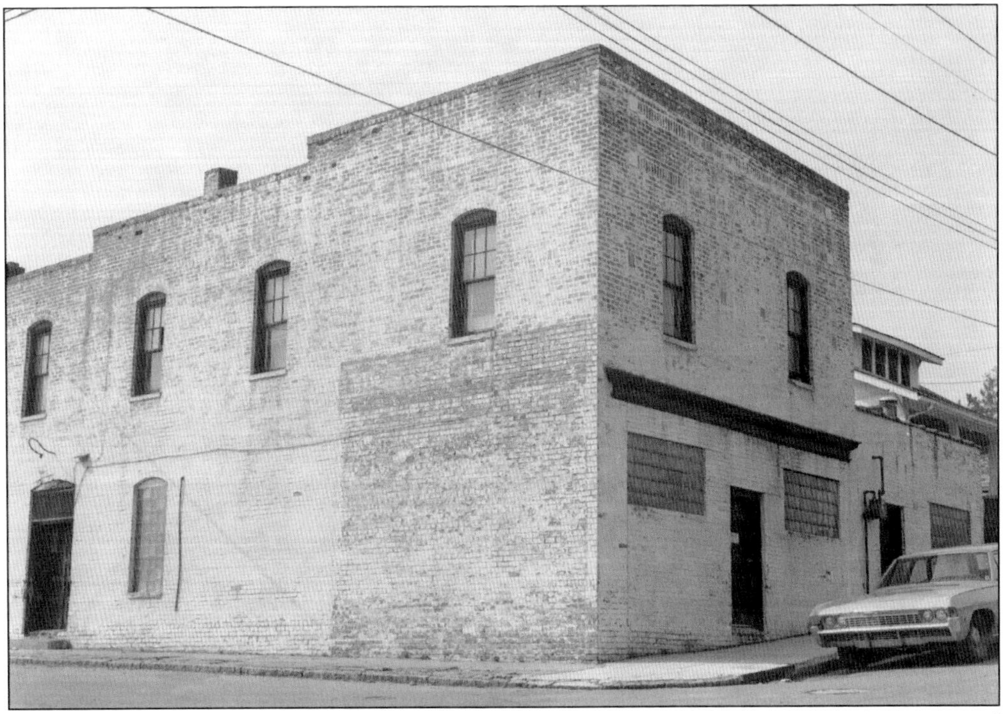

An example of business, science, and industry is found in this Forsyth County building, pictured around the 1970s. It was originally built as a textile mill for Arista Cotton. It was then used as a cigar factory. Later it was a general store, and finally, it was the print shop for the Piedmont Bible College. (Courtesy Piedmont International University.)

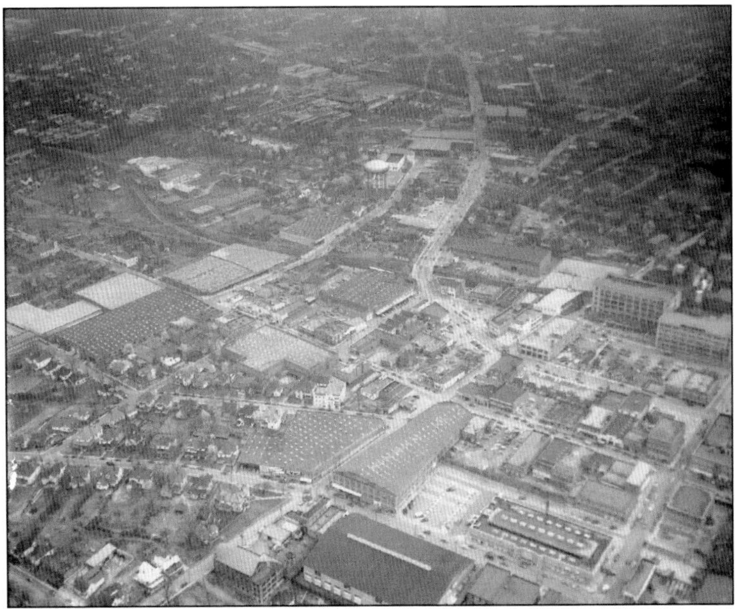

Neighborhoods and towns will continue to be razed if historical preservation is not taken seriously in Forsyth County. Shown here is one old county neighborhood at Cherry and Liberty Streets in the 1950s. Large commercial buildings have taken over previously residential lots, and countless homes have been lost to demolition. (Courtesy FJ/WSHA.)

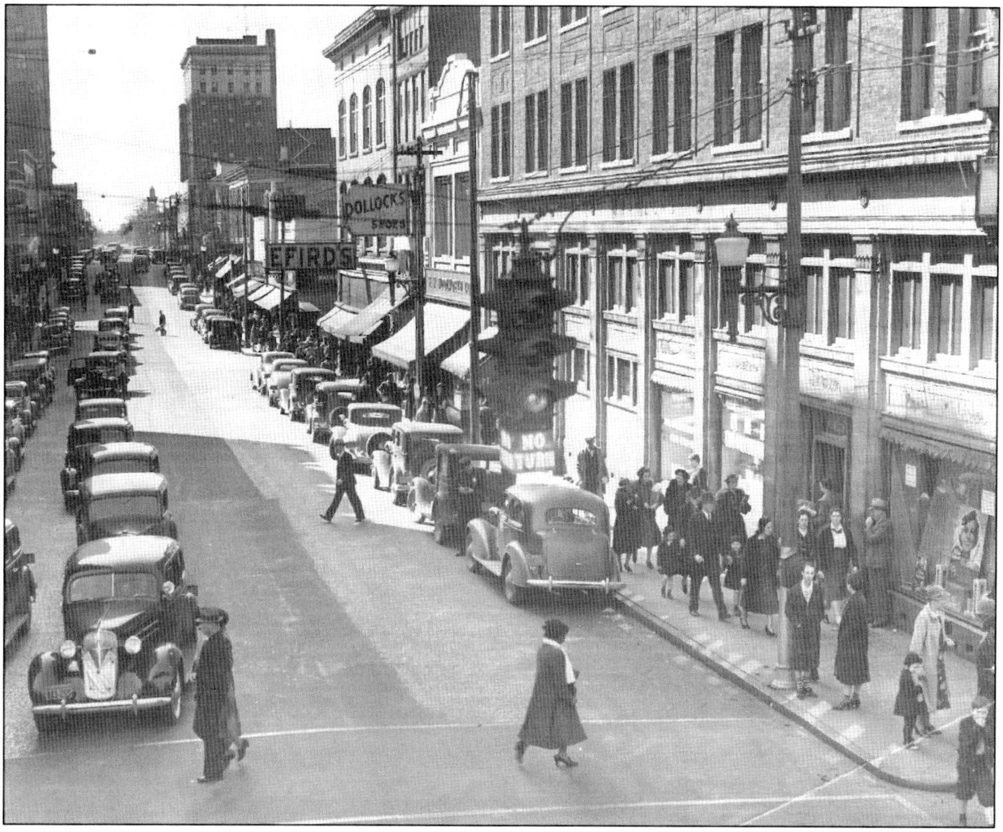

In *Forsyth County, Economic and Social*, printed about 1924, Charles N. Siewers writes, "Forsyth is the country's largest manufacturer of men's knit underwear, the South's largest manufacturer of knit goods, the South's largest manufacturer of woolen goods, and the South's largest manufacturer of wagons." This no. 1 standing was led by Forsyth's no. 1 city, Winston-Salem. On Fourth Street, pictured above in the 1930s, shoppers bought most all products imaginable. Farther down Fourth Street, the former Sosniks Ladies Wear Building is pictured below in the 1930s. The Art Deco Sosniks building later became the elite Thalhimer Department Store. (Courtesy FJ/WSHA.)

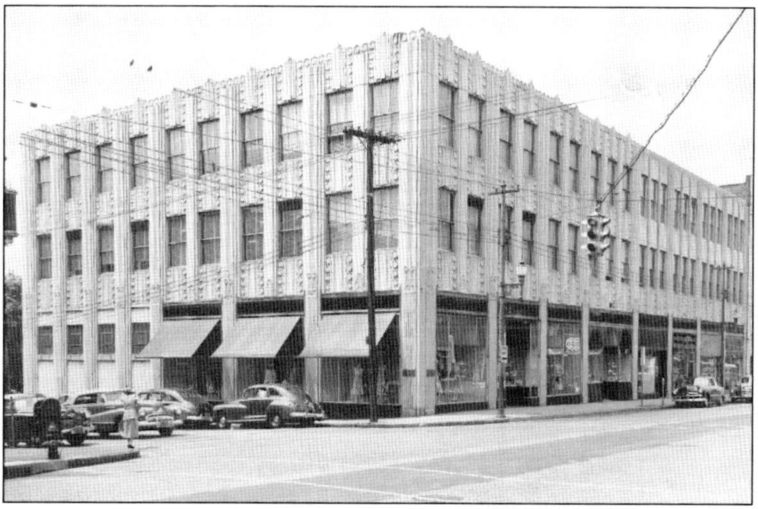

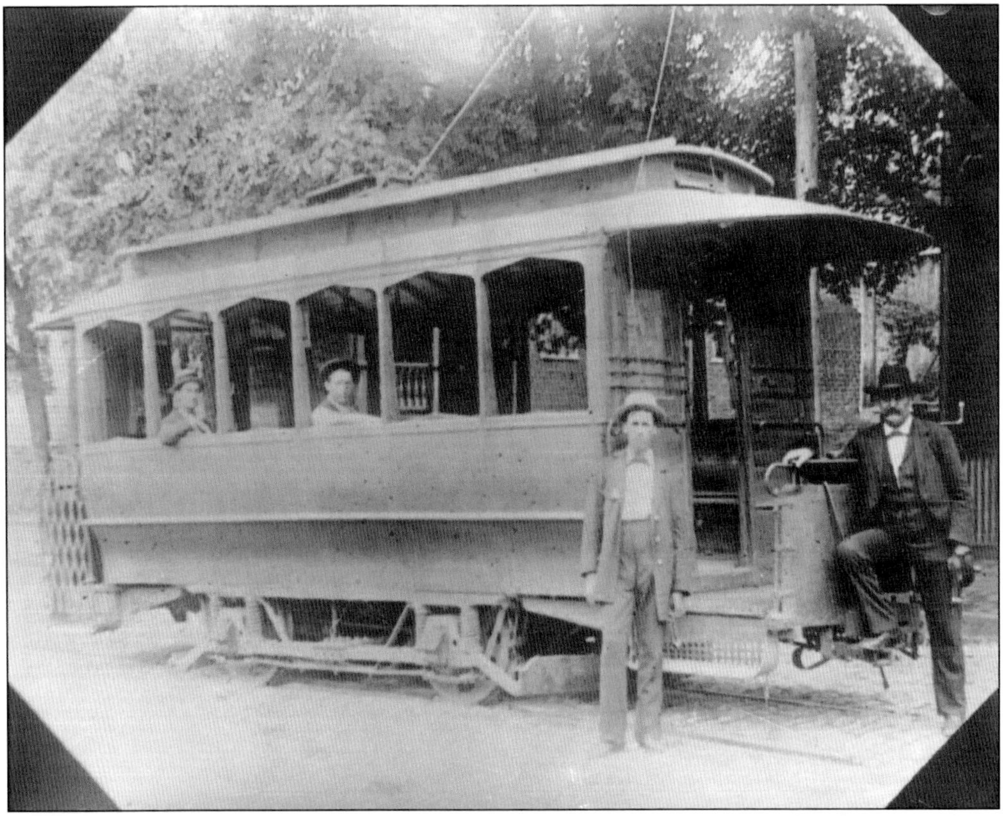

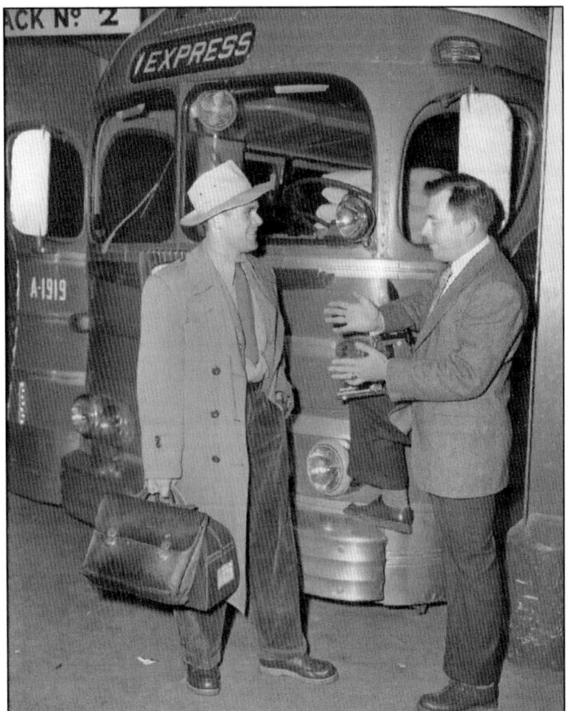

Brother Transou of Bethania taught the art of wagon making to the family's patriarch, Tycho Nissen, in 1771. The Nissen Wagon, popular throughout the 19th century, was manufactured in large numbers. Between 1805 and 1820, wagon trains passed through the post town on their way west, often comprised of local Nissen or Spach wagons. The streetcar arrived in the 1890s, but wagons were still the main form of transportation. Buses replaced the streetcar in the 1950s. At left, Frank Jones, *Winston-Salem Journal* photographer, chats with a traveler before his journey from the Winston-Salem bus station on Cherry Street. (Courtesy FJ/WSHA.)

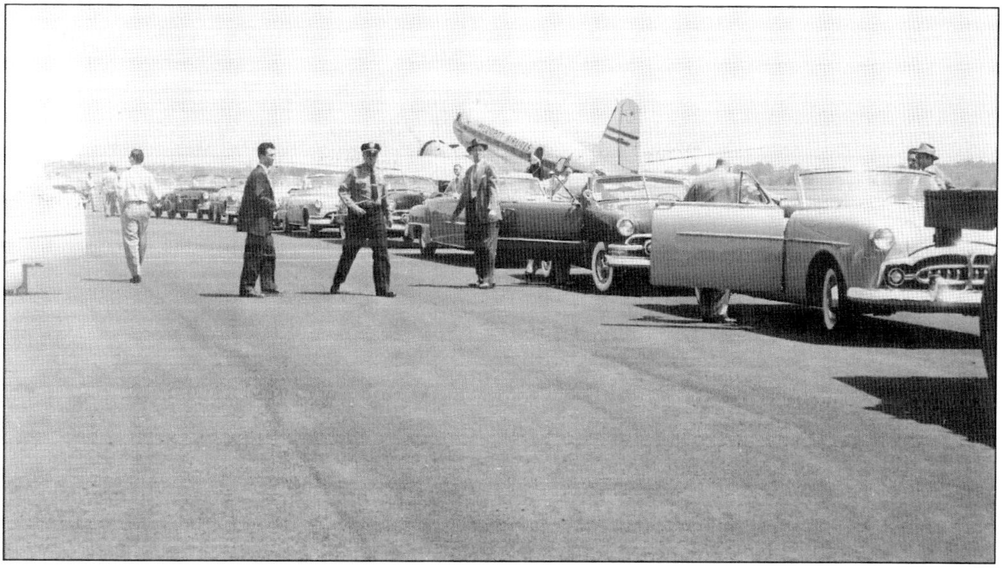

Forsyth dedicated its first airport in 1919 at Maynard Air Field near Kernersville. Charles Lindberg visited here and set the stage for a larger Miller Airport north of Winston about 1927. By the 1940s, the airport had grown to become a commercial airfield, and Smith-Reynolds Airport was born, pictured below in the 1950s. The Bell Telephone Building, built about 1950 and pictured below in the 1950s on Fifth Street, is Forsyth's premier communications center. Telephone communication has come a long way from Winston's first telephone service—two tomato cans and a wax string in the 1870s. (Courtesy WSHA/M. Bricker.)

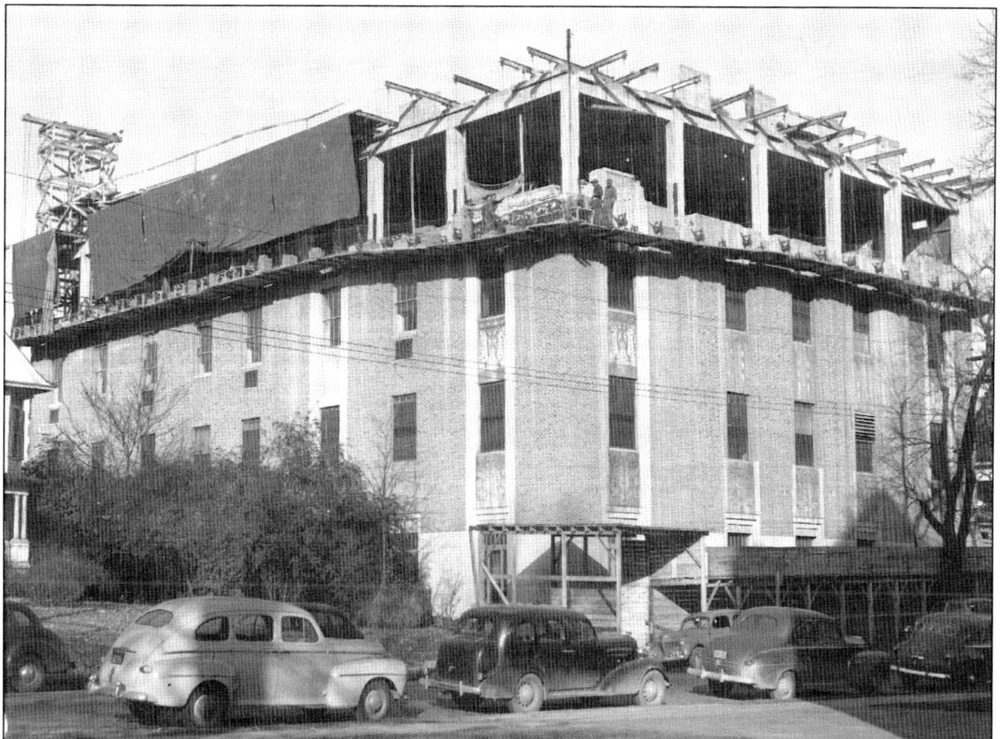

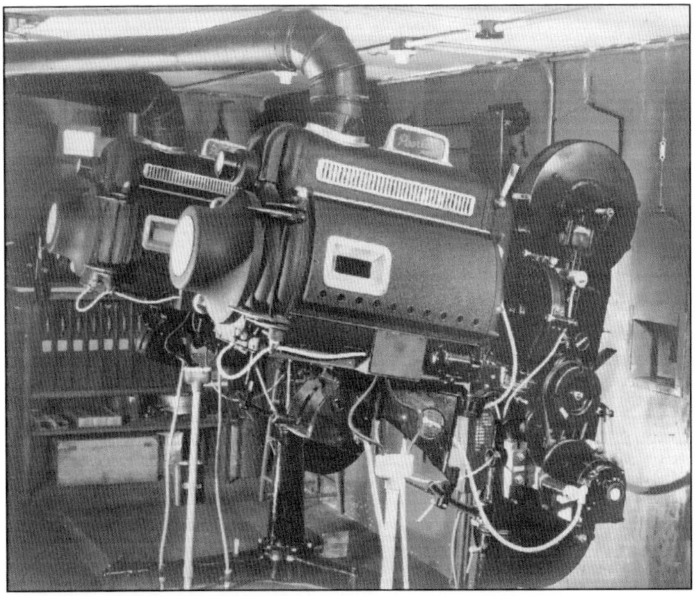

Watching performances—whether in a crowded campground while waiting for the tobacco auctions in the 1800s, or mesmerized by plays and movies in the Grand Reynolda Auditorium or Carolina Theatre in the 1920s—has long been a popular recreational and cultural pursuit. Moving picture theaters in the early 1900s included the Amuza, Elmont, and the Rex. This photograph shows a projector at Carolina Theatre in the 1950s. (Courtesy M. Bricker.)

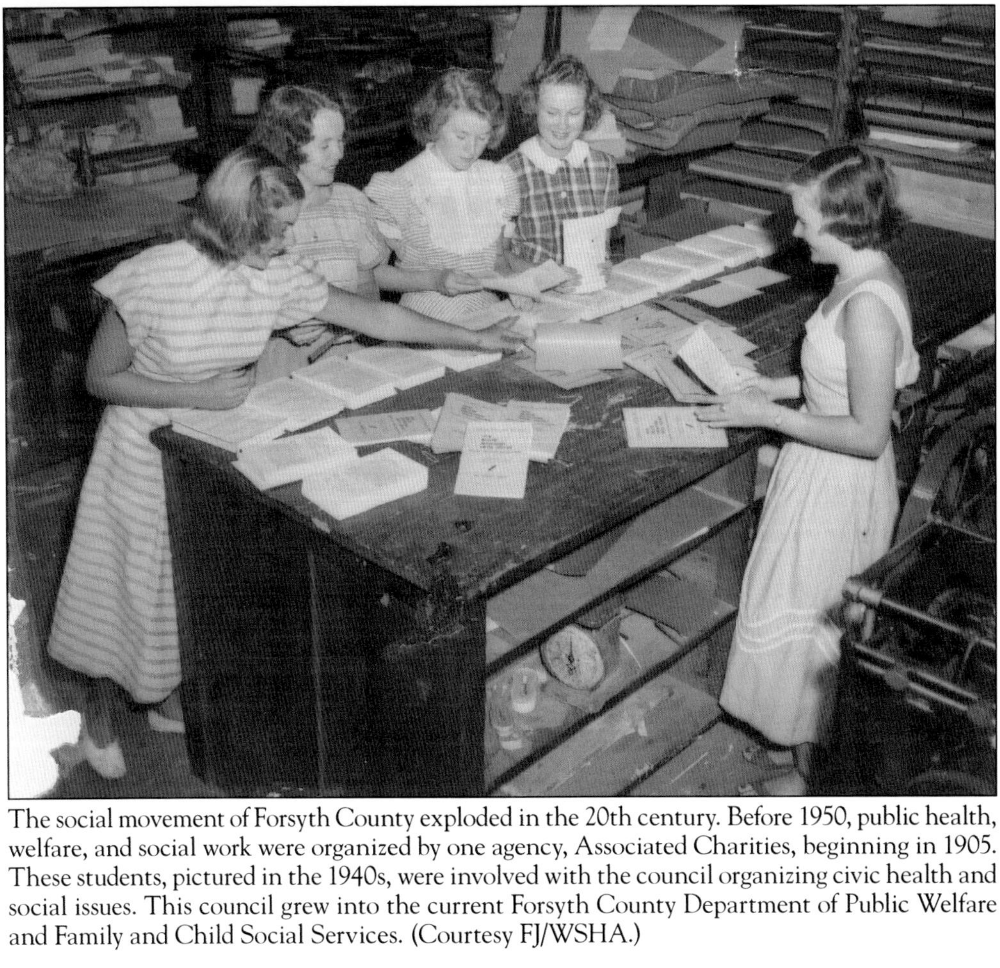

The social movement of Forsyth County exploded in the 20th century. Before 1950, public health, welfare, and social work were organized by one agency, Associated Charities, beginning in 1905. These students, pictured in the 1940s, were involved with the council organizing civic health and social issues. This council grew into the current Forsyth County Department of Public Welfare and Family and Child Social Services. (Courtesy FJ/WSHA.)

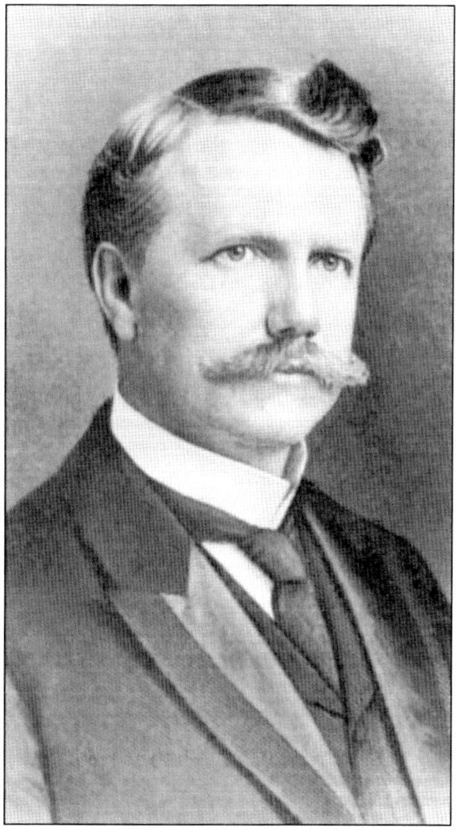

Col. Francis Fries, pictured in the 1850s, helped lead the Fries family into public awareness and responsibility while running the Fries Woolen Mill before the Civil War. The use of slavery in his mill was necessary in his eyes, but later, family members joined with the Reynolds and Hanes families in the 20th century as proponents of social justice. The photograph below shows the R.J. Reynolds House about 1900. Colonel Fries's descendant Dr. Adelaide Fries, along with Annie Grogan, traveled throughout the area doing social work. The Reynoldses' social advocate, Kate B. Reynolds, wife of William N. Reynolds, and Mary Reynolds Babcock, wife of Charles Babcock, gave Tanglewood and Reynolda House for social purposes. The Kate B. Reynolds Regional Hospital for African Americans was also founded in this way. (Courtesy WSHA/M. Bricker.)

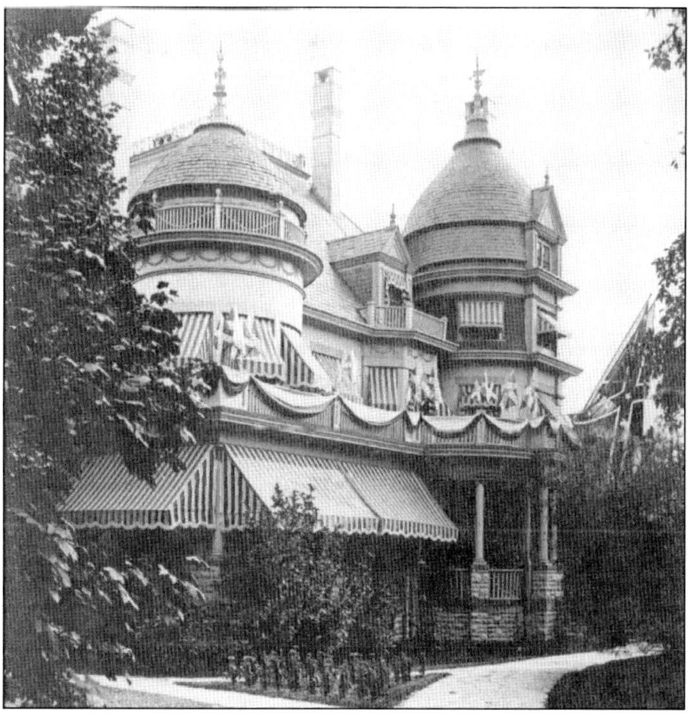

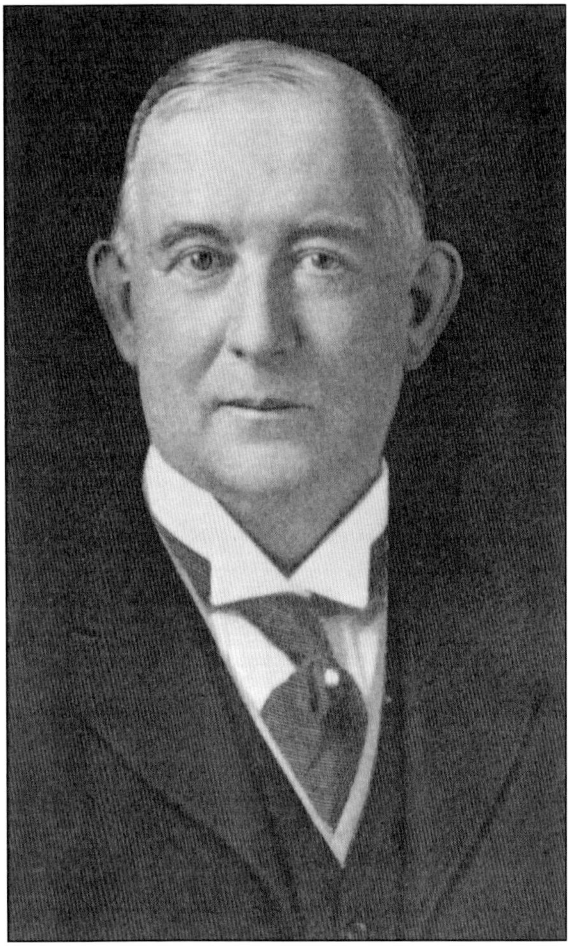

James Buchanan Duke, pictured in the 1900s, sparred with R.J. Reynolds for tobacco domination. The Tobacco Trust, which "Buck" Duke started, was a monopoly on tobacco processing and sales in the open market. The shrewd Reynolds stopped this trust and gained an empire all his own. Both would come together in the 20th century as philanthropists, Duke creating Duke University and Medical Center and the Reynolds family creating Wake Forsyth University. (Courtesy WSHA.)

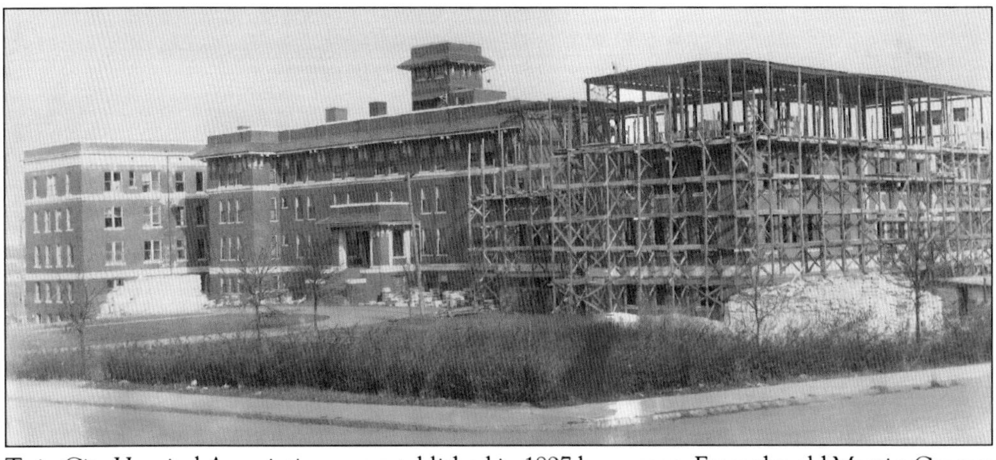

Twin City Hospital Association was established in 1897 by women. From the old Martin-Grogan House, it moved into a more spacious building in Brookstown. It contained one ward and three private rooms with a total of 17 beds. By 1914, a spacious, modern hospital had been constructed. The ladies of the Twin City Hospital Association were still in charge of this large complex. (Courtesy M. Bricker.)

Forsyth Memorial Hospital, shown in the 1960s aerial photograph at right, was built on the former property and farm of P.H. Hanes, textile magnate. Other hospitals in Forsyth County at the time were North Carolina Baptist Hospital and Medical Complex, and the Medical Park Hospital, constructed in the late 1960s. Until 1970, the Kate Bidding Reynolds Hospital, servicing the East Winston community, built a new building, the Reynolds Memorial Hospital. Hospitals in Forsyth have expanded their medical services to keep up with advances in technology. The 1950s photograph below shows a patient receiving state-of-the-art care for the time. (Courtesy FJ/WSHA.)

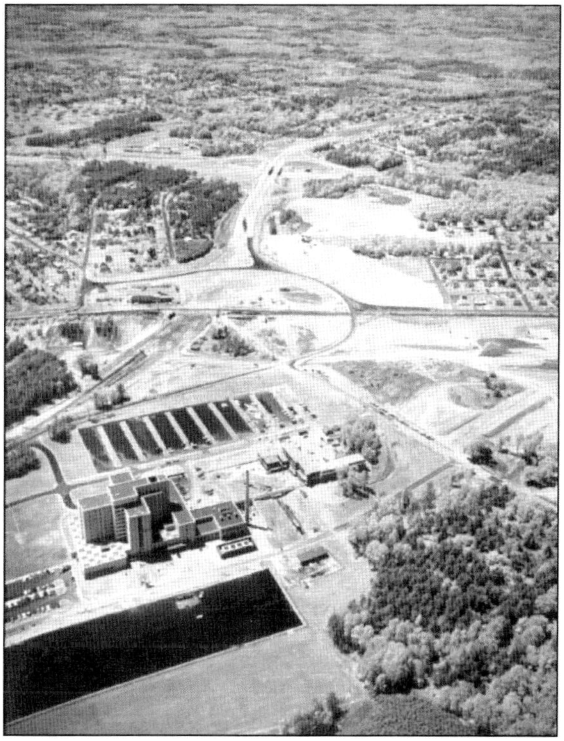

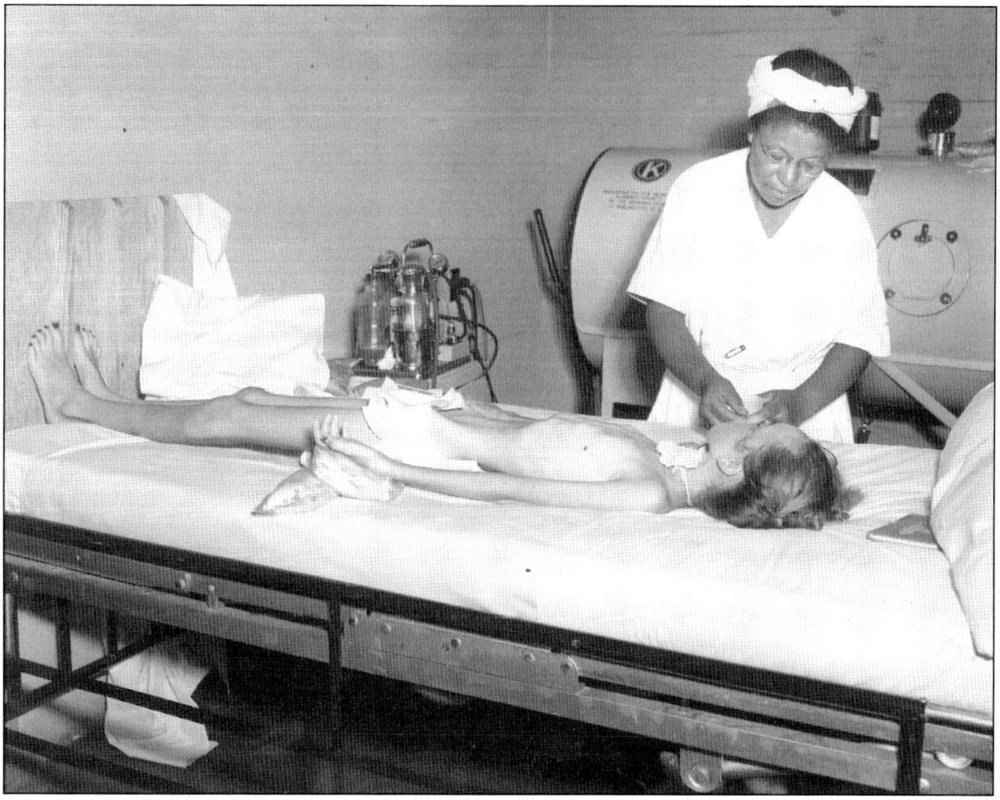

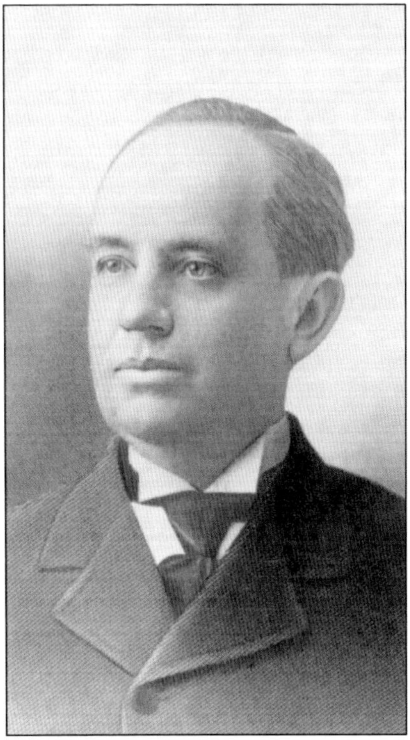

William Louis Poteat, pictured at left, was one of several professors of Wake Forest Baptist College (founded in 1856 in Wake Forest), who moved to Winston-Salem in the 1950s for the new Wake Forest University and College. Wake Forest College is shown below about 1960. The university has grown to encompass business, law, science, and the arts; its Baptist roots have been left behind. (Courtesy WSHA.)

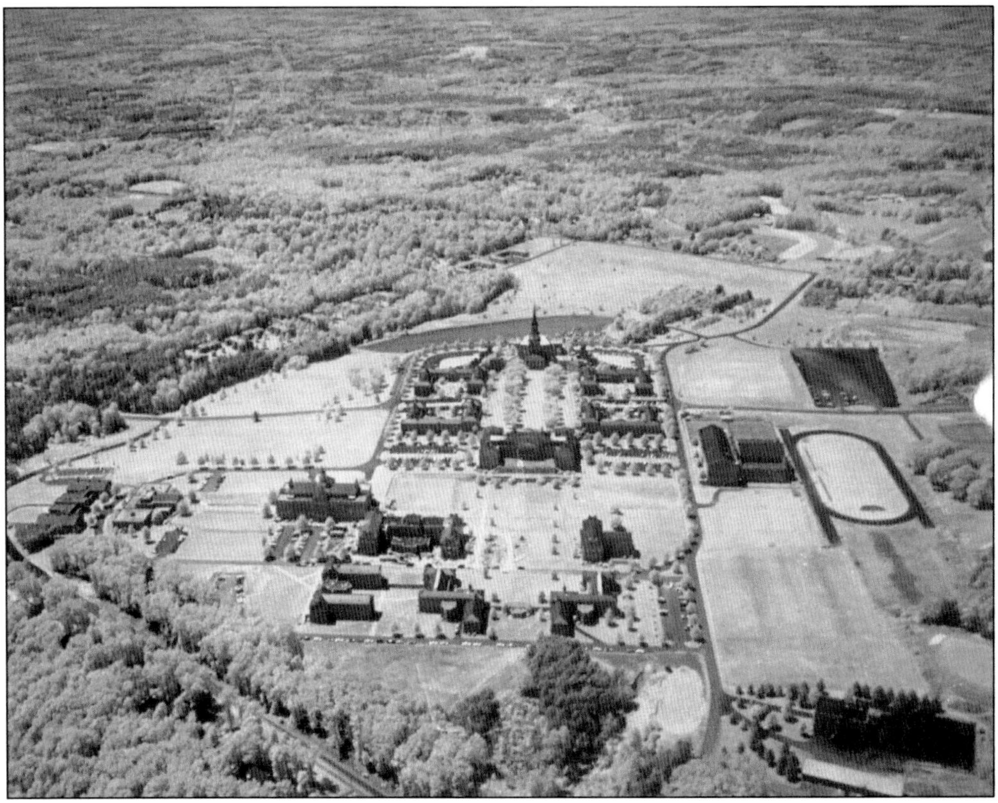

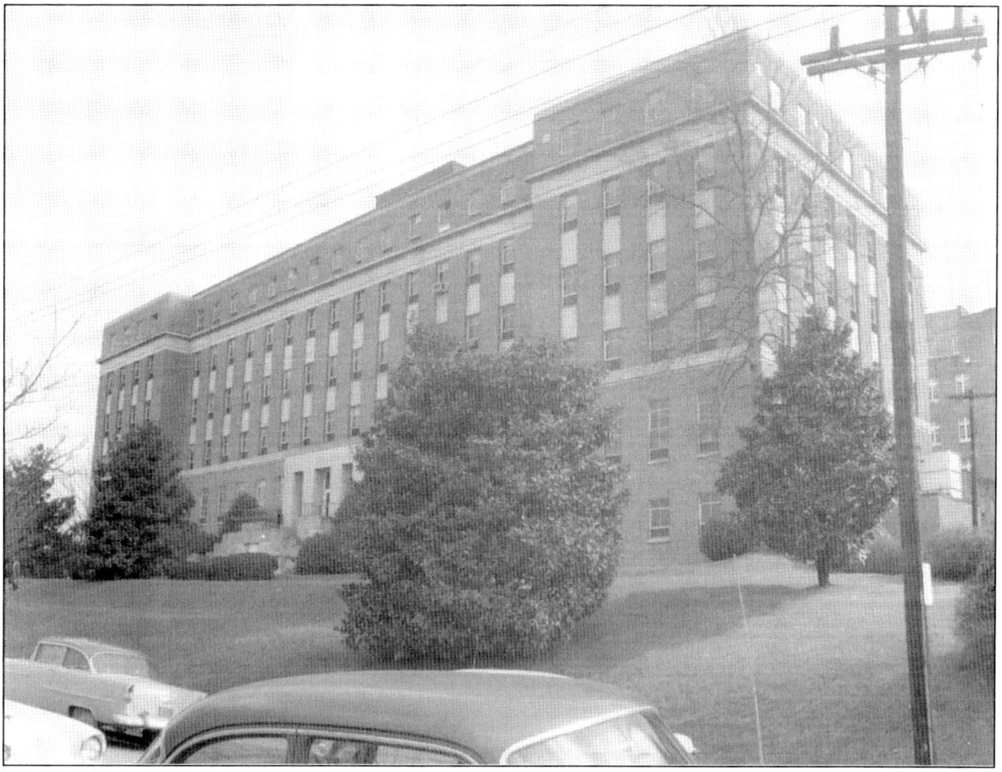

Above, the c. 1920s Wake Forest and Bowman Gray Hospital and School looms atop Hawthorne Hill in 1950. Today, Bowman Gray is rated one of the top medical schools in the country. Pictured at right in a 1920s postcard is the quiet and tranquil Salem Baptist Church. The research park of the new downtown Wake Forest complex stands in contrast to Salem Baptist Church, but both the church and the hospital have more in common than one may think. (Courtesy FJ/WSHA.)

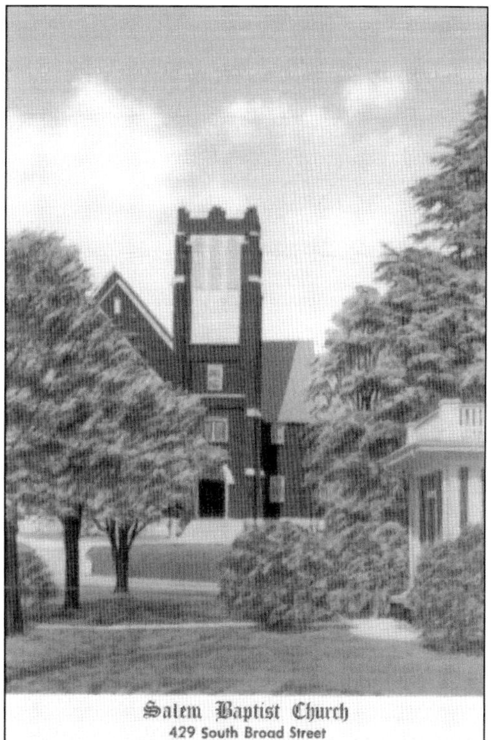

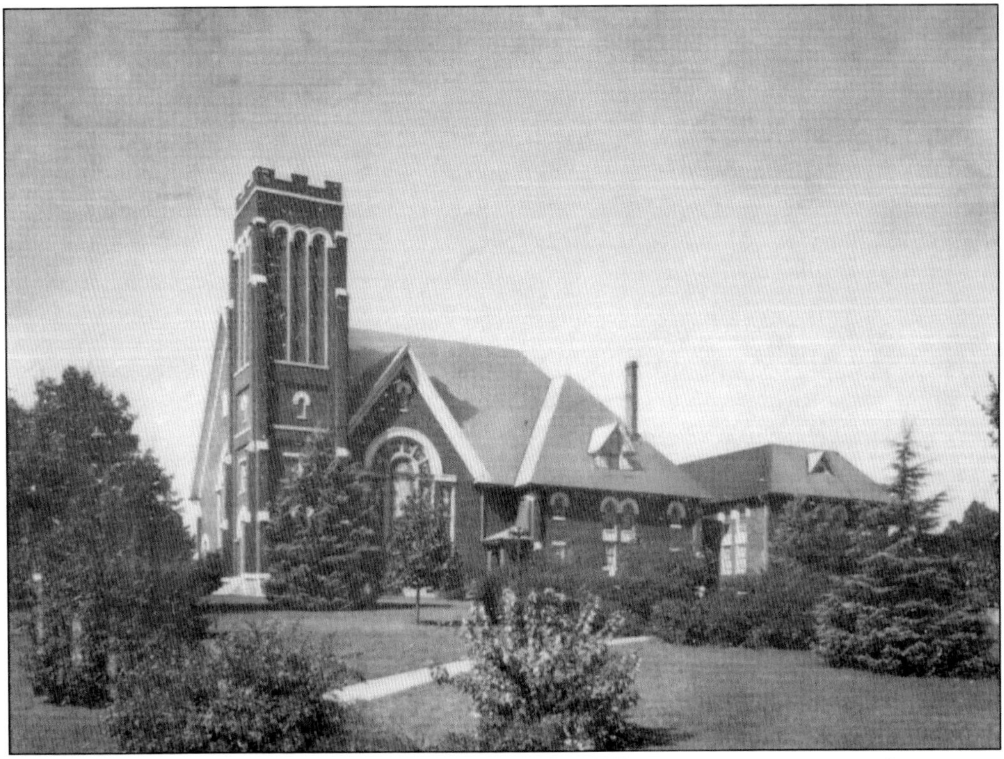

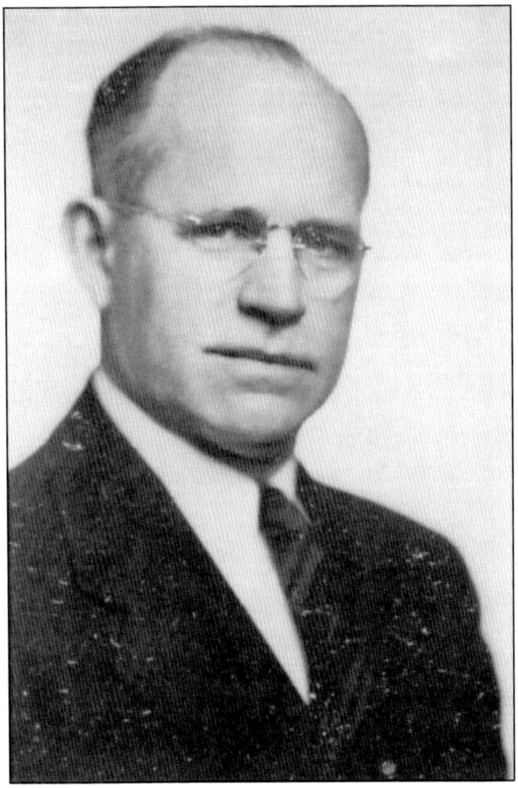

In 1925, a young minister arrived in Winston with the hope of becoming Salem Baptist Church's new minister. The church is pictured above on Broad Street. He found the church struggling with an issue of church versus state—creationism versus evolutionary theory. Salem Baptist Church became the hub where many Baptist church officials met, discussed, and obtained the right to teach evolutionary theory in the public schools. Pastor Charles Stevens, shown at left, left the church disheartened but returned gallantly a few years later and led the church back to its core Baptist beliefs for more than 50 years. (Courtesy to LaNelle Church.)

Seven

A Historical Vision for the 21st Century

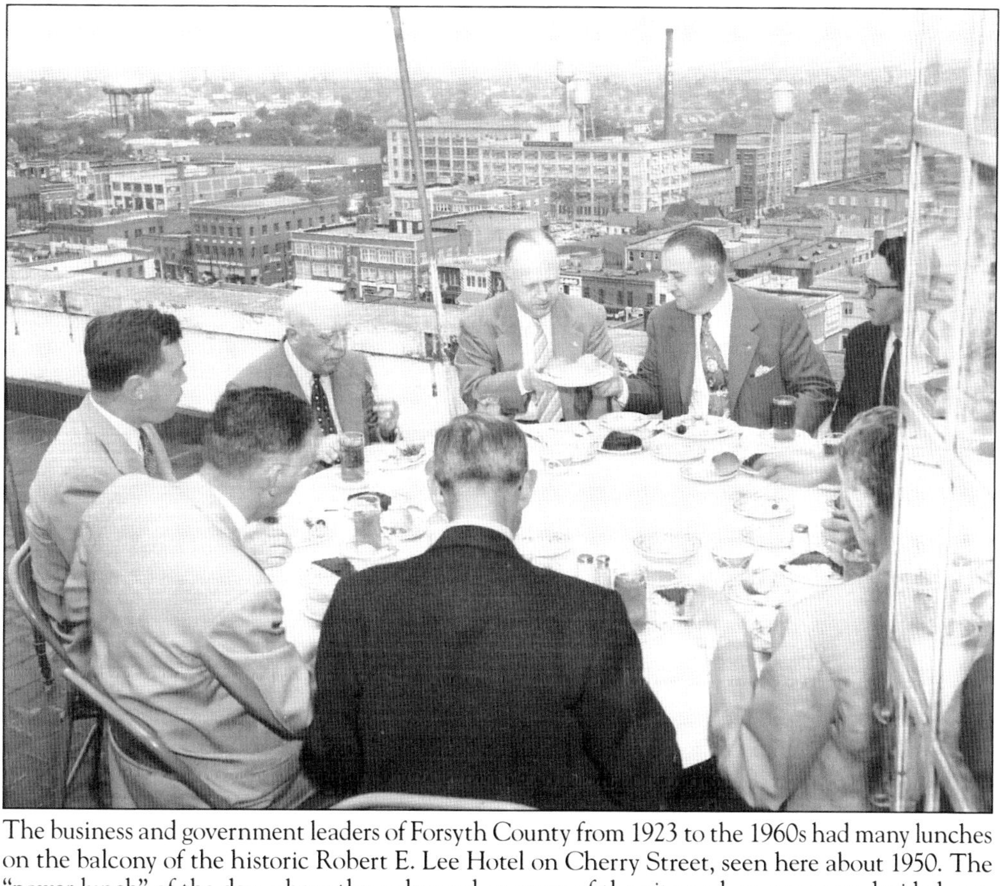

The business and government leaders of Forsyth County from 1923 to the 1960s had many lunches on the balcony of the historic Robert E. Lee Hotel on Cherry Street, seen here about 1950. The "power lunch" of the day, where the pulse and progress of the city and county were decided, was held in an extension of the 12th floor of the downtown Reynolds building. The county's vision for the 21st century began here. (Courtesy FJ/WSHA.)

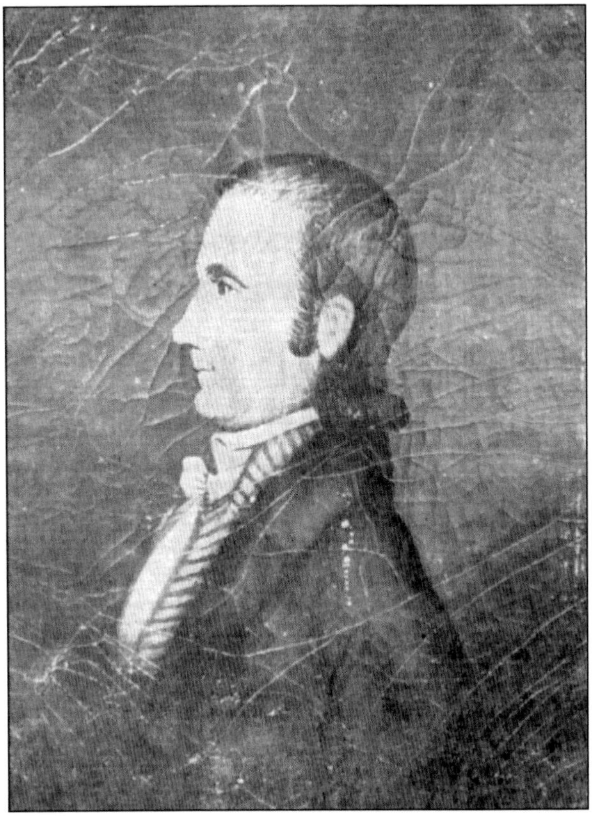

Col. Joseph Winston (pictured) was a distinguished serviceman. He was highly educated, serving North Carolina as a senator and the country as a congressman. His counterpart Colonel Forsyth was elected to the house of commons in Stokes County in 1800. Forsyth lost his life before leading his troops to Canada in the early part of the War of 1812. (Courtesy FJ/WSHA.)

This c. 1970 map of Forsyth County shows the townships and municipalities of today. It is unfortunate that the hero chosen to be the county's namesake left no known pictures of himself. (Courtesy Forsyth County Historic Commission/M. Bricker.)

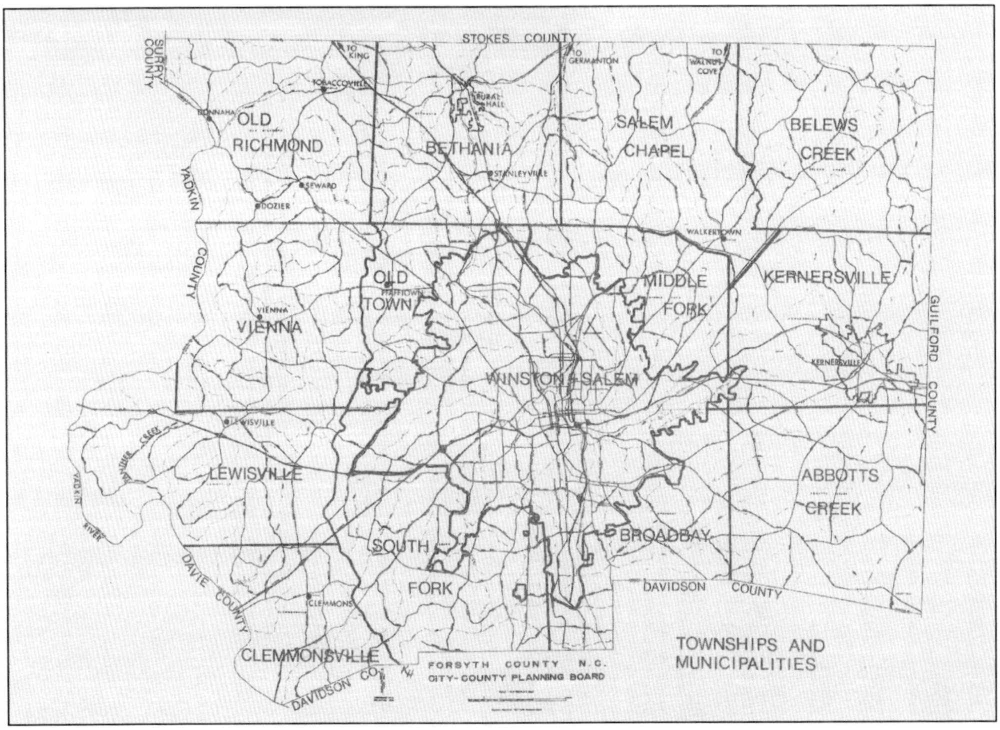

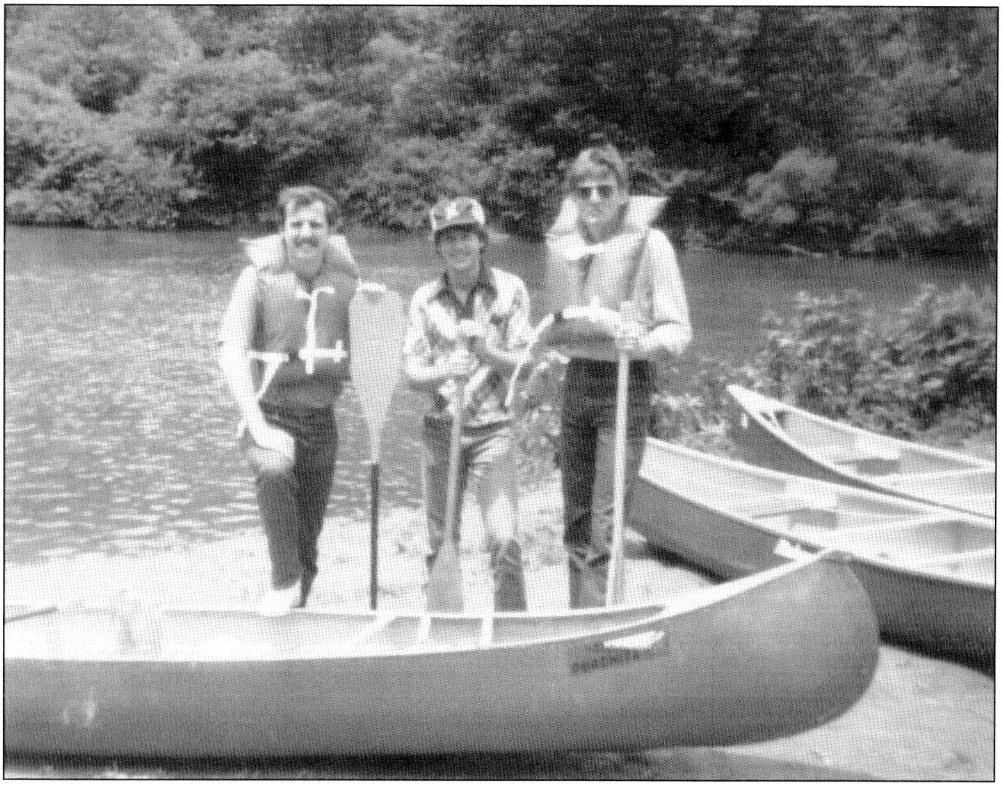

The Yadkin River meanders through the North Carolina piedmont. It was the principal river passage the early settlers traveled to reach the backwoods of the piedmont. This photograph from the 1970s shows the author's friends (Russell Dancy, Harry Nunn, and Bill Wright), who followed an expedition down another piedmont river, the New River. (Courtesy M. Bricker.)

The preservation of neighborhoods and rural towns in Forsyth County remains important for the 21st century. Winston-Salem is credited with having the most historic neighborhoods in the Southeast. Unfortunately, not everything was saved. In this 1950 photograph, Old Cherry and North Liberty Streets were slowly disappearing to progress. (Courtesy FJ/WSHA.)

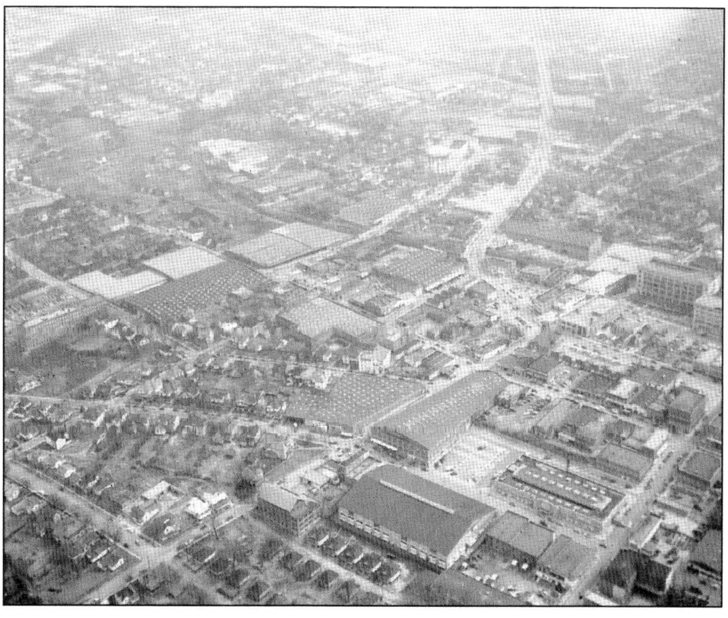

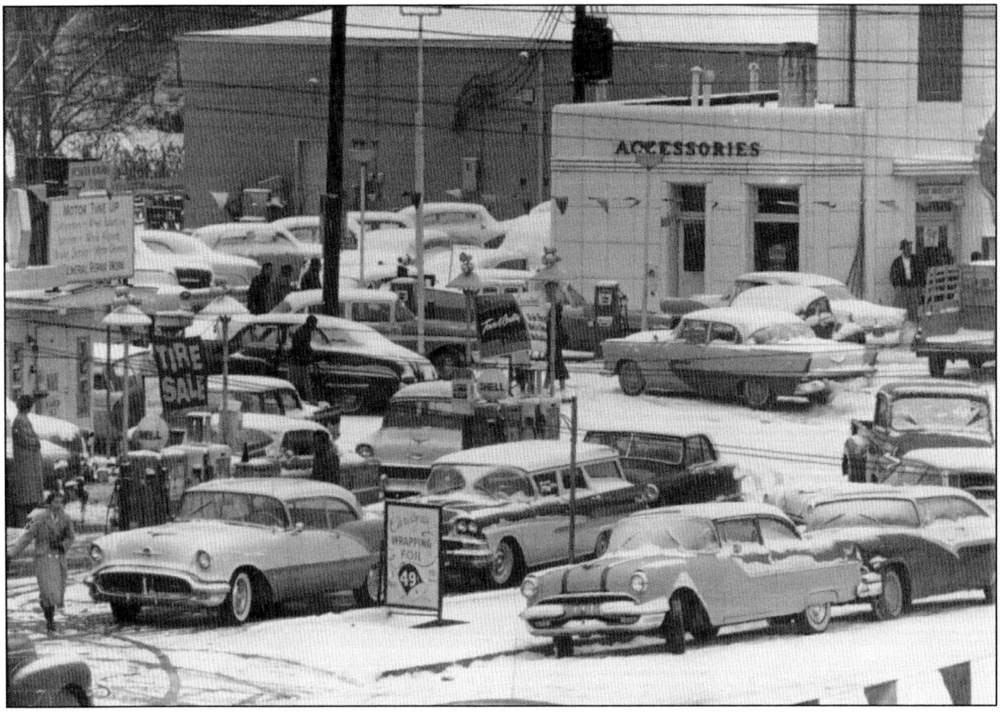

This c. 1950 photograph of a Shell gas station at the intersection of Hawthorne Road and First Street in the West End was taken during the Christmas season. (Courtesy WSHA.)

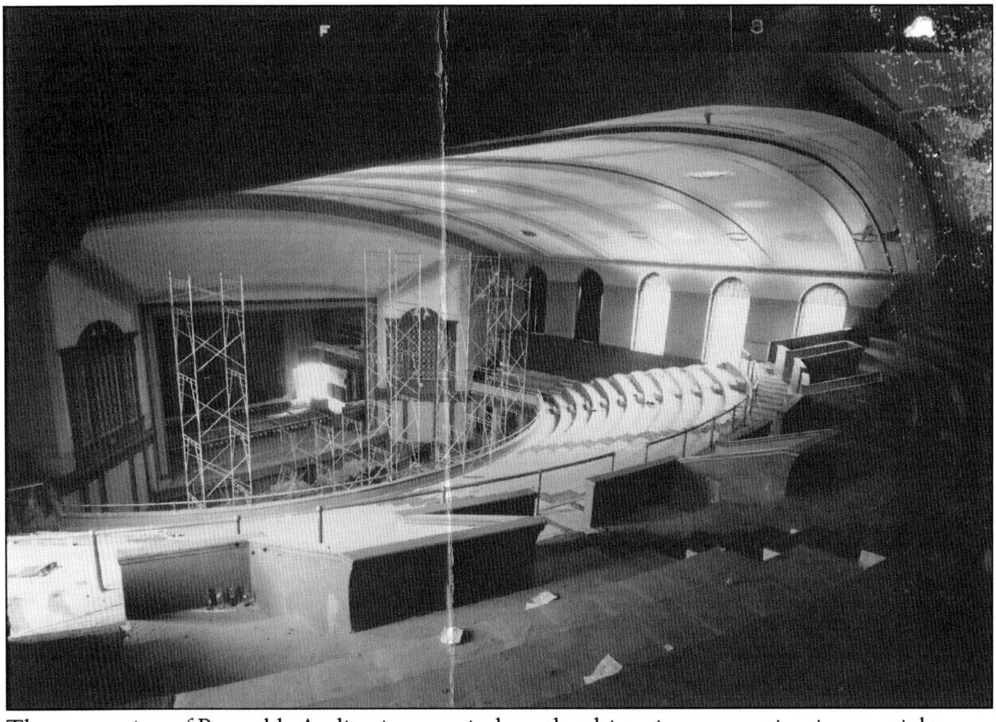
The renovation of Reynolds Auditorium reminds us that historic preservation is essential to our future. The auditorium is an excellent example of 1920s architecture. (Courtesy WSHA.)

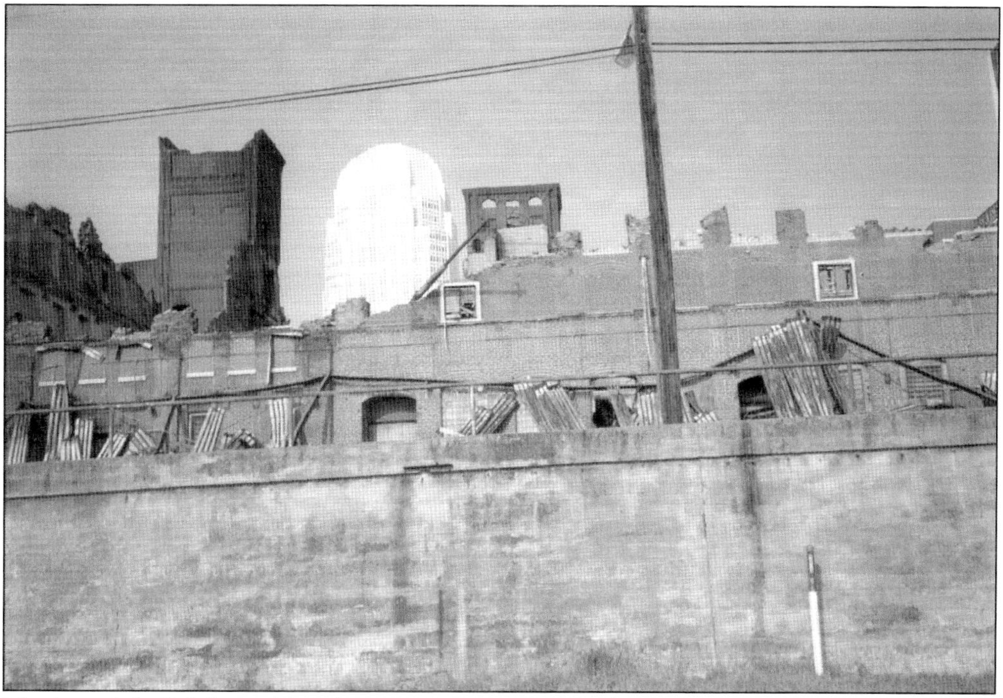

The loss of the R.J. Reynolds Tobacco Factory no. 256 (with the new Wachovia headquarters in the background) shows how two of the most powerful entities in their fields can be gone in an instant, the factory by fire and the headquarters by takeover. (Courtesy M. Bricker.)

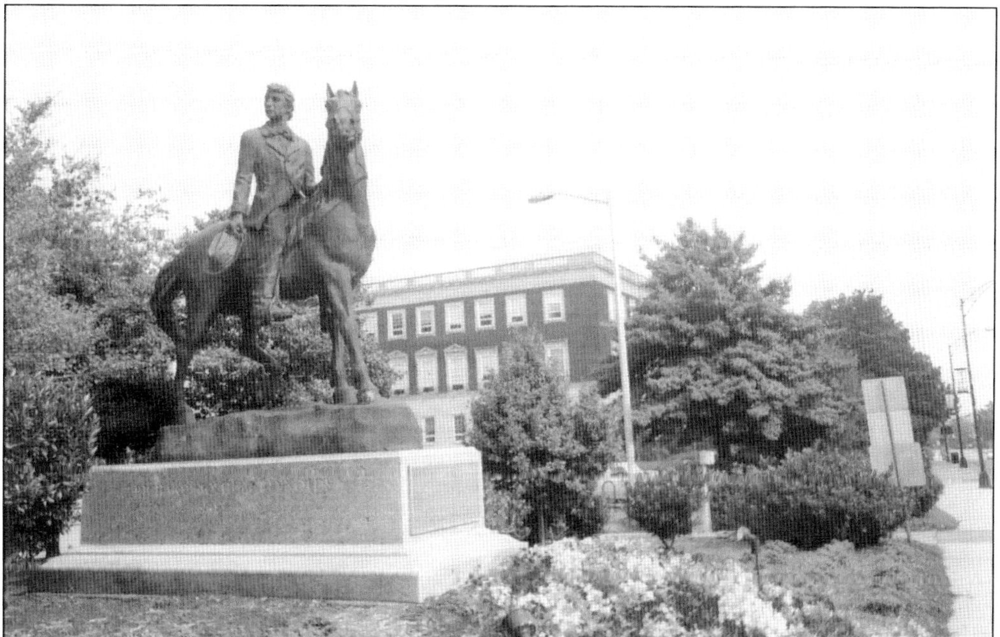

Richard J. Reynolds Sr. is immortalized in this statue at the corner of Main and Second Streets in Winston. He is shown surveying the town of Winston in the 1870s. Could it be he had seen what the Moravians saw when they first set their eyes on this future county? (Courtesy M. Bricker.)

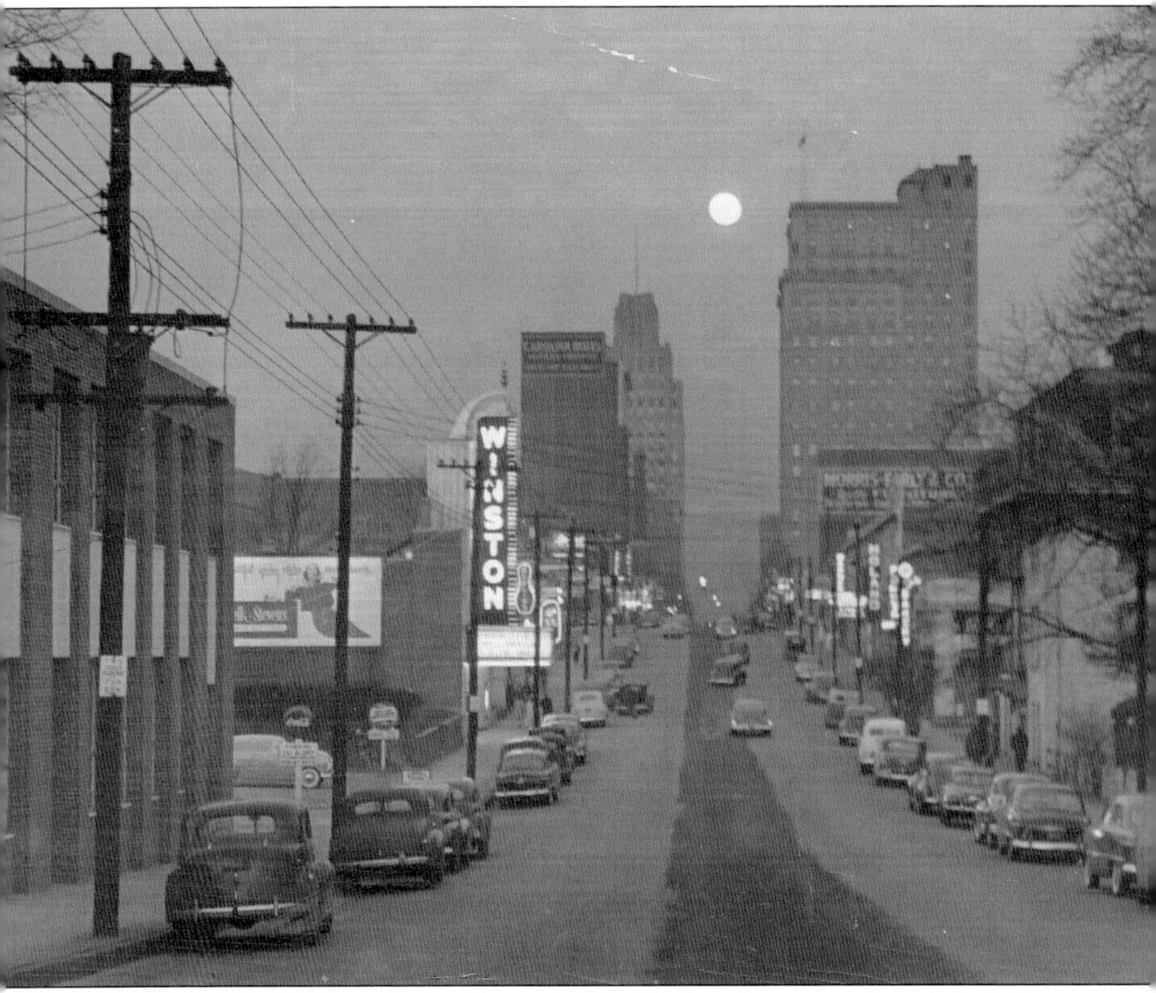

Nightlife was active in Winston in the 1940s. The Woolworth store ran three shifts, 24 hours a day, seven days a week, and employed over 100 people. A renaissance has begun again in the 21st century, with increased downtown living and renewed interest in the arts, music, and theater. (Courtesy FJ/WSHA.)

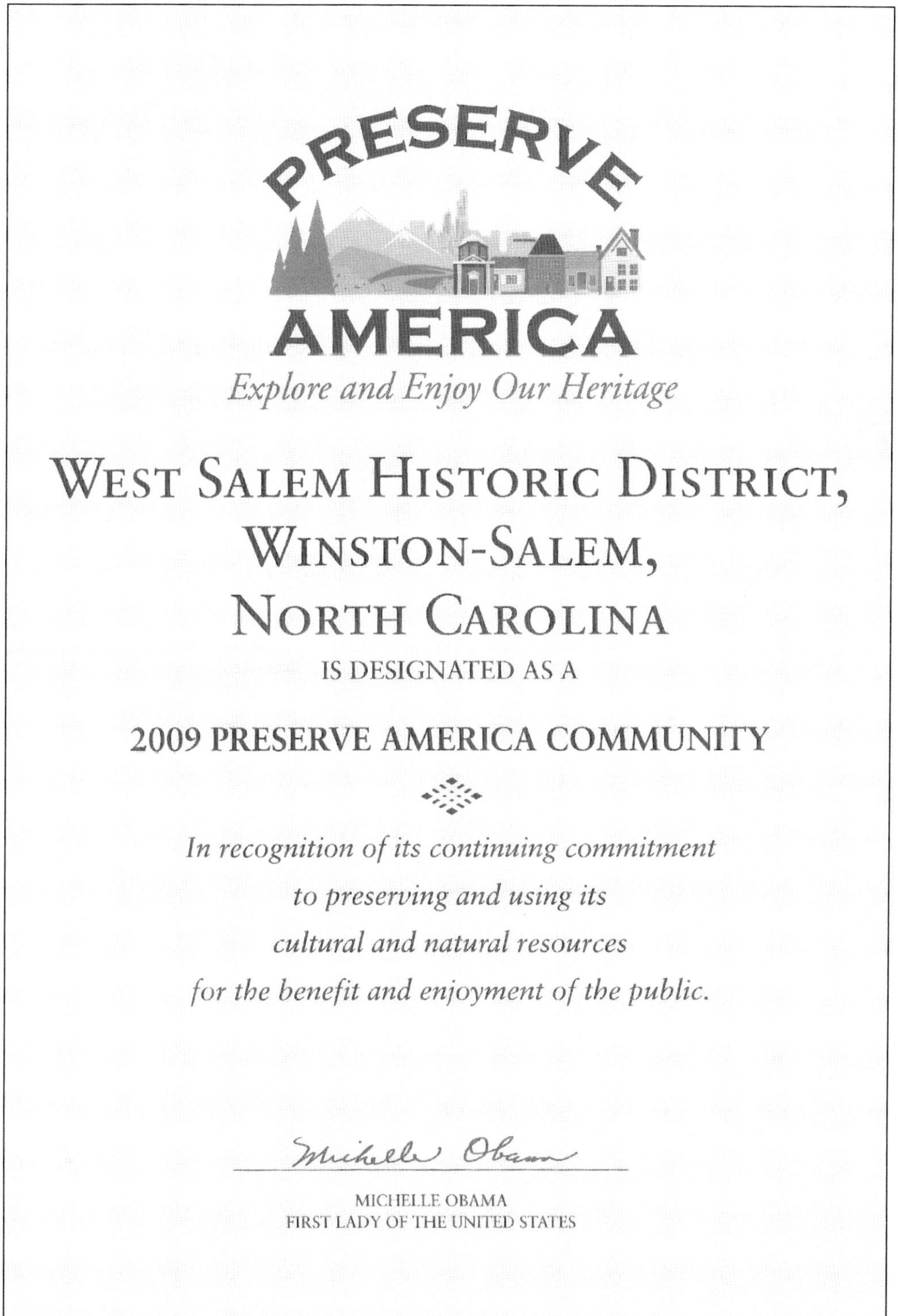

PRESERVE AMERICA

Explore and Enjoy Our Heritage

WEST SALEM HISTORIC DISTRICT,
WINSTON-SALEM,
NORTH CAROLINA

IS DESIGNATED AS A

2009 PRESERVE AMERICA COMMUNITY

In recognition of its continuing commitment to preserving and using its cultural and natural resources for the benefit and enjoyment of the public.

Michelle Obama

MICHELLE OBAMA
FIRST LADY OF THE UNITED STATES

The West Salem Historic District is the only Preserve America Neighborhood in the Carolinas. It is one of only three such neighborhoods in the Southeast.

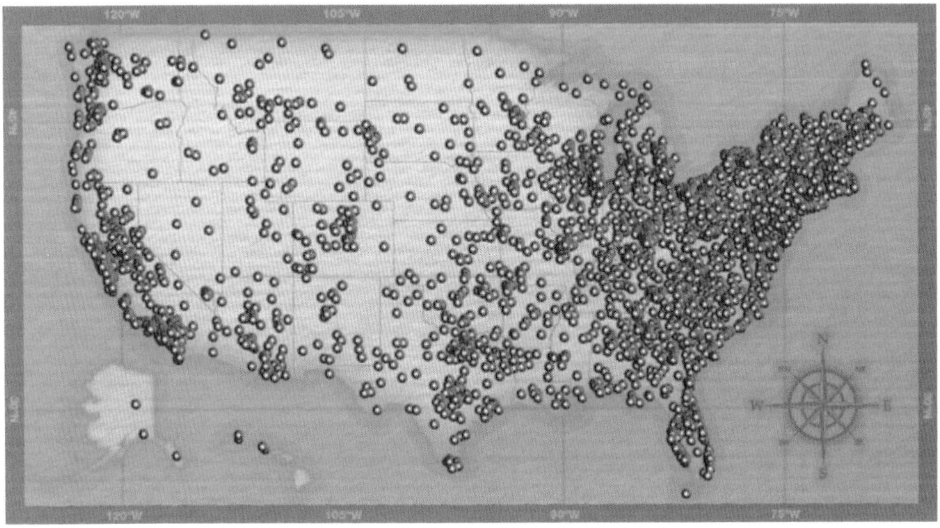

Consistent with our mission to preserve history on a local level, this book was printed in South Carolina on American-made paper and manufactured entirely in the United States. Products carrying the accredited Forest Stewardship Council (FSC) label are printed on 100 percent FSC-certified paper.

MADE IN THE USA